Conscience of a Conservationist

Michael Frome

Conscience of a Conservationist

SELECTED ESSAYS

The University of Tennessee Press
KNOXVILLE

Frontispiece: Rudolph Wendelin

The paper in this book meets the minimum requirements of the
American National Standard for Permanence of Paper for Printed
Library Materials. ∞   The binding materials have been chosen for
strength and durability.

Library of Congress Cataloging in Publication Data

Frome, Michael.
   [Essays. Selections]
   Conscience of a conservationist: selected essays / Michael
Frome.
—1st ed.
      p. cm.
   ISBN 0-87049-602-6 (cloth : alk. paper)
   1. Nature conservation—Appalachian Region, Southern.
2. Frome, Michael. I. Title.
QH76.5.A57F7625 1989
333. 7'2'0974—dc19   88-27659   CIP

To My Editors
Who encouraged, tolerated,
and defended me, when need be,
in the original publication
of these essays.

Contents

Foreword by Paul C. Pritchard / ix
Preface / xi

Part 1 In the Southern Mountains
1   Pisgah: Dawn of American Forestry / 3
2   Why the Rockfeller $5,000,000? / 19
3   The President and I Discuss Tellico Dam / 34
4   A New Age of Walking Americans / 42
5   Weavers and Woodcarvers—
    Soft and Mellow and Rich / 46
6   The World's Greatest Road—
    But No Highway / 54
7   Poison Coverup in Tennessee / 60
8   To Save the Southern Highlands / 70
9   Harvey Broome, My Teacher and Hero / 79
10 Any Wilderness in the East? / 81
11 Protecting the Public Options / 103
12 Panthers Wanted—
    Alive, Back East, Where They Belong / 117
13 If the Panther Can Make It, So Will We / 124

Part 2 Conscience of a Conservationist
14 America the Beautiful—
    Heritage or Honkytonk? / 133

15 Let's Rescue Our Roadsides—Now! / 144
16 On Such Foundations—
    The National Park Service at Fifty / 153
17 The Politics of Conservation / 156
18 A Conservation Ethic / 170
19 On the Day Martin Luther King Died / 176
20 Welcome Back to School
    from the Old Professor / 181
21 A Pacifist Spoke to Me on Earth Day / 185
22 Saving the Wilderness / 189
23 Forestry: Fallacy and Failure
    of Dominant Use / 196
24 To Lucy: "Unlock Your
    Dreams and Courage" / 206
25 When Fishermen Save the World / 213
26 Freedom of the Press—
    For Those Who Own One / 225
27 Forestry: Only God Can Make a Tree, But . . . / 248
28 Thoreau's Glad Tidings / 258

    Epilogue / 265

    Index / 267

Foreword

By Paul C. Pritchard

It is hard to find heroes in our contemporary world. Or at least so it seems. I am not sure why this should be the case. Historically, it may be that the concept of a "hero" was always based upon a perception of reality rather than reality itself. Then came the new reality of "up close and personal" induced by the news media, television in particular, and our intimate familiarity with every public and private figure.

Maybe the loss of heroes derives from "situation ethics"—where everything is based upon the conditions of the moment, and not on any perpetual values. Maybe because virtually all professions, including those once revered like medicine, education and journalism, have been cast as self-serving.

Ironically, Michael Frome has always bathed in these curious contradictions and still emerges as a hero. Michael has a way of following his conscience without fear or favor. He directs the consequence of conscience at foe or friend, as need be. He is a journalist, but he takes few liberties as some journalists do. He is committed to honesty and aggressiveness, but rather than aim at individuals, he illuminates the effect of the individual's actions upon society.

And, unlike the recent survey that said that America's modern heroes are self-serving movie stars and athletic giants, Frome has always made personal sacrifices to ensure that his cause be honest, to maintain his own values and to serve the common good.

Eric Hoeffer in his presentation of the *True Believer* indirectly described Michael Frome better than I can. Frome's *Conscience of a Conservationist* conveys the specific attitudes that Hoeffer described so well. Interestingly, however, there is one Hoeffer quality that Frome does not project, i.e., he is not naive about the cause he serves. Michael has toiled in the vineyard of the environment most of his adult life. He knows its purposes and how to achieve them. That gives him additional strength, for when he writes about saving the free-flowing Little Tennessee River from the Tellico Dam, or about some of the other great natural resources, he does so fully aware of the inestimable odds against his cause. Yet he seems either to relish the challenge, or to believe that all things are possible to him who works at it with dream and desire.

This book is a collection of the road markers of his journey. It spans many subjects, numerous places and much time. Yet, despite all of this diversity, there is the binding common element in the conscience of Michael Frome.

The book is valuable as good reading, and more besides. It is a record of past battles for the environment that deserve review and remembrance. It is a model of how to win and how to take the losses without quitting. In some ways I like it best as revealing the constant commitment of one man, dedicated to the betterment of the world through his own self-responsibility.

Conscience of a Conservationist is an essential statement of how to be a hero in an age searching for constants, for bearings, for enduring values. Michael Frome is one such exemplar, the rare individual who can and does present a timeless piece of guidance.

Preface

In 1959 I began to belong to myself. For ten years I had been writing and doing public relations in Washington, D.C., and then at last was free of the limitations and restrictions of regular employment. It's nice to have an income to pay the bills, but a steady paycheck is enslaving in its own little way. You've got to be there every day, go to meetings, write reports, and smile politely when you don't feel polite at all. In many circumstances the steady paycheck, or even an unsteady paycheck, stifles individuality and creativity. It requires conformity to somebody else's ideas and rules, which I was happy to escape in order to pursue my own goals.

I wasn't exactly sure of those goals, or where they would lead. I thought of myself as a travel writer, but in the course of time I became more interested in protecting and preserving than in promoting. In the mid-1960s, for example, when I went South to write a book about the Great Smoky Mountains, I intended it to be some kind of travel guide, maybe like one of the books in the old Rivers of America series. Just then, however, the National Park Service came out with its plan to dismember the Smokies wilderness with a trans-mountain road and other goodies. That dreadful idea stirred a lot of passions, including mine. Instead of a guide, I wanted every word in the book pointing to one public conclusion: that the Great Smoky Mountains National Park must not be reduced to cheap and easy fare. The park administrators dealt with me as an impertinent intruder—for a time banning *Strangers in High Places* from sale in their visitor centers. But the trans-mountain road was not built and that counted more.

I remember somewhere in that same period being engaged to write the script for a film about the new federal law protecting wild and scenic rivers. It was a joint project of three agencies, the U.S. Forest Service, National Park Service and Bureau of Outdoor Recreation, with financing contributed by Exxon, the big oil conglomerate, but I was responsible mostly to the Forest Service. I did considerable preliminary research in advance of going to Houston to discuss the project with the Exxon people. Just the day before the scheduled trip I met with Forest Service officials directly in charge of their agency's wild and scenic rivers program. Now the way to begin this film, they told me in all seriousness, was at a dam site in order to show how dams benefit wild rivers by releasing water to them. I thought about it for awhile. The whole concept of wild rivers was to *save* them from dam builders. That evening I telephoned the information chief of the Forest Service, who had hired me, to resign from the project. I could have used the money, but had I continued I would have been just another clerk on a payroll, doing what I was told and not what I believed.

Between 1964 and 1971 I wrote a column of opinion in *American Forests* magazine, published by the American Forestry Association. I enjoyed the opportunity for unrestrained self-expression. Ultimately, unfortunately, there came a time when I was warned that I must not criticize in any way the Forest Service, forest products industry or forestry profession, and that my work would be censored in advance of publication to make certain it did not offend timbering or forestry interests. Thus the relationship ended.

I don't want to make myself out as a hero. That isn't the point. During an exciting time of environmental crisis and growing awareness I was exploring what it was all about and trying to identify the weak spots, as I was taught to do as a journalist with social conscience. Moreover, I was able to express ideas freely. Nobody can take away the work I succeeded in doing. James B. Craig, the editor of *American Forests,* was my staunchest defender as long as he was able. So was Clare Conley, my editor at *Field & Stream*—he got fired before I did. When one door closed another would open, if only I would hang tough with strong ideas and write them with clarity and conviction. That the University of Tennessee Press should now choose to publish this collection demonstrates that in our democratic society avenues of communication will always be open, with access to public opinion and public policy.

This collection of essays and articles, dating from the early 1960s through the 1970s is divided into two parts. The first deals with my interest and activity in Southern Appalachia. I spent considerable time and made many friends in and around those mountains. I was with friends when we dedicated the Gee Creek Wilderness in Tennessee and the Sipsey Wilderness in Alabama; when we winter-camped in the Cohuttas in north Georgia, strategizing to save that wilderness and when we hiked down to Slickrock Creek in western North Carolina; when we hiked the high ridge to "Save-the-Smok-ies" and again to save Cataloochee; when we floated the Big South Fork of the Cumberland, on the Kentucky-Tennessee border, and the Little Tennessee, Obed and Upper French Broad; when we went to Mount Mitchell, trying to protect the highest mountain in the East by campaigning, alas unsuccessfully, for a new national park; when we walked in the Monongahala National Forest in West Virginia, hoping somehow to arrest the clearcutting devastation; and when we tried to stop strip mining, the scourge of the southern mountains. We won a few, proving that it can be done, but lost considerably more, I fear. Even so, the genius of people shone through—people like Harry Caudill, of eastern Kentucky, who through his classic book, *Night Comes to the Cumberlands,* and other works did his share and more; Ken Hechler, the West Virginia congressman, who strived not to legitimize strip mining through regulation but to eliminate it alto-gether; plus a lot of everyday folks who stood up to be counted and should not be forgotten.

The second part joins Appalachia with a broader context, through essays relating conservation to the national landscape, forestry, ethics, pacifism, education, social justice and politics. After twenty years or more, I may feel a little differently about some things, but the basic ideas remain. Each of us must be inspired to realize the power of his or her own life and to never sell it short. The timid, the hesitant, the compromisers have failed. The bigger and bolder the program, the greater the chance of success. Individually and collectively, true believers can work miracles, if we have faith and hang together, studying life as well as school books, taking a few splendid risks based on principle about political expediency and glorified professionalism. These convictions remain paramount.

The names of many people who helped me along the way are in this book. I want to add a special word of appreciation to Chris Strom, a student at Northland College in Ashland, Wisconsin, who helped in the preliminary selection, and to Robert S. Brandt, Glenn C. Graber and Paul C. Pritchard, who were asked by the University of Tennessee Press to read and comment on these and others of my essays; their thoughtful critique proved most helpful. I am grateful to my friends at the University of Tennessee Press, particularly Cynthia Maude-Gembler, who worked closely with me from the very beginning. I also acknowledge with appreciation the index by Lisa Friend and frontispiece illustration by Rudolph Wendelin, both caring people.

One final retrospective thought. On February 15, 1959, *Parade* magazine, the Sunday supplement, published an article of mine, "What's Happening to Our Shoreline?" Two days later Senator Richard L. Neuberger, of Oregon, introduced the article in the *Congressional Record*. There was nothing unusual about that— congressmen load the appendix to the *Record* with all kinds of relevancies and irrelevancies—but Richard Neuberger was a man I much admired as a writer with a cause who made his mark in public life. Moreover, in his remarks Senator Neuberger said he was introducing the article in tribute to a former Oregon governor, Oswald West, who still lived in retirement in Portland at the age of eighty-five. The point was that Oswald West, as governor from 1911 to 1915, kept one of the most beautiful seacoasts on earth from being exploited for private greed and gain. He saw to it that the law of riparian rights safeguarded the three-hundred-mile Oregon shoreline for perpetual public benefit, rather than permitting it to be devoured for commercial uses. "That this shore of white sandy beaches and timbered headlands has not been defiled or looted," Senator Neuberger declared, "is due to the foresight, vision and courage of ex-Governor Oswald West." I was struck then, and have been over and over ever since, with the abundant individual opportunity to serve the public good through foresight, vision and courage.

Part 1

In the Southern Mountains

Chapter 1

Pisgah:
Dawn of American Forestry

I love to stand on the beautifully landscaped terrace of George
Vanderbilt's colossal chateau and admire the scene of the Blue Ridge
Mountains sweeping westward to join the Great Smokies. Then I
conjure the youthful, wealthy Vanderbilt standing at the same spot
years ago and saying softly, "All this, that my eye can see, is mine."

One would think today that he chose to acquire this mountain
kingdom because it was forested as a forest should be, wooded to the
summit of Mount Pisgah, and, in his time, free of dwellings built by
any other man.

But it was not that way.

When he came here this land was composed of many holdings,
largely impoverished farms and logging sites. In many places it was
overgrazed by cattle, overcut by lumbermen, burned, slashed and
badly eroded.

Then the theory of forestry was placed into practice, for the first
time anywhere in the United States. Most trees which now grace the
view from the terrace were planted. Others were cut with a plan to
replace them with a new generation of trees, as had never been done
before.

This was the chosen design of George Washington Vanderbilt,
grandson of Commodore Cornelius Vanderbilt and consequently one
of the world's richest young men. He arrived here in Asheville, in
the western corner of North Carolina, in 1890, after considering

From *Whose Woods These Are—The Story of the National Forests* (Garden City,
N.Y.: Doubleday, 1962; Boulder, Colo.: Westview, 1984).

many locations on which to build a great country home. He desired one that would compare with the chateaux at Chambord and Blois, surrounded by a landed estate of equal grandeur that would match the Black Forest.

It was not a matter of calculated ostentation. George Vanderbilt had no need to prove his wealth, although some of the one-room cabin dwelling mountaineers believed the richest man in the world had come to settle in their midst, in his thousand-foot long castle, deliberately to show how poor they really were. But such incongruity worked both ways. One Negro farmer, owner of a small place in the center of the estate, refused to sell out for many times the value of his land. "I have no objection," he would calmly and repeatedly advise the land agents, "to Mr. Vanderbilt as a neighbor."

Vanderbilt was slender, wore a well-trimmed black mustache that made him look like a Frenchman, and was still a bachelor in his early days at Asheville. His primary interests were not hunting, fishing or ladies. As an aesthete of means, he devoted himself to literature, interior design and landscape architecture. Thus, he sought to create a proper environment for his collections of furniture and furnishings, of tapestries, paintings and books. For his estate, he wanted formal gardens close at hand; an arboretum; then naturalistic landscaping; a model farm of the finest domestic animals, and, finally, covering most of his 120,000 acres, a forest in which timber would be managed and harvested, and game protected. He named it Biltmore, from *Bildt*, the Dutch town from which the family's forebears came, and *more*, an old English word for rolling, upland country.

To lay out the estate Vanderbilt engaged Frederick Law Olmsted, the slight, lame genius then at the very peak of his career in landscape architecture. Though most associated with the design of public parks, including Central Park, New York, and university grounds, it was he who recommended that forest management be instituted here. To develop the practical plan, he advised Vanderbilt to engage young Gifford Pinchot, lately returned from his study of forestry in Europe and eager to prove it would work in America.

Pinchot arrived in 1891. Initially, he found, the estate covered about 7,000 acres of rolling hills and bottomland on both sides of the

Conscience of a Conservationist

French Broad River. It was composed of some fifty small farms and ten country places which had been owned by impoverished Southern landed aristocracy. The condition of tree growth was very poor. There were defective, fungus-ridden shortleaf pine and remnants of chestnuts, which must have been the leading hardwood in earlier times. But most had been killed by forest fires set by farmers to improve their pastures.

Then Vanderbilt purchased other land in the mountains, including Mount Pisgah, over a mile high, which someone had named for the Biblical mountain. ("Get thee to the top of Pisgah," Moses was told, "and lift up thine eyes.") This was to be a great wildlife preserve at a time when there were no game laws to protect wildlife in North Carolina, when deer herds were decimated by uncontrolled hunting with dogs, unregulated timber cutting and repeated burning. Vanderbilt stocked the woods with deer and turkey, and the streams with trout. Their descendants are still thriving. Elk and buffalo were brought, too, but they are all gone. Four game protectors, or wardens, like those of the Black Forest, were hired to tend about 25,000 acres each, cutting trails through the laurel for access and keeping poachers out—when possible. Vanderbilt also built a handsome lodge at Buckspring, on the slope of Mount Pisgah, in the style of a Black Forest hunting lodge. The walls of the lodge were hewn and built from a thousand immense chestnut logs; a wagon road four miles long had to be completed first to haul them up from the valley. The lodge remained in family hands until recent years, when it was presented to the Blue Ridge Parkway, which now runs along this right-of-way. For a time the Park Service considered transforming it into a museum, but decided it would be too expensive a project.

Where the western North Carolina forest had not been cut it was a wonderland to delight the most learned of botanists and the most unlearned of travelers. Flowers and shrubs were everywhere, in the densest woods, the open clearings and on the treeless, tangled heath balds of the higher mountaintops. In early May, after gradual spring thawing of winter's chill, the pent-up forest would come rapidly into bloom. Dogwood arrived to brighten the barren woods, like a milky way, with its profusion of white blossoms. The four large, petallike leaves—chalky white, sometimes pink—surround the true flowers, a small bouquet of greenish white or yellow. The moist ground beneath the dogwood would turn white, too, with snow trillium, the flower of the trinity, bearing three leaflets, three green sepals and three petals, and the curious local name of "Stinking Willy." Another early flower was the pink azalea, which the mountaineers called wild honeysuckle; the blossoms do resemble those of the honeysuckle vine but are larger and more vivid. Soon they were joined by the blazing flame, or fire, azalea, which William Bartram described as "the most gay and brilliant flowering shrub yet known." He said that a long time ago, but anyone who has seen the brilliant Southern Appalachian springtime show of these tall and vigorous shrubs, with their clusters of large, trumpet-shaped orange or red flowers, would agree it is still true.

There were flowers in the branches of tall trees, too. By mid-May the clustered creamy-white blossoms, long, thin and ever erect, of the Fraser magnolia studded the mountain hollows. This giant of magnolias, growing to eighty feet tall, was called the "cucumber tree" by the mountain people because of its small cucumberlike fruit, which swells and opens to scatter reddish seeds. Although magnolias are generally found in warm, humid climates, the hardy cucumber tree adapted itself to the coolness of the mountains.

To the exploring botanist and early forester the genius of the Southern Highlands was in the incredible variety of its vegetation. Here the Fraser magnolia of the South was found thriving on the same mountainside as the red spruce of Canadian forests. Professor Asa Gray, of Harvard, said he encountered a greater number of indigenous trees within the thirty miles west of Asheville than could be observed in traveling from England clear across Europe to Turkey, or from the Atlantic Coast to the Rocky Mountains. On dry, exposed slopes at low and middle elevations, Professor Gray met scarlet and black oaks and pines, with some sourwood, black gum and locust. In sheltered coves, with depth of soil, below 4,500 feet, he found America's great hardwood timber tree, the fast-growing chestnut, with trunk diameters of nine and ten feet, together with oaks, yellow poplar, buckeye, basswood, ash, sugar maple, beech and cherry. Along streams, lower slopes and ridges up to 5,000 feet was the hemlock forest, with a mingling of maples, birches, beech, yellow poplar and holly. At higher elevations he journeyed through the northern hardwood forest, mantled in New England species like yellow birch, mountain ash and red maple, into an island of green Canadian vegetation dominated by red spruce and Fraser fir, or balsam.

The botanist and forester both recognized the great variety and size of trees was due largely to moist, warm winds from the Gulf of Mexico combining with the highest altitude in the East. Fog and cloud would hang in the gaps, following rainfall, dripping plant-enriching moisture and making these mountains the region of highest precipitation this side of the Pacific Northwest—higher in precipitation than even the Rockies, with their deep snowfall.

In Pisgah Forest, Pinchot found no less than seventy kinds of trees. He and Vanderbilt considered the Pink Beds, a huge bowl of 20,000 acres, a specially favorite section. It derived its name from the pinkish color of the kalmia, or mountain laurel, called ivy by the local folks. They would ride out in late May or June, when the mountains were tufted with white and rosy laurel. On each shrub tiny tea-cuplike blossoms clustered with oval leaves at the ends of the twigs. The exposed ridges from rim to rim overflowed with purplish-pink thickets of rhododendron (laurel, in mountaineer lexicon). Where fire had not taken its toll were giant virgin yellow poplar, oak, hemlock, hickory, black walnut and beech.

In 1892 Pinchot began to make working forestry plans. He felt the first needs were to exclude cattle, reduce the fire hazard and conduct improvement cuttings, harvesting old and unsound trees that were shading out young growth.

He discarded the old way of logging. No longer would any and all trees, including young growth, be cut in order to bring out the desirable ones the easiest way, leaving erosion and fire hazard behind. Henceforth, "conservative lumbering" would be conducted in Pisgah Forest to assure a new generation of trees growing to maturity.

As the first process in selective logging, Pinchot and his assistant cruised the timber and chose the trees they wanted cut. These they blazed (that is, branded) with a marked ax bearing the stamp of a

Circle V. Part of the immediate goal was to have the timber fall where it would harm the future forest the least. They learned that a sound straight tree could be thrown in any direction, a sound leaning tree anywhere in a half circle. Part of the greater problem was to demonstrate that the added cost of caring for the land was relatively small, for Pisgah was to be the proving ground of theoretical forestry for practical lumbermen everywhere in America.

"I knew little more about the conditions necessary for reproducing yellow poplar than a frog knows about football," confessed Pinchot. He was feeling his way in cutting Big Creek, a deep valley directly under Mount Pisgah. There was no previous record in the United States for comparison. But, after poring over his French and German textbooks, he believed natural reproduction would follow cutting if damage from cattle and fire could be minimized. This was contrary to the lumberman's belief that yellow poplar, or any tree, once logged would not grow lumber again. Pinchot was right. He achieved the first known successful effort to gain natural reproduction of a particular tree through scientific forestry: Forty years later he would walk through Big Creek and find yellow poplar growing more abundantly than when he blazed it for cutting.

Lumbering in denser forests, which came a little later, was more complicated. Trees had to be selected with the greatest care, roads had to be built and kept roughly in order. After the better parts of the trunks had been cut into logs and as much of the rest as possible into shingle bolts (round sections of the tree from which shingles are split), they were skidded by mules to the roads, loaded on wagons and hauled to the mill. The mill was a small portable circular with fifty-two-inch saw, operated by a twenty-horsepower steam engine. From the saw the lumber went to the Vanderbilt lumberyard. After the available logs about the mill had been sawed up, the engine was used to run a shingle mill, and when all the bolts had been disposed of, the whole plant was moved to another site. The first year's work in 1893 showed a balance of $1,220—plus a growing forest behind it.

The forestry project grew in size and attracted national attention. Secretary of Agriculture J. Sterling Morton visited Biltmore and observed, "Mr. Vanderbilt has more workers and a larger budget for his forestry projects than I have at my disposal for the whole Department of Agriculture." Young men attracted to forestry as a career came to take their places as Pinchot's assistants. Among them was Olmsted's own son, Fritz; instead of following his father into landscape architecture, he followed the magnetic Pinchot into the Forest Service.

Once the Pisgah project was well underway, Pinchot elected to set forth to conquer other fields, continuing here only as a consulting forester. In 1895 he brought in his successor, Carl Alwin Schenck, as chief forester to manage the lumber operations, experimental areas and planting.

Schenck, who became a legend in the mountains, acted and dressed the Prussian. He was slender, wore a Kaiser Wilhelm mustache. He sported a German forest-service uniform, polished leather boots and spurs, and a feathered Tyrolean hat. It was inevitable that he came to be called The Kaiser.

Schenck was a logging forester first and foremost. "The best forestry," he said, "is the forestry that pays most." This was the basis on which he managed the 112,000 acres of Vanderbilt land under his charge. Possibly he was right, for his time, considering that "conservative forestry" was yet to be sold to the lumber industry.

"Naturally, forestry must be remunerative," he said, "if it is to exist anywhere on a large scale. To that end, the products of forestry, the trees, must command a price sufficiently high to make their production remunerative, and the future of tree investments must look bright and must be reasonably free from reckless competition, forest fires and other hazards.

"Is forestry itself not a business? If it is not, it has no room in a country as businesslike as is the United States. And where in the world of the woods is lumbering not a legitimate part of forestry?"

Despite these commercial pronouncements, he conducted painstaking experiments in forest regeneration. He started in 1895 on the steepest slope, which had been cleared for farming sixty years before and subsequently abandoned. This area and many other worn-out fields, pastures and orchards became outdoor laboratories in which Schenck tested twenty species of hardwoods and twelve of softwoods.

One badly eroded plot, for example, was transformed into a

plantation of three species of pine (shortleaf, Norway and Virginia). In another, he tested Douglas-fir, Colorado blue spruce, European spruce, silver fir and white pine and learned that white pine was superior to all in that setting. Elsewhere, in the midst of a hardwood plantation, he planted 5,000 white pines, the first two-year-old seedlings on American soil. And on another plot he tried alternating two-year-old white pines raised at Biltmore with four-year-old white pines brought from Germany.

In 1908 he invited lumbermen, foresters, state officials, botanists and newsmen to a three-day Biltmore Forest Fair, showing the results of his work in sixty experimental plots. Eighty-five came. It was a large and enthusiastic rally. "Many of the visitors declared that they have learned more about forestry during the past days than they could possibly have learned in a lifetime had this opportunity not been afforded them," reported the Asheville *Gazette-News.* And Schenck, of course, was proud to show that his lumbering operations were profitable.

Schenck trained many future leaders of his profession at the Biltmore Forest School, which he operated from 1898 to 1913. Students came from all over the country and found him an inspiring teacher. He would lecture three or four hours a day at the little schoolhouse in the Pink Beds. For the remainder of many days the students would be strung out on horseback behind him, traveling full speed while he tended to his duties as forest manager, which he explained to them at frequent stops. The Vanderbilt estate covered 200 square miles and apparently Schenck, with his coattails flapping, was determined to lead his saddle-weary embryo foresters over every mile of it.

The curriculum, however, covered a wide range. Dr. Homer House taught botany. Government and university lecturers came to speak on timber preservation, geology, entomology, zoology, climatology, economics and law. Field studies included forest nurseries, transplanting, surveying, logging, furniture manufacture, fish and wildlife and, of necessity, how to kill and skin rattlesnakes.

Schenck solicited the support of lumbermen for his school but they turned instead to the Yale School of Forestry (originally endowed, ironically, by Gifford Pinchot's parents) and other universities, which thoroughly frustrated the Prussian.

In time, he and Pinchot developed sharp differences. Schenck claimed the "infantile maladies" of American forestry were due largely to agitation led by Pinchot in establishing a distinction between forestry and lumbering. But possibly their primary point of difference was in their judgment of the human species. Recording a trip they made together in the Pink Beds, where they found a number of farmers squatting in the most fertile sections, Schenck wrote, "It dawned upon me that the real owner of Pisgah Forest was not George W. Vanderbilt, but these mountaineers, who were using his property for farming, pasturing, and hunting at their own pleasure. Pinchot apparently took these inroads on the rights of the proprietor for granted. To my own European feeling they were equal to theft and robbery."

Pinchot, on the other hand, noted that Schenck, "being a German with official training, had far less understanding of the mountaineers than he had of the mountains and woods. He thought of them as peasants."

Pinchot was endowed with a consummate faith in people. It was the source of his strength, in the same sense as with Winston Churchill, who would write, "I was brought up in my father's house to believe in democracy. 'Trust the people.' That was his message." Thus, Pinchot, who had heard such a message, too, believed in the mountaineers, despite their impoverishment, backwardness and sheer abuse of the land.

In a way, these mountain folk, through their very mistreatment of the land, were responsible for establishment of national forests in the East.

Many a mountaineer and his family slept and dwelt in a one-room cabin, which he had built himself, alongside a stream, hugging the mountainside against the wind. He believed in the family as the all-important unit in social life and might have had ten children within this single room. The cabin had one door and no windows, or at best an open window covered with split boards. Within, an open fireplace served as cookstove and furnace. Homespun was the common wear and anyone under the age of nineteen in shoes was either moving to the city or getting married. Hookworm, typhoid and tuberculosis were rife through hills and hollows.

These people, who lived in isolated poverty for generations, started drifting down before the Revolutionary War and in the early 1800s. Some were Scotch-Irish Presbyterians, who left Pennsylvania to find religious and civil liberty. Others came from Maryland and Virginia at a time when those colonies were growing more tobacco than was profitable and only the cheapest kind of labor, that is, slave labor, could make it pay. The yeoman farmer could not compete and drifted farther and farther into the southerly backwoods.

They brought a manner of speech with them, a direct carry-over of old English, almost as it was spoken in the times of Elizabeth and Shakespeare. It survived into our time, a combination of a language hundreds of years old with the freshness of the raw frontier. A bag was a "poke," a comical person an "antic," a sweetheart a "donna," and when a man gave notice of a meeting by word of mouth he "norated." They spoke with a lyric softness and utility of words. "I thought shorely undoubtedly of a sartin hit war so," one might say. Or, "I didn't fault him for hit."

The mountaineer lived off the land, hunting deer, bear, rabbit, squirrel, turkey, and fishing in the streams. He used forest wood for building his log cabin, for his fuel, the butt of his rifle, his furniture and the cover of his still. But he knew little, or absolutely nothing ,about care of the land, as he cleared the mountainside to raise corn, fatten and feed his hogs, cattle and mules. After the Civil War, he tried tobacco. It required rich new ground and for a while paid high prices, till the market dropped and the ground gave way, seamed with gullies.

"Ordinary farming on these mountain slopes cannot exist permanently and should never exist at all," Secretary of Agriculture James Wilson warned in his report of 1901, which Theodore Roosevelt transmitted to Congress with a strong recommendation for national Forest Reserves in the Southeast.

"No more than 10 percent of the land of this region has a surface slope of less than 10 degrees (approximately 2 feet in 10), while 24 percent of it has been cleared," Secretary Wilson continued. "In this region land with slopes exceeding this cannot be successfully cultivated for any considerable time, because its surface is rapidly washed into the rivers below by the heavy rains, and the same agency leaches out and carries to the sea its more soluble and fertile ingredients."

Already the valley lands had largely been cleared, and the farmers were advancing up the mountain slopes, clearing patches nearly to the summits. They planted a field in corn, grain, then grass, then within five or ten years abandoned it to weeds and gullies. A forest which took centuries to grow perished in less than a decade. Soil which accumulated over a thousand years was cleared, cultivated, abandoned and on the downward road to the sea. From one of these thousands of cleared fields more soil was sometimes removed by a single heavy rain than during the preceding centuries while it was densely forested.

As the streams flowed toward the sea they removed the soil of valley farms, too; they widened and plowed new channels across the fields, damaging thousands of acres of the most productive valley land.

"It is only a question of time, to be measured not in centuries but in years," the Secretary warned, "when, unless this policy is changed, there will be no forests in this region except on the small remnants—say 10 percent of the whole—where the mountain slopes are too precipitous and rocky to make the cultivation of the land possible, even by an Appalachian mountaineer and his hoe."

This point contributed to the ultimate enactment of the Weeks Law in 1911. For ten years Secretary Wilson's report, in which Pinchot's hand was strongly evident, was a principal source of arguments to bring the national forests east. It proposed to protect the mountain slopes of the Southern Appalachians within a Forest Reserve, in this way safeguarding the valleys and gentler slopes for cultivation by the native farmer, who would continue to own the bottomlands. Secretary Wilson called it a national problem since, "The dangers growing out of the policy now in force are national in character, as are also the benefits of the policy now advised."

On passage of the Weeks Law, this area outside Asheville was established as the Pisgah Purchase Unit. Five years later two other units, the Mount Mitchell and Unaka, were merged with it. It was not the first National Forest in the East, but was the first one composed of land not originally in the public domain. That is, here for the first time the Federal Government invoked its new authority to purchase private land for the protection of river headwaters and define it as National Forest.

Within Pisgah National Forest, which extends over an area roughly one hundred miles long and forty miles wide, the most historic section is the Pisgah Ranger District. More than half its 160,000 acres were given to the government by Mrs. George W. Vanderbilt in 1916, following her husband's death. The remainder was purchased over the years until the late 1930s, mostly from lumber companies, which felt they were quite through with the land after once logging it. The largest tract was acquired from the Sunburst Lumber Company; the National Forest obtained 36,000 acres, while other land and the mill at the town of Sunburst were bought by the Champion Fibre and Paper Company, which is generally highly regarded for its forestry practices.

Today second-growth timber is harvested on land once managed by Gifford Pinchot and Carl Alwin Schenck, without damaging the forest or really interfering with the enjoyment of visitors, who total over a million yearly on the Pisgah District. During May and June it becomes a vast flower garden, rhododendron and azalea, immense kalmia, dogwood, redbud and cucumber magnolia blooming mile after mile. During summer clear, cold mountain streams with numerous cascades and tumbling falls add to the forest beauty, while the cool woods offer a haven to campers. And in autumn the purple haze and blaze of color in the foliage form a panorama to rival New England.

Speaking of camping, or of sight-seeing, one of the choice spots is in the Pink Beds, just off Route 276. It is about eighteen miles from Asheville via the valley of the French Broad River and about the same distance from Brevard. A plaque marks the site of that first forestry school started by Dr. Schenck. You are almost at the base of Looking Glass Rock, a massive forested boulder and a landmark of these mountains. Within a couple of miles you can picnic or swim at Sliding Rock Falls, where youngsters love to slide over the watery rocks. Also nearby, Looking Glass Falls cascades 276 feet over a rocky precipice.

Here, too, you are just below Wagon Road Gap, joining one of the newest links of the Blue Ridge Parkway, which follows the crest of the Blue Ridge Range through highly scenic parts of the National Forest as it journeys westward to the Great Smoky Mountains.

Crossing the Parkway onto Route 112, you will reach Frying Pan Campground, over a mile above sea level, the best spot for cool nights and mountain hiking.

If you are not a camper, there is still a place for you, and a fine place, too, at Pisgah National Forest Inn, on the slope of Pisgah Ledge, elevation 5,120 feet. In lieu of tennis, golf or swimming are the restful atmosphere, excellent American food, prepared by Leslie and Leda Kirschner, and leisurely walking trails through wildflowers and woodland. From here you can climb the summit of Mount Pisgah and see the world—well, five states, anyway.

When the Vanderbilt land was acquired by the Forest Service, it was designated as a National Game Preserve and remained closed to hunting from 1916 to 1932 in order to stock up deer herds. At one period the Forest Service ran a "fawn farm," raising about 200 fawns yearly on bottle feeding. As the herds grew in number, Pisgah deer were made available to game departments in other Southern states and their descendants are now scrambling over the countryside from Virginia to Oklahoma. Since 1932, game hunts have been held for deer, bear and smaller animals every fall, except during a four-year period when a severe epidemic of shipping fever killed about half the deer herd.

Mrs. Vanderbilt shared her husband's interest in the mountains and was drawn to the problems of the mountain people. Observing that most homes had looms, she inspired the establishment of Biltmore Industries in order to widen the opportunities open to them. Their weaving proved successful not only as a craft but as a business venture which is still thriving. Another pioneer in stimulating pride and profit in craftsmanship was Miss Frances Goodrich, a social worker. Early in the century she started Allanstand Cottage in Asheville to bring "healthful excitement" to mountaineer ladies. It became evident to the people, who had hand-hewn and hand-made almost everything they owned, that they could not only use and swap such products, but sell them. Other shops arose. In 1930 the Southern Highland Handicraft Guild was formed to preserve the better traditions and to encourage creative use of materials. It has done these jobs well. Allanstand in Asheville is the Guild's chief display and marketing center; you will not go wrong shopping there for jewelry, wood carving, pottery, wrought iron or weaving. For five days every summer, at the Craftsman's Fair in Asheville, craftsmen set up their looms, benches and wheels en masse to whittle, sew and carve in full public view.

There is another mountain craft deftly practiced, though not in such full view. The character of the country and the character of some of these talented folk being what they are, western North Carolina has ranked for many years high among the moonshine centers of the universe. This probably started when a few of the mountain men considered the yield of their steep land in bushels was mighty poor and decided a measurement in gallons would be more profitable. Or when others allowed that, while they didn't dislike work, exactly, outwitting the law would surely add zest to it. Moonshine, being tax free, has a flourishing market. It costs less than storebought whisky, if you can stand the taste.

Is moonshine brewed in our national forest? Ted Seeley, who is now ranger of the Pisgah District, won't say that it is, but won't say it isn't, either. However, during the thirties, one still was discovered by the district ranger about every two weeks. In those days, before galvanized iron pots and portable oil burners, revenuers would track their way in by following telltale wood smoke curling up from the forest. But the ranger (whose functions do not include revenuing) had a silent, unwritten agreement with his constituents not to wreck a still unless he had to. In a way, he hesitated about interfering with the economic life of the community; besides, he knew that his moonshiners might fire the woods if he acted rashly. So whenever the ranger discovered a still he would tack up a sign, "Get this still out of here within ten days."

Speaking of present practices, let us not overlook the Carolina caged-bear routine. Gracing the foreground of the historic gateway to Pisgah National Forest on Route 276 is a roadside souvenir and refreshment stand. Here you can buy a Coke, hand it to a bear through the bars of his cage and watch him drink it. The purpose of his presence is to attract your interest and trade.

Western North Carolina has a variety of such crude attractions. One is the reptile "garden" on Route 19, which everyone who loves wild creatures should see—not because it is good, but to observe how the animals, assorted scraggly deer, a bear and snakes, are cared for. There are the "Twin Yona" (Cherokee for twin bear) caged on the roadside in the Indian Reservation between the National Forest and Great Smoky Mountains National Park. And like displays of wildlife before gift shops and gasoline stations in Maggie Valley.

How are these creatures captured? And how are they cared for? I asked the State of North Carolina for its policy on such things and received a copy of the application for a permit to trap an animal, along with the regulations for holding it legally in captivity. "North Carolina law prohibits the taking of cub bears at any time or in any manner," the State Wildlife Resources Commission advised. "Most of our roadside bears are purchased from Indians who can take them legally on their reservation. The sentiment of the Commission is strongly against keeping bears or any other wild creatures in captivity—outside a zoo." (Responsible persons in the Smokies, however, seriously question whether the Cherokee Indians are indeed responsible—or simply are the easiest to blame.)

I discussed this with the Humane Society of the United States. It considers this frightening handful of gas stations, gift shops and zoo-owning North Carolinians as the worst in the country for mistreatment of wild creatures.

Enough of this unpleasantness. Write your Congressman. Write the governor, if you live in North Carolina.

Let us proceed to the Biltmore estate, the remainder of the vast Vanderbilt holdings, 12,000 acres of sheer Southern and worldly glory, commingled to form a showpiece of America. The approach road winds three miles through planted pine, hemlock and hardwoods, rhododendron and kalmia, landscaped by Frederick Law Olmsted. Before the house was built a three-mile spur had first to be erected from Biltmore station to transport construction materials to the site. Then a thousand workmen, including many artisans from Europe, were engaged; they worked five years, 1890 to 1895, cutting and fitting the Indiana limestone and executing the detailed carvings which rise to the peaked slate roofs and lofty chimneys. On the interior, the 250-room house contains a treasure of paintings, tapestries, statuary, porcelain, furniture from early Renaissance through Empire, and portraits by John Singer Sargent of personalities associated with this house.

Part of the estate is occupied by Biltmore Dairy Farms with its

1,200 purebred Jersey cattle. George Vanderbilt was interested in improved methods of breeding and brought the finest stock from the Isle of Jersey. At one time sheep, horses, chickens and pigs were raised here, too.

The Biltmore grounds were managed by Chauncey Delos Beadle, who came to work under Olmsted in 1890 and remained for sixty years as superintendent of the estate. His artistic touch is most evident in the Italian garden and its formal aquatic pools, the four-acre English walled garden, and the azalea garden, with specimens which he collected all over the world.

These are probably the finest gardens in America, and perhaps in the whole world. Yes, we are dealing in superlatives. And if the sun must set on these Appalachians, let it set gently while we stand on the terrace, bordered with wisteria and trumpet creeper, and admire the view to the south and west of Pisgah and its healthy, growing forest.

Chapter 2

Why the Rockefeller $5,000,000?

Franklin D. Roosevelt, the President whose physical infirmity prevented it, would have loved to hike, climb, and romp in the Smoky Mountains. Although a subtle and sophisticated man, he treasured the simplicities of nature and the out-of-doors, as even the casual visitor can tell by learning of his way of life at Hyde Park, New York, and especially at Warm Springs, Georgia. He took a considerable interest in the Smokies and had an idea about establishing a herd of roe deer from Europe, which he continued to suggest almost until the outbreak of World War II.

The President agreed to participate in ceremonies officially dedicating the new national park. Over a period of many months tentative dates were scheduled, then canceled because of depressing international developments. In June 1940, word was received that the event might have to be carried out on a few hours' notice, but in early August the President himself suggested that he would like to dedicate the park on Labor Day.

The Roosevelt entourage arrived by car from Chattanooga, where the President had dedicated Chickamauga Dam. It was a hot drive through the valley that had once been the Overhill Cherokee country, and then it was cool in the mountains, almost too cool for summer clothes. The presidential party was three quarters of an hour late arriving at Newfound Gap, which Harold L. Ickes, the tempera-

From *Strangers in High Places: The Story of The Great Smoky Mountains*
(Garden City, N.Y.: Doubleday, 1966, Univ. of Tennessee Press, 1980).

mental Secretary of the Interior, blamed on the sad miscalculation of whoever had made up the itinerary.

Ickes was there and so was Arno B. Cammerer, whom he disliked intensely. Senator Kenneth McKellar was there and so was Superintendent J. Ross Eakin, whom *he* detested. Governor Prentice Cooper, of Tennessee, and Governor Clyde Hoey, of North Carolina, were there. Newton B. Drury, scholarly San Franciscan long the champion of the redwood forests, who had already succeeded Arno B. Cammerer as Director of the National Park Service, was there. So were Colonel David Chapman and Mrs. Willie Davis. (Her husband and Mark Squires were dead.) Ten thousand cars rode up the mountain bumper to bumper, carrying a tremendous throng of 25,000 to hear the President and see the park officially opened.

The ceremonies were held at the crescent-shaped masonry wall and platform, straddling the boundary line between Tennessee and North Carolina, where the bronze plaque bears this inscription:

> For the permanent enjoyment of the people—
> This Park was given One-half By the Peoples and States
> of North Carolina and Tennessee and by the United States
> of America and One-half In Memory of Laura Spelman
> Rockefeller by The Laura Spelman Rockefeller Memorial
> Founded by Her Husband John D. Rockefeller.

The minister who delivered the invocation irritated Ickes. The Secretary became nervous and impatient. The reverend continued to warm up to his subject before the illustrious audience and the vast crowd. "One of those pests who thinks that the whole nation wants to hear him harangue God ad lib," was how Ickes described him later. Finally Ickes could contain himself no longer. He touched the minister on the arm and brought him to a halt. Worst of all, he had to cut his own remarks to four minutes. The two Governors spoke, and the President delivered his speech on the international situation and its threat to American liberties. Then the official party descended the mountain into Knoxville and pulled out by train. It took the 10,000 cars until dark to disperse, despite all efforts to control and channel the flow of traffic.

Only John D. Rockefeller, Jr., was not there. He was the missing witness.

Although invited to attend, he had declined politely, writing to Secretary Ickes as follows (on July 11, 1939, when plans for the dedication were first being formed):

Dear Mr. Secretary:

Since I am just leaving for an extended absence, I greatly regret that it will not be possible for me to be present at the dedication of the Great Smoky Mountains National Park in which important ceremony you kindly invited me to participate. That the President of the United States is planning to honor the occasion with his presence is indicative of the high value which he places upon this newest park. That the governors of Tennessee and North Carolina are also to take part in the program is peculiarly fitting in view of what they and the commonwealths have done so generously and so untiringly, to make possible this noble result.

As president of The Laura Spelman Rockefeller Memorial when it pledged five million dollars to the Great Smoky Mountains National Park and as the son of my mother in whose memory the gift was made, I rejoice profoundly in the opening of this great area of outstanding natural beauty for the permanent enjoyment of the people of these United States. May the beautiful spirit of my mother, who was a loyal and devoted wife, a wise and loving parent, and an earnest Christian woman, descend upon those who visit these mountain fastnesses, who find refreshment in the shaded valleys and new courage by the side of the sparkling streams! May the peace of the Father of mankind, the Creator of all this beauty, to Whose service my mother's life was dedicated, dwell in their hearts and make beautiful their lives.

Very sincerely,
John D. Rockefeller, Jr.

"You see, this was the extent to which he felt that he should participate. He did not want the spotlight," said Kenneth Chorley when he showed me this letter from the files at the Rockefeller headquarters in New York. Chorley was Rockefeller's close associate for forty years, and served as president of Colonial Williamsburg, as emissary to the two states of the Smokies, and as a confidant. "He didn't feel entitled to it. He was the most modest human being I've ever known."

I never met John D. Rockefeller, Jr., and therefore have been unable to ask him what he was thinking when he decided to go ahead and contribute $5,000,000 to the cause. Once, at Williamsburg, I overheard a visitor comment to his wife, "Rocka-fella could afford to do all this, with his millions. He had to spend that money somewhere and didn't care where." Well, that was one theory expounded by a curbstone expert.

Writing about Rockefeller, or any man of immense wealth, is difficult, because you find yourself currying favor with his establishment or currying antifavor with the disestablishment (from the servilely subsidized to the carpingly critical, as James Warner Bellah once characterized the range of writing about the Du Ponts). But I want to treat John D., Jr., in terms of the Great Smokies and areas related to them, without concern for where he got his money, whether he had too much of it, or where he spent the rest of it.

This is not easy either, for he has often been dealt with and portrayed as an institution rather than as a human being. His own phraseology doesn't make it easier. The purpose of his benefactions to Acadia National Park in Maine was to make accessible "one of the greatest views of the world." When he made a gift of Forest Hill, outside Cleveland, it was so the people of the community could enjoy, "as I did during the happy days of my childhood and youth, the beautiful area comprised within the park." When he came away from the Redwoods, he was "speechless with admiration at anything so beautiful as the forests we came through today." He gave funds to preserve Linville Falls in North Carolina because it was "that beautiful area." He gave the $5,000,000 for the Smokies in memory of "the beautiful spirit of my mother."

He was a man who indeed felt a natural love for beauty, in architecture, painting, nature, and the landscape, a love that he wanted to share. I have seen this demonstrated time and again in the course of my travels over the years—in the Smoky Mountains and Acadia, the Grand Tetons, the Redwoods in California, Williamsburg, the Cloisters in Manhattan, Tarrytown on the Hudson, the old

Baptist Church in Providence, and at Versailles (he contributed millions after World War I to preserve and restore the palace and gardens).

Many places where he expressed his interest in restoration and conservation reflect his personal taste and touch. A Rockefeller road is always built with native material; the borders are landscaped naturally and never look ugly—they're not allowed to. He wanted and had things done right, well ordered, never left raw nor displayed too loudly, but always neatly. He was meticulous to a fault and wanted the national parks to which he contributed kept as clean as his own development at Williamsburg. Once, after fire swept over Bar Harbor and Acadia in 1948, Park Service naturalists wanted to leave the burned and downed timber to serve as a breeding place for insects, which in turn provide food for bird life, but Rockefeller shuddered at the unsightliness and paid to have nature's messiness tidied up. It is also true that he personally selected the site of Jackson Lake Lodge, in the Tetons, though it otherwise would have been located at a less conspicuous setting.

If these incidents indicate flaws in his viewpoint, they were minor flaws, negligible when weighed in the balance. Rockefeller came on the scene with great wealth and clear vision at a time when relatively few Americans were concerned with conservation. He plunged into projects concerning endangered areas, as Chorley recalled, or projects that might never have been undertaken. Sometimes these were daring in size and concept, and stirred fierce opposition. At the same time he was involved with the Smokies, Colonial Williamsburg was just getting started; there he was not interested in restoring a single building in inappropriate surroundings, but in reviving an entire segment of the past. And concurrent with the Smokies and Williamsburg, he was active in Jackson Hole, Wyoming, where he bought up 30,000 acres between 1926 and 1950, despite the wrath of local ranchers, and assured preservation of one of the most beautiful mountain valleys in the world.

As for the Smokies, he didn't write a check for $5,000,000 as a contribution to a worthy charity. He knew exactly what he was buying—it was virgin primeval wilderness to be safeguarded for generations hence—and he insisted through Cammerer, then director of the National Park Service, that the states block timber cutting before it went too far.

He respected North Carolina and Tennessee. Maybe they wouldn't have been able to raise their matching funds, or sell their bonds, without the stimulus of his $5,000,000 gift, but it was overwhelming to him that the people of the two states should have the foresight and courage, in the midst of a depression, to spend their money for the national park and for their children's children.

In short, above all others involved in the Smokies, John D. Rockefeller, Jr., who could not, because of his immense wealth, have experienced much intimate contact with the common man, demonstrated his faith in the people and faith in the future. He believed in them both. In his own way, these ideas must have been in his thinking when he decided to contribute to the cause.

"No fuss and feathers about young John D.," wrote O. O. McIntyre, in his newspaper column (in the *New York American*) of October 8, 1930. "He walks up the avenue window-shopping every evening he is in town to his home around the corner in West Fifty-fourth Street. Many in his neighborhood do not recognize him. His home is not particularly pretentious. Around his doorway or loitering nearby are always two guardsmen in plain clothes. Mr. Rockefeller often stops to talk to a street sweeper in his block. He is seldom seen leaving his home after dinner.

"Those who know say John D., Jr., is the most dutiful of sons. He phones his father wherever he may be daily. He visits the family home at Tarrytown twice a week and father and son take long walks together about the Pocantico Hills estate."

He had a fixation about his parents. He was trustee, not owner, of the Rockefeller fortune—that was his father's money. Everything he did was in the name of his father, or of his mother, as in the case of the Smokies.

He developed his lifelong interest in landscaping as a boy on the family summer estate outside Cleveland (which he later presented as a city park). When he was sixteen, Rockefeller became involved in clearing underbrush, resurfacing roads, and planting scores of trees. If he had had to work for a living, he might have become a landscape architect (much later he was awarded honorary membership in the

American Society of Landscape Architects) or a nurseryman. He surprised the park naturalist in the Smokies, Arthur Stupka, with his knowledge of trees and shrubs and his close examination of the veins of leaves. Not so the people who worked for him at Williamsburg. They became accustomed to his recognizing trees not only by species, but as individuals; whenever he visited Williamsburg he could tell where a tree had been cut and wanted to know the reason.

Rockefeller's first association with national parks was at Acadia. He was among the elite Bar Harbor summer residents who responded to George B. Dorr's appeal to preserve Mount Desert Island, leading to the establishment of Sieur de Mont National Monument in 1916. He not only donated 2,700 acres of land, but offered to build and maintain a road system. Acadia was a bit of prelude to the Smokies, for it had been well scarred with resort developments, logging mills, and a cog railroad to the summit of Mount Cadillac, all of which are gone today.

However, it was his meeting with Horace Albright in the summer of 1924 that marked his full entry into philanthropy for conservation.

He had contacted Stephen Mather, though he didn't know him personally, asking for aid in planning a tour of the western parks with his three oldest sons, John, Laurance, and Nelson. Mather instructed the superintendents to make themselves available, but to restrain themselves from talking about their financial problems unless the gentleman of means asked specific questions. This, apparently, was precisely what John D. had in mind. At Mesa Verde, the shrine of the cliff dwellers, he asked Superintendent Jesse Nusbaum a few questions and before he knew it, he was giving money to help establish a park museum because Congress had given nothing to house and display the treasures of the ancient culture.

Then he proceeded on to Yellowstone. In those early years Horace Albright was there each summer as park superintendent, then he would return to Washington to pick up legal and administrative problems of the whole park system as Assistant Director under Mather. At the moment of their meeting before the railroad depot at Gardiner, Montana, John III, eighteen, was recording in a notebook the amounts paid in tips to Pullman porters, while Nelson, the future governor of New York, then sixteen, was engaged in helping porters transfer baggage from the train to Yellowstone Park buses for a group of tourists. As the superintendent guided the Rockefellers over the park during the next few days, John D., Jr., was disturbed to observe timber that had been slashed years before, in the 1870s and '80s, to open the way for park roads, stacked and rotting along their route. He later corresponded with Albright about whether it could be cleaned up, and how much it would cost, and in the next three years contributed $50,000 toward a tidier Yellowstone.

In 1926 he returned to the West to have another look around, but perhaps to see Albright more than the sights. They began their long period of association based on mutual respect and trust. "I felt close to Mr. Rockefeller from that year until he died in 1960," Horace Albright told me. "He regarded me as his adviser on conservation problems and affairs and I often had visits with him in his office and at lunch." (Albright left the Government in 1933 to become general manager, then president, of the U. S. Potash Company, with headquarters one building removed from Rockefeller's office in Rockefeller Center.) Rockefeller was reticent, cautious, alone. For all his wealth and generosity he could be cautious with his money, too. When his wife wanted to restore the interior of their house at Williamsburg, he resisted at first. "They can use the money elsewhere," he said. Finally, he gave in but quipped in his wry manner, "Just so you don't take in tourists." Albright had the gift of penetrating with sound advice in questions of principle, policy, and ideals, of suggesting where money must be spent in the right places. In the course of thirty-five years his advice and judgment influenced the expenditure of millions of dollars to acquire historic and natural treasures for the public.

Rockefeller placed his trust in people like Albright. And Chorley, who joined the inner organization as an assistant to Colonel Arthur Woods, educator, industrialist, and first president of Colonial Williamsburg, whom he succeeded when Woods became Herbert Hoover's director of unemployment emergency relief in 1930.

It was in 1924, as the records studied by Chorley show, that Rockefeller became aware of the campaign to establish a national park in the Great Smokies. And it was Willis P. Davis who made a pilgrimage from Knoxville to New York in order to talk with one of

Rockefeller's associates, in the hope of enlisting financial support. Davis went away empty-handed, but later that year Director Mather sent Rockefeller a request to join him in making a contribution toward the expenses of the Appalachian National Park Committee. He contributed $500, as I have written earlier.

"In 1926," according to Chorley, "the treasurer of the Great Smoky Mountains National Park Purchase Fund Campaign wrote Mr. Rockefeller requesting a subscription to express his interest, but the request was declined. Actually, the National Park Service and others interested had told the local people that, if they would meet certain conditions, help would be given them in getting citizens throughout the country to support the effort, and Mr. Rockefeller's declination was doubtless based on the fact that he would be called on in the later effort and therefore was not inclined to contribute at that time."

In August 1927, after the legislatures of North Carolina and Tennessee had taken action to furnish funds, Cammerer wrote to Rockefeller with an eloquent plea. It would require some $9,316,000 to establish the park, he advised, of which $4,950,000 had been raised or pledged. The two states had done all they could—now public-spirited men all over the nation must be counted on for the remaining $4,400,000.

It is possible that Cammerer came to New York for a conference later that year, at Rockefeller's invitation. "Mr. Rockefeller respected Cammerer's judgment highly and liked him personally," recalls Horace Albright. "When it comes to discussing who convinced Mr. Rockefeller of the importance of the project, and who furnished him with the information necessary to make a decision, I feel we must give credit to Cammerer. It was he who did the big job of making financing certain."

Rockefeller at first pledged $1,000,000. He interested Edsel Ford in pledging $50,000. By early 1928 the campaign for public subscriptions had made no other headway; only the Rockefeller and Ford pledges had been received. Then he decided to contribute the whole amount. He would do so through the Laura Spelman Rockefeller Memorial Foundation, a relatively small foundation established by his father. Surely, as Rockefeller said, preserving the beautiful Smokies would have appealed strongly to his mother. At a meeting of his staff in February 1928, he discussed his plans. "Gentlemen, this is something that interests me. I hope it interests you."

The first week of March, Chorley went south to review the precise terms of agreement with the Governors and other officials of both states. The announcement of the gift was made simultaneously in North Carolina and Tennessee on March 6. It was greeted in Knoxville with the sound of whistles and bells throughout the city at 4 p.m. Across the mountains, two days later, the *Raleigh News and Observer* (whose editor, Josephus Daniels, and Rockefeller were in correspondence about the national park) commented thoughtfully: "It must give large satisfaction to the two Rockefellers to make the $5,000,000 donation in the name of wife and mother and thus associate her with the loftiest of God's creations, which for all time will be the resort of those who seek sweet communion with nature."

However, on March 27, still finer words were written by an unforeseen correspondent, the president of the Bank of Lenoir, a North Carolina mountain community.

Dear Mr. Rockefeller:

I note from the papers that the Governor of North Carolina and probably other officials in some way connected with the Great Smoky Mountains National Park have written you in acknowledgement of your recent magnificent contribution to that great project. This you of course expected, but I am wondering if it would not be even more gratifying to you to know of the very deep and sincere appreciation on the part of a warmhearted southern people—the rank and file of a great deal of just plain "everyday folks." It has occurred to the writer that, while this sentiment of gratitude for so munificent a gift exists and is freely expressed among the thousands, it may occur to all too few of them to tell you so, therefore I am, without authority, taking the liberty of acting as spokesman for this individually unknown and un-numbered multitude in conveying to you this expression of unbounded admiration for your generous act.

Very sincerely,
J.H. Beall

The reply was dated March 31:

Dear Mr. Beall:

Your gracious letter of March 27 is received. Nothing in connection with the gift to the Great Smoky Mountain Park in memory of my mother has touched me so deeply as the warm-hearted and sympathetic appreciation of the people of the South of the memorial aspect of this gift. Your letter only emphasizes that appreciation, and in so doing adds to the satisfaction which my father and I feel in the making of this gift.

Please accept my thanks for the friendly spirit which has prompted you to write me so delightful a letter.

Very sincerely,
John D. Rockefeller, Jr.

Having committed himself to the Smokies, Rockefeller decided that summer to go and see the region for himself.

He and his wife stayed at the Mountain View Hotel in Gatlin-burg, attended the First Baptist Church, and visited Cades Cove. It was the first of several visits. After his wife died and he remarried, he took the second Mrs. Rockefeller on a honeymoon trip in 1954, traveling down the Blue Ridge Parkway by motorcar to the Smokies. Always he tried to plan these trips quietly (on his 1924 tour of the western parks he traveled with his sons under his middle name of Davison), with arrangements through Horace Albright and the park superintendents.

Long after he had assured the future of the Smokies, he paid a friendly call in 1950 with his youngest son, David, that cost him $100,000 to acquire a parcel of Blue Ridge scenery he would never see personally.

Grandfather Mountain by then was a lost cause for the Park Service. The Service had hoped to manage it as a unit of the Blue Ridge Parkway, together with Linville Falls, ten miles southeast, where the Linville River pitches over a towering outcrop of rock, then tumbles between the dark walls of Linville Gorge. In the early 1940s, the McRae family, the owners of the mountain, had granted the Government an option to purchase its 5,500 acres for $165,000. Another 14,000 acres was to be transferred from the surrounding

Pisgah National Forest. Under this plan, the 6,700 acres in Linville Gorge were to remain under the Forest Service to be administered as a wilderness area, the first in the East, devoted to a completely primitive environment, with a simple trail system down into the gorge and into side canyons.

True to its ancient policy, Congress would appropriate nothing toward the purchase of Grandfather. True to his tradition, Rockefeller had offered to pay half the required amount, if the other half could be raised through other sources. When the option expired, the McRae family granted a renewal, raising the price to $180,000. Harlan P. Kelsey, the conservation leader who had played a key role in the Appalachian Park study of the 1920s, arrived on the scene and barnstormed North Carolina on a fund-raising drive. Not one cent was pledged in the entire state. "What's wrong with Grandfather the way it is?" Kelsey was asked. "What makes you think they'll spoil it?" Although Asheville people in the twenties had urged Grandfather-Linville as a national park, in the forties they turned their backs on the same cause. Finally, in 1948, the option was canceled, Grandfather no longer was for sale. The finest mountain of the Blue Ridge chain was lost to public ownership, where one day it must properly find its place.

This was not, however, the end for Linville Falls. From New York, Albright telephoned Superintendent Sam P. Weems, of the Blue Ridge Parkway, that Rockefeller wanted to tour the southern mountains on a quiet father-son vacation with David. It was the hope of both Albright and Weems, a man known and admired throughout the mountains, to interest Rockefeller in the appealing beauty of Linville Falls, whose primeval environs had never been logged.

The reservations were made in Weems's name. The first night the Rockefellers and their chauffeur stopped at a hotel in Shenandoah Valley, adjacent to the Parkway in Virginia. The second day they continued south through Roanoke. David was now driving, with his father in the front seat and the chauffeur in the rear—so the park rangers reported by radio to their superintendent. Weems and his chief ranger, E. M. Dale (later superintendent of Chesapeake and Ohio National Monument), departed from Roanoke in cautious pursuit of the three-year-old Cadillac with New York plates.

At Floyd Plateau, near the Virginia-Carolina border, the Rockefeller car pulled off and parked on the shoulder of the road. David clambered down a steep hillside in the direction of a cabin far below. He was carrying a large bundle. A green-painted official ranger vehicle came along and stopped behind the Cadillac. The two men in uniform got out and approached the big car.

"Oh, are we in violation of some regulation?" asked John D. Rockefeller, Jr., looking just like any other citizen (and perhaps secretly hoping to be apprehended).

"No, Mr. Rockefeller," replied Superintendent Weems, with a laugh. He introduced himself. "I just happened to be driving down today. The chief ranger and I thought we'd see how you're getting along."

"Well, you had that hotel pack such a large picnic lunch for us that we decided we'd share it with some needy family. That's why we've pulled off here. David has just gone down to that cabin with the basket."

In a few minutes David returned with a proud announcement that they had found just the right place, the home of a poor widow with several children and a "fantastic story"—of how her husband died in the middle of one night and she didn't know he was dead until she happened to touch his feet under the covers and they were cold.

The two cars traveled down the Parkway. Rockefeller was deeply impressed with its management. "I want to compliment you on doing a fine job," he told Weems at one stop. "This is the most picked-up park I've seen."

The entire party stopped for the night at the lodge at Doughton Park, one of the loveliest settings in all Appalachia (located in Wilkes County, celebrated for mountain music and moonshine). Rockefeller, as always, showed his interest in landscaping and road construction. "How can you afford such fine stone curbing?" he asked. "Why, it looks like the entrance to a private estate." When Weems explained that, with native materials and local labor, the Government paid ten cents a foot, delivered, Rockefeller replied, "Do you know how much this would cost at Tarrytown? At least ten times as much."

Next morning Weems proposed that Rockefeller and David ride in the Government car, with the chauffeur following. They carried a basket of food, complete with linen, for a picnic lunch. Superintendent Weems was determined to make his play for Linville Falls, where a lumber company was then cutting virgin timber on the ridge top and endeavoring to obtain the rights to the property directly surrounding the Falls.

After a generally pleasant morning (during which the chauffeur became lost on a side road in the hills and had to be rescued by a ranger), Rockefeller asked where they would stop for lunch. Weems checked his watch, calculated thoughtfully, and announced that the logical place would be Linville Falls—where else?

They stopped under a big old hemlock and unloaded the basket.

"Before lunch, Mr. Rockefeller," suggested the superintendent, "wouldn't you like to walk up and see the falls?"

"I'd better not. It looks like a steep climb. My doctor cautioned me against overexertion. David, you go with Mr. Weems."

They climbed the hillside. David asked about a little heath plant, the Allegheny sand myrtle, questioning whether it might grow at Tarrytown. He stood briefly at the brink of the watery chasm in the wilderness and took but one photograph with his camera.

While they lunched, Weems told the Rockefellers about the logging encroachment and the possibility of saving the beauty spot. His hope rose when Rockefeller asked, "How much could it be bought for?"

"The asking price is much higher, but I think one hundred thousand dollars would do it."

"That's very interesting."

The superintendent reached in his brief case for a folio of photographs, maps, and descriptive material on the Falls. Rockefeller accepted it without comment, or even looking at it, but passed it to the chauffeur to be filed in the luggage. The superintendent's hopes fell.

That evening in Asheville, after dinner at the Battery Park Hotel, Rockefeller said that he wanted David to have a suit made of the famous Biltmore Industries homespun cloth. The Industries shop itself was then closed, Weems advised, but the hotel gift shop carried a rack of bolts of Biltmore homespun.

They went to the gift shop across the lobby, where David bought dolls for his children and his father selected four or five hundred dollars' worth of cloth, while the young girl clerk stared at the slight, average-looking man picking out all that merchandise.

"May I write a check for the amount?" he asked her.

"Well, I'm not sure," she hesitated. "You've spent an awful lot of money. I don't know whether I can take a check for that much. Do you live in Asheville?"

Superintendent Weems came forward and volunteered his good confidence, as a Government official in uniform, in the gentleman's honesty and the integrity of his check. When she accepted the check rather reluctantly, the girl looked as though she was going to ask Weems to endorse it with his signature. But when she read the name, she turned purple, looked faint, and gasped.

The next morning, at their parting, Weems thought he was bidding farewell to his dream of acquiring Linville Falls. It appeared so hopeless that he did not even mention the area.

Six months later, Albright wired: "If you can buy Linville Falls for $100,000, Mr. Rockefeller agrees to contribute full amount."

And so he spent his money. Though probably he had more of it than any one person should have, he spread it where it was needed in behalf of all people, filling a deep void during a period of Congressional indifference, and asking little personal recognition. Mr. Rockefeller foresaw his responsibility. He was, by all odds, a man worthy of his role in the Great Smokies.

As for his purchase on the Blue Ridge Parkway, when he returned in 1954 on his honeymoon trip with the second Mrs. Rockefeller, Sam Weems served as his guide once more.

"Would you like to go to Linville Falls, Mr. Rockefeller?" the Parkway superintendent inquired.

"Oh, that's right. I did buy something down here for you."

"Yes, Mr. Rockefeller, you sure did."

Chapter 3

The President and I
Discuss Tellico Dam

President Lyndon B. Johnson and I have met only once. It was a brief encounter in the cause of conservation and natural beauty. His expression was one of deep interest and concern.

Presently, in the lines below, we shall conduct a fuller dialogue. Our subject is specific: the proposed Tellico Dam across the Little Tennessee River.

This project has the endorsement of Mr. Johnson's Administration. The first $3.2 million to begin construction was appropriated by Congress last year, 1966, in a monstrous piece of pork barrel legislation.

Along with a great many others, I consider it morally sinful, sheer sacrilege against land and people. My hope in this interview is to learn how it can be halted and thus spare us all from the disgrace of future judgment.

The discussion, you understand, is imaginary. However, the words of Mr. Johnson are his own, taken from public statements with full respect for the context of their meaning.

The President: "For over three centuries the beauty of America has sustained our spirit and enlarged our vision. We must act now to protect this heritage."

Frome: This is precisely why I have come to you. Centuries of beauty and our heritage are in grave danger on the Little Tennessee.

The President: "I can inform you that in response to this request your Government has taken hundreds of steps—large and small—to

From *American Forests*, March 1967.

increase natural beauty. We still have a long way to go, but I am determined that this Government in all of its activities shall be a model and pacesetter for the entire Nation."

Frome: I pay serious attention to your words about the fate and future of our resources, and have the strange notion that others should do likewise. I don't mean the average citizen, who feels the urgent need to safeguard the environment for his family and the future. He looks hopefully for leadership to all levels of government.

But I do mean officials of the Tennessee Valley Authority, who exemplify bureaucracy unleashed, unresponsive to the people, embarked on a ruthless, ruinous adventure. I mean leading members of your own party in Congress, who measure achievement in terms of public works projects for their individual districts—hardly a comprehensive view of total conservation needs. I mean the Bureau of the Budget, a branch of government directly responsible to you.

The President: "The importance of natural beauty cannot be easily measured. It cannot be coded for computers or calculated by economists."

Frome: But the Bureau of the Budget told me that neither conservation nor natural beauty had been considered in the Tellico project, that it would not consider natural beauty as a factor, that only economics were important. Can this possibly fit in with your conservation program?

The President: "Its object is not just man's welfare, but the dignity of man's spirit. . . . I think it is going to demand that all of our private citizens be constantly alert to stimulate, to inspire, and to stem new danger to beauty. For it is the quality of our lives that is really at stake."

Frome: Your words will be heartening to the opponents of the Tellico fiasco, an encouragement to continue the fight, for they share your feeling.

Who are these people, Mr. President? They represent the broadest spectrum of public opinion. Every major national conservation organization, from the American Pulpwood Association to the Wilderness Society, despite their divergence of views, are united in opposition. So are the great majority of business and professional leaders of the area, county governments, civic clubs and property

owners. So are the Tennessee chapters of the Daughters of the
American Revolution, Farm Bureau Federation, Livestock Association, Federation of Garden Clubs, Society of American Foresters.
They all are rallied behind the leadership of the Association to Save
the Little Tennessee.

When I talked with Mr. Carl H. Schwartz, Jr., Chief of the Resources and Civil Works Division of the Bureau of the Budget, he
dismissed them lightly, asserting, "There is always somebody
opposed to a water development project." But these are responsible
people, Mr. President. They understand watershed protection and
wise utilization of water resources; they do not blindly oppose all
dams on principle.

The President: "The same society which receives the awards of
technology, must, as a cooperating whole, take responsibility for
control."

Frome: This is what these people seek. What they receive in
return is the height of irresponsibility. Representative Richard
Ottinger, a courageous young Congressman of New York State, arose
on the floor of the House last year to expose Tellico as "purely and
simply a pork barrel project that will have the taxpayers of the
United States footing a $42 million bill for a risky 5,000-acre real
estate speculation." That opening price tag has already been increased officially by $6 million. Conservationists believe in frugality,
Mr. President, the expenditure of federal funds where they are really
needed, not scandalous waste of this nature.

Tellico is represented by TVA as a "multipurpose river development." "It is not justified by power production needs," as the
Chattanooga Free Press editorialized. "It is not justified by navigation
needs. It is not supported as a flood control measure. The only
significant argument is that it would open new industrial sites. This
is a poor argument when (1) there are many, many industrial sites in
the area that are not yet in use, and (2) it is not the business of the
federal government to take the role of real estate developer. It
appears that the real reason behind the Tellico Dam is that its
proponents just have run out of something else to do for the time
being."

The President: "Private citizens own or manage three-fourths of the land that makes up the United States. We look to them as producers of the abundance that flows from American agriculture—and as the preservers of our farmlands and their resources."

Frome: Under the guise of "general economic development," TVA would use the powers of condemnation to acquire all shoreline lands, then resell the 5,000 acres for a profit, controlling both the buyer and seller markets. More than three hundred families would be displaced. No landowner could obtain a trial by jury as redress. This scarcely sounds like respect for the private landowner, Mr. President.

The Tellico Dam would flood 14,400 acres of fertile bottomland. In this valley are lovely Tennessee farms (producing substantially over one million dollars in dairy products yearly), woodlands, campsites, hunting areas, scenic roads and historic landmarks. Here, too, is a major tree nursery with a capacity to produce thirty million seedlings a year—and with nine good years of experimental tree culture, highly significant to pulp, paper and wood industries throughout the nation.

Furthermore, these sites are hardly necessary. TVA already has available thousands of acres going begging nearby.

The President: "When land is ruined, we blight the future of people as well as the face of America."

Frome: I think we have here an example of a Federal agency perfectly qualified and eager to ruin land. As the National Wildlife Federation commented: "Unless TVA can produce a whopping big profit on the land sale—at the expense of individual landowners—the margin of profit over cost is too small to risk destroying a beautiful valley as a monument to this 'Big Brother' brand of bureaucracy."

Personally, I feel that TVA deserves close scrutiny by Congress and yourself.

Despite all its press notices of benefactions to the people, I understand that a total of 103 of the 210 counties of TVA country today are included in the Appalachian poverty program. Its record in strip mining is one of abysmal neglect of responsibility. "The few conservation and forestry practices that the TVA may have put into effect," comments the *Lexington* (Kentucky) *Herald*, "in its own or maybe some nearby areas are far outweighed by the massive destruction wrought in other areas where low-priced, inferior coal is supplied by stripping and auger mine operations." TVA buying practices have contributed directly to the fantastic mining havoc of Appalachia.

The President: "When land is used in harmony with our needs and the requirements of nature, it rewards us with beauty and riches."

Frome: Precisely the issue in the Little Tennessee. Twenty-two impoundments surround the Little Tennessee in a 50-mile radius. The Little T itself is regulated by seven major dams. Now we have only thirty-four miles left in free-running condition—this portion would be destroyed by the Tellico dam. No real need for another dam has ever been shown. It is a beautiful clear stream rippling over the rocks——

The President: "I remember when I was a very young man . . . those hills and those fields, that river was the only real world that I really had in those years . . . We were not a wealthy family, but this was my rich inheritance."

Frome: As you rightfully regard the Pedernales, so others feel about the Little Tennessee and the marvelous surrounding mountains. A moving river is a living, vibrant part of our heritage. Though we may be able to place a man on the moon, we cannot replace a living river. The waters of the Little T are cold and clean. No other stream in a large radius provides the same superlative canoeing and float-fishing opportunities—in a scenic and historical setting. It provides miles of superb trout fishing in its upper portions; the habitat conditions are ideal. With its unique qualities, it could be one of the finest recreation streams in America—an economy in its own right—complementing the adjacent regions of the U.S. Forest Service, National Park Service, and TVA lakes. This would really be using land "in harmony with our needs and the requirements of nature."

I haven't mentioned yet the archaeological impact of the dam, how it would destroy treasured sites of the early mountain people, the Cherokee Indians——

The President: ". . . 161 years have passed since President

Thomas Jefferson charged his countrymen to treat the original inhabitants of our country 'with the commiseration their history requires.' As President Jefferson pointed out, our European ancestors found the American Indian 'occupying a country which left them no desire but to be undisturbed.'

"That desire was thrust aside by history and Jefferson's plea was ignored. We cannot turn back the hands of time, but after 161 years of neglect we can honor Jefferson's plea."

Frome: Mr. President, if that pledge is genuine, then your honor and the honor of the nation, are at stake along the shores of the Little Tennessee.

The Eastern Band of Cherokee Indians, who hold alive the torch of their people in the mountains of Western North Carolina, have entered a plea that this dam not be built. Their brethren, the Cherokee Nation, Tribe of Oklahoma, whose forebears were uprooted from their homeland over a century ago and driven across the continent, have joined in this plea.

"I understand there are some Indian graves or something down there," Mr. Schwartz of the Bureau of the Budget said to me.

To the Cherokee, the area to be flooded is hallowed land. Here along the Little Tennessee is the site of their ancestral capital and city of refuge. Echota, or "Chote the Metropolis," headquarters of their illustrious chieftains, Kana-gatoga, or Old Hop, and his nephew, Attakullakulla, the Little Carpenter, who saved white men from annihilation; and also, the sites of other villages, including Tuskega, or Tuskegee, which we believe to be the birthplace of Sequoyah, the genius who created the written Cherokee language. We honor him by the use of his name for a great American tree, but shall we dishonor ourselves by destroying the soil over the remains of his homeland?

If the dam is built, the archaeological sites would be permanently lost. You should realize that they may be the most important in Eastern United States. We do not know how far back the culture of man reaches in these hills and valleys, or what secrets they hold of the movement of man.

Besides the Indian sites, let us consider the fate of Fort Loudoun. This was the first English fort west of the Appalachians. It played a key role in the struggle that determined this nation would be an English- rather than French-speaking land. It was restored with loving care over a period of many years by patriotic Tennesseans. If this dam should be built, Fort Loudoun would not quite be destroyed. It would be accessible only by boat or bridge, a mockery of its historical context.

Mr. President, it is difficult to believe that you or the Congress could have been aware of all the factors we have discussed.

The President: (pays tribute to) "the vision of a truly great conservation Congress led by men who are conservation minded and who are knowledgeable in that field."

Frome: I feel my obligation to point up the voids. The Little Tennessee is no shining example of knowledgeable administration or Congressional leadership in conservation.

I admire the efforts to save the river made by Representative Ottinger, whom I mentioned earlier. Representative John Saylor of Pennsylvania understands the issues well. As part of his Scenic Rivers Bill, the future of the Little Tennessee would be studied, as it should be. However, if we consider the positions of Senator Albert Gore and Representative Joe Evins, we have two Tennesseans who spoke loudly last year against excessive federal spending, but were quite eager to pick their share of pork from the barrel. Then we have the key man, Representative Michael Kirwan of Ohio, the chairman of the Public Works Subcommittee of the House Appropriations Committee. He is one of your Congressional leaders. At hearings of his subcommittee, opponents of the Tellico Dam were well represented, but scarcely given a chance by Mr. Kirwan to identify themselves, let alone to state their case.

Possibly Mr. Kirwan was preoccupied with his pet project, a canal from the Ohio River to Lake Erie, the ultimate cost of which is estimated at between one billion to three billion dollars. The chairman of the Public Works Committee, Representative George Fallon of Maryland, has said there would be no real benefits and that the proposal was economically unsound. Now consider this comment last fall from the *Knoxville News-Sentinel*: "When some House members tried to delete this liberal outlay of taxpayer money in honor of Kirwan, they were shouted down; too many others had projects in the bill for their districts." And so Tellico became part of the package of Congressional horse trades.

Would you, perhaps, consider recommendations in the matter?

The President: "I will immediately give careful consideration to any that require immediate Executive action and that can be taken without legislation."

Frome: The Administration budget for this year carries an additional $7 million for the Tellico project. Many opponents, organizations and individuals, have been writing earnest letters to you, pleading for your help; they have urged that you eliminate this item from the budget and bring the sham to a halt. In return, they receive acknowledgment from the Executive Office of the President, a form letter signed by Joseph Laitin, Assistant to the Director of the Budget Bureau.

I telephoned Mr. Laitin for clarification of a phrase regarding "the project's merits in light of other important efforts in which we are engaged." Mr. Laitin is the press officer of the Bureau, admittedly no expert on Tellico. He referred me to Mr. Schwartz, who said the decision had been reached, would not be reconsidered, that opponents had not spoken up early enough. Do you feel that a decision of this nature should be irrevocable, especially at this early stage?

The President: "At times we have paid a heavy price for this neglect. But once our people were aroused to the danger, we have acted to preserve our resources for the enrichment of our country and the enjoyment of future generations."

Frome: That comment is extremely pertinent. I appreciate this discussion. One final word, perhaps?

The President: We must preserve what remains of the natural beauty and tranquillity that was here long before man came . . . I want to be judged as we judge the great conservationists of yesterday as benefactors of our people and as builders of a more beautiful America."

Frome: We shall all be judged by the outcome of the Little Tennessee River.

Chapter 4

A New Age of Walking Americans

We are entering a new age of walking Americans. The figures show it—that walking for pleasure has become the nation's most popular form of outdoor recreation. More important, conditions of the times demand it. A people whose everyday lives are circumscribed by mechanization and urbanization clamor for respite, a return to native ways. In order to survive and prosper as a race of thinking beings, we need to exercise our bodies in natural surroundings, for man is no synthetic creature, but a living offspring of the earth.

Some officials of our Federal and state public land agencies haven't caught up to the new age. They misread the aspirations of their clients and misjudge their own responsibilities. Instead of devising new techniques to introduce nature to people and people to nature, they tend to follow the easy way, pouring concrete for more and wider highways, congesting visitors on treeless, barren camping suburbias—the kind of facility that could as well be located on private land—and utterly insulating them from the environment. In the process, they destroy the natural features that people have come to enjoy.

We need look no further for an example than the Great Smoky Mountains, the country's most popular national park. The ill-conceived transmountain road, proposed to link Bryson City, N.C., and Townsend, Tenn., across The Appalachian Trail, is only one of a sequence of major desecrations projected for the Smokies, which

From *Appalachian Trailway News*, September 1967.

now would well be under way were it not for the strength of the Wilderness Act and the voice of shocked public protest.

The "master plan" for the Great Smokies is a bizarre document, a design of roads gutting the wilderness, and of massive campgrounds of 200 or 300 or 600 units that rob the camper of a true park experience and take up priceless national real estate for sheer bedroom space.

The present park superintendent promotes this course of destruction. "None of us is getting younger," to quote his statement from the *Knoxville News-Sentinel* of November 2, 1966. "In fact, we're all getting older. So we can't all hike, visit the waterfalls or camp out. We must open new roads for visitors who are growing older. Many can't hike anymore." This in a time when people of all ages—not to forget future generations—crave and need the stimulation of foot trails, and the guidance to pursue them.

Then we have the effort of the chief park naturalist. On page 22 of the Student Conservation Program Newsletter for Spring–Summer 1966, issued by a private organization for a group of young people who had visited the park the preceding summer, we find a letter from the naturalist. He endeavors to elicit public support for the program with the following statement:

"Since the National Park Service is a people-serving agency, we must consider all aspects of preservation and visitor use. If the people did not visit the parks and use them, the Service would not be here. We must carefully weigh each decision between use and preservation before it is made."

This may sound like bare-faced bureaucratic opportunism. It may sound like willingness to downgrade the traditional quality of a national park experience, or to sacrifice the inherent values of the Great Smokies. But his title, after all, is "naturalist." So he continues to present his case:

"A cross-mountain road such as proposed is needed to divert the heavy traffic we now experience. Nearly six million people visited the park in 1965 and if some of these visitors could be diverted to other areas of the park this congestion could be relieved for several years if not forever. Secondly, the proposed route would provide several loop trips, using existing state roads of considerable distance, which we believe visitors would take. Visitors would then be in their cars several hours longer driving and as long as they are in their cars, no damage to the natural features can be done."

One is wise when he learns never to look down or to think down to the American public, especially not to the young. Unfortunately, the chief naturalist of the Smokies and other public officials are not quite that wise. As if in response to him, a lad named Andy Maloney, who was sponsored on the Student Conservation Program by the Westmoreland Sanctuary of New York, wrote this report:

"While I was in the Smokies and even now a great battle is being fought to save the Park from a second transmountain highway. The National Park Service and business people favor it. Groups such as the Wilderness Society, Appalachian Trail Conference, Sierra Club, and other conservation groups are fighting to preserve the area as a wilderness. From what I have seen, I certainly hope the latter are successful and that I myself have helped in a small way as a part of the Student Conservation Program."

The National Park Service knows better. It knows from its proud 50-year history that the park superintendent and naturalist are wrong and that Andy Maloney is right. The management of the park may have lost perspective, but even the master plan begins by enunciating the good conviction that ". . . the park will perpetuate the natural resources of these magnificent mountains so that existing and future generations of mankind can continue to benefit from and enjoy the intangible values associated with the forests, the landscape, the wild country, the mountain streams, and the wildlife for human experiences that are enjoyable, educational, healthful and inspirational."

The Service, furthermore, knows what must be done to accomplish these goals. The master plan touches the principle of regional planning and a circle-the-park loop road in these words: "The Service should encourage and cooperate with TVA, U. S. Forest Service and other agencies in development of recreational facilities on Fontana Lake and environs. . . . The circulation system of the park is closely allied to the state roads near the boundary of the park. Improvement of existing roads and construction of new roads by either Tennessee or North Carolina will affect park circulation. The concept of the circulation in the Great Smokies is to develop spur roads from a circumferential belt to the developed areas in order to preserve the natural character as much as possible."

This portion of the plan was written by someone with knowledge and vision, someone in step with the recently expressed views of Interior Secretary Stewart L. Udall, who declared, "Experience of the postwar years tells us that the motor car, with its fumes, noises, and accompanying clutter, is a paramount blighting influence within parks. If we had an opportunity today to replan the development of Yosemite, we would unquestionably keep the automobile on the park's fringes."

But the balance of the plan is devoid of this spirit. So is its practical application in the management of the national park. Road building is on the march. Provisions for hiking are on the decline.

Friends in the Park Service say to me, "We can't encourage *everybody* to hike on the trails. They would hurt the wilderness. Therefore, we have to keep them in the visitor centers and build more roads."

I object to this line of thinking. I object to the continued reduction by the Park Service in the number of guided overnight walking trips and to the reduction of daylong trips of seven hours to four or two hours. There should be more, and better, guided walks and hikes. There should be no apology for wilderness, no reluctance to introduce people to it on wilderness terms. For hiking adventure breeds enthusiasm, idealism, love of life, and the hiker champions enlightened use and appreciation of quality.

The walker, the amateur naturalist, the student of birds and butterflies, the person to whom identification of plants and trees is important—these citizens associate themselves with patriotism of the highest order. They should be regarded as staunch allies by the National Park Service, the U. S. Forest Service, the administrators of state parks and forests in fulfillment of their long-range missions.

In some places, by some officials, this is well recognized. But there is no substitute anywhere for enlightened public participation in determination of principles and policies in order to assure that this generation of walking Americans, and the next generations, will have adequate trails in the wilderness to follow.

Chapter 5

Weavers and Woodcarvers— Soft and Mellow and Rich

Whenever I go into the Southern Highlands and watch a wood-carver, weaver, or maker of pots, dolls, or dulcimers at work, I ask myself, "Is this person an artist or craftsman? Where does one leave off and the other begin? Can someone of country stock working with country materials create a piece so individualized that it deserves to be considered an art form?"

The answer I find in the application of universal rules. Art is shaped by the hand, heart, and mind. The artist finds his reward by giving of himself, or herself, expressing innermost talent through work. Therefore, the hillsman, in whatever medium he or she works, can produce an original piece of lasting quality as worthy of being called art as the paintings of an Andrew Wyeth or a Ben Shahn.

Rural arts of the Appalachian Mountains bespeak a regional tradition, the culture of a people. They offer an answer to the technology and sameness of our times. Their significance is scarcely related to the formal brand of training or education in art, but the significance is there.

This is illustrated to me in the experience of Miss Lucy Morgan, who founded the Penland School of Crafts in western North Carolina and directed it until her retirement a few years ago. As an exemplar of teaching and social work, Miss Lucy has asked little during her lifetime but to associate with humble mountain people, to believe in them and to reveal to them their own creativity.

From *Southern Living*, June 1968.

"There was nothing harsh in Aunt Susan's colors," she wrote in her autobiography, *Gift from the Hills*, of a mountain lady she once visited. "All were soft and mellow and rich. For me her coverlets were the greatest attraction; I fairly ogled them, I felt their softness and perfection of texture. I marveled at their color. I yearned to know how to create such materials and such patterns. All the way home I thought of those beautiful specimens, each worthy of immortality in some museum, and of what a tragedy it would be were the art of creating such things lost to succeeding generations."

On a song and a prayer, Miss Lucy began the Penland School in order to perpetuate native skills and to provide the people of the Toe River Valley a means of livelihood. After she herself had mastered the art of weaving, she would walk the hills to the homes of her weavers and teach them. One cold winter's afternoon she stopped at the home of a mountain woman who had been weaving scarves requiring only two harnesses; but Miss Lucy wanted her to try a four-harness operation.

"Law," the mountain woman sighed, looking hopelessly at the draft. "I never could learn to do that."

"Yes, you can. You're a smarter woman than I and I learned to do it."

"Why, Miss Lucy," she insisted. "I hain't had no education."

"Education doesn't put brains in your head."

"Well, I reckon it don't. But it helps you use what you got. Don't it?"

"Sometimes, I suppose. You can do it, though, and I know it."

And the woman learned not only to thread the new draft, but to solve many intricate loom problems. To be told once was all she needed.

Appalachian arts and crafts are deep-rooted in the ways of people who dwelled for generations in the world of magic sunsets and misty solitudes. Almost everything they owned was handhewn and handmade. In the day before cottons appeared at crossroad stores (to be bartered for eggs, nuts, honey, herbs, or a poke of water-ground meal), the woman of the house was obliged to manufacture the family clothing. She started by shearing the sheep, then picking, washing, carding, and spinning wool, linsey for underwear or dresses, jeans cloth for men's clothing (with chain of cotton, filling of wool). Dyes were derived from materials of the forest, field, and garden: indigo for deep blue; madder root for red; maple bark for purple, if the material was cotton. She would also use the hulls, roots, and barks of walnuts, or "warnut," sumac berries, and laurel leaves. Weaving with heddles and treadles was serious, creative work, a quiet art demanding time and patience, particularly in making coverlets, or "kiverlids," in traditional patterns.

The mountain man, meanwhile, in the early days was likely to be his own smith, cooper, cobbler, and carpenter, working seriously and slowly. In the course of slow community growth, artisans developed. One man became a specialist at chairmaking and carpentering; another at pottery, making churns, crocks, bake pots, and dishes; a third at shingle cracking, deftly riving several hundred shingles a day. People came from miles to the blacksmith to have tools mended and horses shod and to pick up hinges and other items fashioned from worn horseshoes and mule shoes. In due time a tub mill operated in every community, running on certain days of the week to grind meal, with the miller getting a "toddick," or small amount as a toll. Barter was the common exchange.

The ancient ways have faded, but they do not die. Mountain people still rive shingles in some places. Old crafts are followed by young people, who refuse to surrender to the factories or to take their families into crowded cities, preferring the home ground and the spirit of their elders.

The best example of perpetuating native skills relates to the oldest people of Appalachia, the Cherokee Indians of North Carolina, and to basketry, the oldest art form in America.

Years ago the secret of making the complicated double-walled baskets was dying out, known to only one old woman. She agreed to teach it up to a certain point to Lottie Stamper, a slender, soft-spoken but extremely determined native of the town of Cherokee in the Great Smokies. Lottie struggled until she mastered the craft, then undertook to teach it to others, showing them how to collect their own materials—river cane, split oak, and honeysuckle—and how to use roots and leaves for dyes. Consequently, a few Cherokee women once again make fine double-walled baskets as did their mothers'

mothers. Nor did the potter's art perish; old Cherokee patterns have been reborn, based on museum research and the willingness of the people today to use them. A lot of trinkets and trash are sold to visitors on the reservation, but the Qualla Arts and Crafts Mutual, a cooperative of more than 200 members, offers articles both traditional and modern—and really worth owning.

An amazing variety of crafts is produced in the Southern Appalachians by people holding to their heritage. In southwest Virginia, a man like D. S. Miller reminds us of the old specialty of making knives out of files and saws, which he learned from his blacksmith father. Today he makes his saw-blade knives with beautiful two-piece cedar handles held together with babbitt metal. In east Tennessee, Taft Greer works at the same loom at which his grandmother died at the age of 101. At Bybee, Kentucky, members of the Cornelison family turn out stoneware in the same pottery where their fathers have worked since 1845.

Pottery is found everywhere throughout the hills, but no two pieces are alike—there are as many kinds of pots as people and personalities making them. Some slip-decorated earthenware, made by descendants of the Staffordshire potters who came to this country in the 18th century, bears resemblance to the "rimmed pan" work described in early logbooks. Other pieces, marked by new shapes and elegant simplicity in black and white, could as easily come from the contemporary potters of Scandinavia. Appalachian pottery is immensely popular today, for it embodies a living tradition. A problem, alas, is that the workshop of the country potter is apt to take on the aura of the studio potter; on the other hand, the same man may become even more of an artist by cultivating his talent wisely.

The mountain people have been singularly blessed by a cadre of thoughtful outsiders who asked only for the right to encourage them to revive vanishing crafts, like weaving, to perfect their work in basket making, and to show them how to make a living in a changing world. Berea College in Kentucky was an early vital influence 60 years ago when it first offered students from eight Appalachian states the chance to "barter for larnin'." That was the beginning of the Berea College Student Industries, a choice stop on anybody's crafts trail today. Visitors are welcome to tour the shops as well as the sales rooms that merchandise everything from beaten biscuits and mountain sweets to dolls, brooms, candlesticks, and a complete line of quality furniture.

In Tennessee the sisters of Pi Beta Phi, one of the first national college fraternal organizations for women, chose Gatlinburg in the Smokies as their special place that needed book learning and social welfare. When they established their settlement school in 1912, two hundred families dwelled in log cabins and shacks along the creeks that spilled down from the mountainside and in the tiny fertile coves that turn up unexpectedly at the bend of a mountain stream. From the beginning, the school urged the mountain people to sing their old folksongs and the teachers introduced an arts and crafts program as part of the effort to foster home industries. Old looms were hauled out of the attics and reconditioned. Forgotten drafts—the patterns handed down from mother to daughter for a century or more—turned up on yellowed and wrinkled paper. Women were eager to learn.

The men were willing too. In 1922 O. J. Mattil began to conduct classes in shopwork, demonstrating how to remodel furniture and make new pieces, how to use tools more sophisticated than the saw, plane, and hammer.

In time, Mattil set up his own shop, the Woodcrafters and Carvers, where dozens of talented mountain cabinetmakers have studied and worked, learning to produce quality furniture and how to price it for sale.

The Great Smoky Mountains National Park and mountain crafts have grown up together, not solely in Gatlinburg and in Cherokee, but in the entire Appalachian environs. The roads brought visitors who were exposed for the first time to the craftsman's wares at Pi Beta Phi's Arrowcraft Shop and many other shops. Mountain people in substantial numbers found markets for handwork they loved to do. There are now more than a thousand looms busy in the Gat-linburg area, producing about a million dollars' worth of coverlets, towels, table linens, handbags, and petticoats. In 1923 the Pi Beta Phi ladies were overjoyed when the sales reached $1,000 a year.

Across the mountains in North Carolina, Miss Frances Goodrich, a social worker, started Allanstand Cottage early in the century as a crafts center in Asheville in order to bring "healthful excitement" to mountaineer ladies—who presently learned they could not only barter their products, but actually sell them for cash. Mrs. George Washington Vanderbilt (whose husband built the great Biltmore mansion at the edge of Asheville) was another who was deeply social conscious and drawn to the problems of the mountain people; she inspired the establishment of Biltmore Industries in order to widen the opportunities open to them. Their weaving proved successful not only as a craft, but as a business venture that is still active. Then there was Mrs. Olive Dame Campbell, who organized the John C. Campbell Folk School at Brasstown, near Murphy, North Carolina, in memory of her husband, director of the Southern Highland Division of the Russell Sage Foundation. This school continues to be a splendid operation, with no entrance requirements and no academic procedures, but offering a world of pleasure in wood carving, country dancing, folksongs, and dulcimer.

The Penland School, tucked away in the Blue Ridge Mountains, has also achieved eminence since Miss Lucy Morgan began her work in 1929. On many occasions the Department of State has sent students and official visitors from other nations to observe teachers and students in weaving, ceramics, metal, jewelry, enameling, and woodworking. The greatest accomplishment, however, came in connection with the restoration of Independence Hall, when Penland was asked to handweave the green tablecloths as the Founding Fathers might have known them.

Bea Hensley, of Spruce Pine, is another whose work has been shipped to distant places. Bea is one of the few remaining blacksmiths; his forge produces artistic ornamental wrought iron, including chandeliers, andirons, candle holders, and fire screens. He has demonstrated his talents before Lady Bird Johnson when she visited the Peaks of Otter (on the Virginia portion of the Blue Ridge Parkway) and before thousands of visitors at the Smithsonian Institution in Washington. His specialty appears to be his ability to play a tune with his hammer as it taps along the anvil, but there is far more than showmanship involved. A finished wrought iron leaf almost seems to have the touch of the painter, so delicate are the veins of the leaf made by his hammer strokes.

Some of the most interesting products of this region of North

Carolina are at the Wee Loch Craft Shop, at Elk Park, run by Harold Winters, who is known for fine dulcimers of his own design and for his habit of playing folksongs for visitors. He carries folksong records for the dulcimer, folklore books, folk toys, pottery, and woodcrafts. Then there is the Goodwin Guild at Blowing Rock, run by brilliant and perceptive John Goodwin, the master weaver, age 78, whose great-grandfather operated a silk-weave shed in Bolton, England, before bringing his trade to Virginia and starting a family tradition. As a manufacturer of woolen goods, before settling in Blowing Rock in 1950, John roamed the hills of Kentucky, North Carolina, Virginia, and East Tennessee with bolts of cloth, collecting, as he went, coverlets and ancient drafts and patterns that might otherwise be lost. Now his daughter and grandson are learning everything he knows in order to insure that a century and a half of family weaving-and-wool history will continue.

Mountain crafts are far from dead or dying. They seem to me to be reaching to new heights, often against odds. The machine age is upon the free-spirited people of the highlands. Some government aid programs thrust upon Appalachia are devastating to individualism. Other programs, operated by the Office of Economic Opportunity to encourage native handcrafts, have been thwarted by the Department of Labor on the grounds that these cottage industries do not comply with wage-hour laws. One of the best of the programs working with an OEO grant, the Kentucky Hills Industries, run by Mr. and Mrs. Smith Ross at Pine Knot, Kentucky, is well worth a visit to see the fine work being done with cornshuck dolls, end grain cutting boards, handhewn dough trays, and quilting. The program is just getting under way; the people of the region and the nation need it to advance.

Appalachian craftsmanship is here to stay, as a way of life and as a gift from the hills to the world. The Smithsonian Institution now holds four-day folklife festivals on the Mall in Washington, D.C., over the July 4th weekend. Southern mountaineers have been the star performers. They instruct and inspire; they teach the learned how much there is to learn. I have mentioned all too few of them by name.

In summary, I think of the words of Edsel Martin, the wood-carving artist of Swannanoa, North Carolina, who lost one leg in World War II, but exercises the full genius of his hands, heart, and mind in expression and details: "You can drown an awful lot of sorrow in a piece of wood." This may be, Edsel, but you can bring an awful lot of joy in a piece of wood.

Chapter 6

The World's Greatest Road—
But No Highway

The Blue Ridge Parkway is a road that is not really a road. It is a park that is not really a park. It was begun as a make-work project of the deep Depression and as a device to resettle farmers from the impoverished hills of Virginia and North Carolina into the valleys below. Hardly anyone in those years could seriously have foreseen its ultimate completion atop the rough, rugged mountain crest, or have predicted that it would ever become consequential in the American scheme of things.

Yet this Parkway today is the greatest road in the world. It bears scant resemblance—indeed, it provides the happy alternative—to the super-super freeways and highway death traps which scar the countryside and cityside. As a unit of the National Park System, it outdraws all others, having attracted over seven million visitors in 1968. If numbers mean little to you, it's also the best run unit in the entire National Park System.

I speak from personal experience, having traveled over every major recreational road in this country and over many of those in other lands, and having observed the operation of the National Park Service from Alaska to the Virgin Islands. There is nothing on earth to compare with the Blue Ridge Parkway, in design, landscaping, and simple opportunities to enjoy a day, a weekend, or longer of tranquillity. And it lies just a long hoot and holler from Washington, across the rising Piedmont and foothills of Virginia.

For me this Parkway is more than a road. It is a garden of

From *Washingtonian*, April 1969.

flowering trees, shrubs, and herbs; a park, with nature trails, picnic grounds, and camping in exceptional, well-spaced sites; a museum of the Southern Highlands culture, expressed at restored mills, weathered cabins, and farms bordered by split-rail fences; a wildlife sanctuary for deer, bear, bobcat, skunk, and more than 100 species of birds; and a center of mountain handicrafts that evokes the true pride of Appalachia. The Parkway also is a special kind of resort, with three excellent lodges and the core of a broader vacation country that is attractive in three seasons of the year.

The Parkway was designed as a connecting link between the Shenandoah and Great Smoky Mountains National Parks. From its northern end, at Rockfish Gap, Virginia, between Charlottesville and Waynesboro, it winds gently for 469 miles to a point near the Ocon-aluftee Visitor Center on the North Carolina side of the Great Smok-ies. For this entire distance there's not a truck to contend with, not a billboard to blight the trees, flowers, farms, and mountain vistas, and scarcely an urge to rush through this wonderland without taking it all in. For the roadway is designed with gentle curves and grades (and a patrol of rangers) that encourage comfortable driving at 45 miles per hour—an experience that grows on most speed-weary motorists until they enjoy it. All others will quit the parkway at the nearest exit.

It's an easy mistake to confuse the Blue Ridge Parkway with Shenandoah National Park, until you know them both. I have introduced my friend, Sam P. Weems, the Parkway Superintendent, to scores of people who have nodded knowingly and said, "Oh yes, the Skyline Drive, isn't it?" This is almost as bad, to the principals, as calling a park ranger a forest ranger, or vice versa.

Shenandoah, with its Skyline Drive, is a slender national park, two to thirteen miles wide, extending from Front Royal south to Rockfish Gap, where the Parkway begins. Skyline Drive follows the mountain crest for 105 miles. The crest of which mountains? The Blue Ridge, of course, and not the Shenandoah, which only com-pounds the confusion.

The Blue Ridge constitutes the eastern rampart of the Appala-chian Mountains, the oldest mountain system in North America, a broad composition of parallel ranges and cross ranges reaching from

Maine to Georgia. From atop the Skyline Drive one can look west-ward across the Shenandoah Valley and see waves of mountains, including the near Massanutten and Shenandoah. A very good national park, Shenandoah; though it may lack the spectacular quality of the western areas, it provides excellent hiking trails, motel-type lodges and cabins, and fine opportunities for nature study.

Shenandoah, established in 1926, and the Skyline Drive came first, opening the way for the Blue Ridge Parkway and its builders of the 1930s, '40s, and '50s. They benefited from lessons in design and construction while they reached into higher mountains above the narrow coves and valleys. The Parkway varies in elevation from 500 feet to above 6,000 feet, in some sections running along a narrow, knife-like crest, opening vistas on both sides far below, and in other sections running through a dark forest; and always it imparts the feeling of being a long corridor in a gallery, its alcoves lined with the living arts of Appalachia, unfolding a story of plants, trees, people, and wild creatures.

This is for leisurely travel, riding awhile and stopping awhile—at the overlooks, museums, trailside exhibits, and picnic tables. Among the many self-guiding nature trails some are short leg-stretchers that anyone can do in ten or twenty minutes round trip; others take the better part of an hour or more, while the celebrated Appalachian Trail, which parallels the Parkway for 103 miles on its way from Maine to Georgia, affords some of the choicest hiking in America for an hour, a day, overnight, or longer.

Heading south from Rockfish Gap, Humpback Rocks is the first in a sequence in Appalachian life exhibits. It consists of a group of typical log buildings of pioneer farming days, complete with bear-proof pigpen, spring house, stable, and cowshed. Most of these, and the main cabin, were built about 1880; they were assembled here from original sites in the surrounding area. Another stopping place, the James River, a historical American waterway deep blue in color, reminds one of the mountain-set beauty of the Rhine. Exhibits and one restored lock tell the story of the old canal system that served as the gateway from Richmond to the western mountains before the coming of the railroad.

The Peaks of Otter, near Roanoke, are twin mountains that

constitute the core of a recreation complex which, in one form or other, has drawn visitors since Thomas Jefferson's day. In the pre–Civil War days, Mrs. Polly Woods operated a log cabin inn (which still stands near the picnic grounds), where she bedded tourists for the night and served them bear steak, wild turkey, buttermilk, and biscuits. She was succeeded by one hotel, which guests reached in a red spring wagon driven by a liveryman, and then by another which achieved some fame as a resort and honeymoon spa—until fire swept it away. The newest addition, the 54-unit Peaks of Otter Lodge, operated by a private concessioner under Government regulations, is two years old, with a beautiful setting at the edge of a man-made lake surrounded by forested mountains. Peaks of Otter, an easy day's drive from Washington, is an outstanding destination.

Hiking trails wend over the Peaks, Sharptop (3,875 feet) and Flattop (4,001 feet), once considered the highest points in Virginia (Mount Rogers, 5,719 feet, near Marion, is now undisputed king), and an old but effective bus ascends Sharptop the easy way, affording one of the best scenic views in the Virginia Blue Ridge, over the Piedmont foothills to the East and the Great Appalachian Valley, the route of the pioneers, to the West. A hiker may glimpse a ruffed grouse or catch the disappearing white of a fleeing deer. Chards and arrowheads recently unearthed, are considered evidence of ancient aboriginal culture, the oldest dating back at least 7,000 years. Park Service archaeologists believe the aborigines roamed in small bands while they hunted for deer and turkey, wintering in the Piedmont, summering in the high places. The artifacts are on display at the Peaks of Otter visitor center, while further digging goes on nearby.

The Parkway blooms like a mountaintop flower garden. Dogwood and wild flowers open the season in late April. Gradually the trees leaf out, each day widening the band of green. From mid-May, or a little before, flame azalea blazes in the hills, the finest display in the high mountains west of Asheville occurring about mid-June. About the same time comes mountain laurel, followed by purple and showy white rhododendrons from the end of June to late July, when the Parkway is a cool retreat.

From now until the end of October, when the lodges close, come vivid oranges, soft browns and yellows, the brightness of red berries and the brilliance of the red maple, the "color king of the Appalachians."

Even these are a result of intent and design. Over four hundred leases have been issued to neighboring farmers granting them the right to farm on lands administered by the Parkway. Thus they are encouraged to practice crop rotation, contour farming, reforestation and soil conservation on their own lands, as well as on the Parkway, improving the visual landscape of both. And for many miles the Parkway is blessed by its border of national forests, Washington and Jefferson in Virginia and the Pisgah in North Carolina, which seal it from mechanically modern diversions and enhance the traditional mountaineer scene.

The Parkway spans a longer distance than between Washington and Boston, yet it achieves a sense of unity, not only in purpose but in its personality. Craft demonstrations at key points and the finest souvenir shops in the entire National Park System reflect the integrity of the mountains more than the standard spurious trinkets and gimcracks. At the Northwest Trading Post, near West Jefferson, North Carolina, the visitor can purchase anything from homemade mountain cheeses and jellies to handsome five-string banjos, or "banjers," of curly maple. At the Parkway Craft Center, located in the former summer estate of a textile industrialist, he can see demonstrations of weaving, basketry, rug making, gem cutting, and wood carving by members of the Southern Highland Handicraft Guild.

Nearby Doughton Park is one of the Parkway's notable areas in North Carolina, with the 24-room Bluffs Lodge providing a handy stopping place. Another lodge, Pisgah Inn, is located west of Asheville on one of the most recently completed Parkway sections, at the base of pyramid-shaped Pisgah Ledge. Lofty Pisgah, over a mile high, was part of the 100,000-acre estate which George Washington Vanderbilt acquired in the late 1800s.

Such men of taste and wealth have appreciated deeply the appeal of the Blue Ridge. The late John D. Rockefeller, Jr., landscapist, lover of natural beauty, and benefactor of parks, considered the Blue Ridge Parkway a special favorite. In 1950 he chose it as the route for a father-son vacation with his son, David, and in 1954 he returned for a honeymoon trip with the second Mrs. Rockefeller.

But the Blue Ridge Parkway belongs to everybody, regardless of station, and to each offers the chance to interpret its marvels in his own image. For myself, my favorite portion is at the southernmost end, where the Parkway approaches its climax with the Great Smokies, through the heart of the Balsams, a mighty range in its own right. It rises over 6,000 feet to become the highest motor road in eastern America, sometimes coursing through wispy clouds, and between spires of Fraser fir and red spruce, remnants of the "Canadian" forest that once covered the higher Appalachians.

The most sweeping view of all unfolds from the open crest of Waterrock Knob, a superb 360-degree vista over the main ranges of southern Appalachia. Southeast, the misty Blue Ridge outlines its route into Georgia, and straight ahead rise the Smokies, a mountain wall of 70 miles, the greatest height and mass in eastern America. The ancient mountaintops are green, their slopes are contoured, in contrast to the younger sharp peaks of the Rockies and the Alps and the glaciated rock exposures of New England. At this point one feels that even the finest road and man's best achievement must have their end, before the higher, wiser wonders of the wilderness.

Chapter 7

Poison Coverup in Tennessee

In the fall I went down to Tennessee to talk with sportsmen and mountain farmers about the condition of wildlife in the hills and about the effect of poison programs on the game and the ecosystem. I went because these are my constituents, the host of "little" people who love the American earth and are part of it. And I felt that all was not well.

In *Field & Stream* of last July (1969), I reported receiving word from concerned citizens that the Tennessee Game and Fish Commission had blessed Bowaters Southern Paper Corporation and its subsidiary, the Hiwassee Land Company, with permission to spread poison grain in a ten-county area for the benefit of a pulp-producing monoculture, while eliminating native hickory, oak, and other hardwoods. Bowaters is a considerable landholder in Tennessee, though an absentee-controlled rather than southern corporation. In February, as I noted, members of three hunting clubs had taken separate inspection tours of Signal Mountain, outside of Chattanooga, and all had declared the area a terrible tragedy.

This evoked an anguished letter of protest from the public relations manager of Bowaters, Clarence Streetman, accusing me of "misleading statements and fabrications."

The grain, he wrote, was poisoned with a pesticide called zinc phosphide and scattered by helicopter to eradicate voles—rodents of field and forest—from plantations of Virginia pine, not to eliminate native hardwoods. Only members of one club visited the area. They

From *Field & Stream*, January 1970.

found two dead dogs and one dead rabbit, but the rabbit was never analyzed to determine cause of death. Three State game biologists then spent a full week studying the treated area and found no dead animals, no dead birds. Their findings were confirmed by another weeklong study by game biologists from the Nashville and Atlanta offices of the Bureau of Sport Fisheries and Wildlife (earlier, and later, called Fish and Wildlife Service). Furthermore, my column carried the first mention he had seen anywhere of dead honeybees. "If all the dead animals described by Mr. Frome were found," he summarized, "it was the best kept secret in the history of the State of Tennessee."

Mr. Streetman generously provided *Field & Stream* the names of ten experts capable of providing further testimony. It would almost appear that I had concocted the whole story out of thin air, or that my sources on the ground were completely haywire.

Another witness arose to be heard. Soon after my column appeared the American Forest Institute, a public relations front of the wood products industry, issued a report of a survey on the widespread damage caused by the pernicious voles throughout America. On inquiry I learned that the principal source of the "survey" was Bowaters Southern itself. This might be expected considering the Chairman of Bowaters and the Chairman of the American Forest Institute are named V. J. Sutton—one and the same. Another principal source, however, was the Bureau of Sport Fisheries and Wildlife, a public agency, three of whose experts were quoted as follows:

"Zinc phosphide is widely used and in general does not present undue hazard to other wildlife in the affected areas."

"It is not a threat to wildlife and I honestly don't feel there will be trouble caused by it."

"Its black color and odor are deterrents to birds. It is not a hazard to other wildlife and is not considered serious."

Then I wrote to several of the experts recommended by Mr. Streetman, who unanimously gave Bowaters a clean bill of health. The State Game and Fish Commission straightened me out on the "permit" question. The Commission not only had not granted a permit for the vole eradication, but had no authority to do so. Its obligation was strictly to determine that the control program would not cause appreciable loss to native wildlife—and this obligation had been met fully and forthrightly. As for approval of zinc phosphide, "Who could anticipate," wrote the Commission, "that there would be such a hue and cry over the use of a material no more toxic than the 'No bugs M'lady' that millions of housewives line their kitchens with daily?"

John Oberheu, responding for the regional office of the U. S. Bureau of Sport Fisheries and Wildlife, headquartered in Atlanta, heartily agreed, advising that all its recommendations had been followed; that risks to the total environment were slight and of a temporary nature, that all complaints had been carefully investigated but had proven groundless or insignificant.

Dr. Ralph Dimmick, who had been hired through the University of Tennessee as a consultant to Bowaters, concurred also. He told me the areas treated were 4- to 6-year-old Virginia pine plantations established on generally infertile marginal land with little food available to wildlife. Referring to zinc phosphide, he noted, "The substance has absolutely no herbicidal qualities and thus cannot alter wildlife habitat in any fashion."

They were all reassuring. But one point stuck in my mind: Expressions in behalf of the economics of pulpwood production far and away transcended concern for the biological and ecological resource. In the course of widening research, I presently came upon a pertinent report written by a team of distinguished British wildlife authorities who had been invited for an extensive tour of the country by the U. S. Air Force. Henry Langton, a specialist in game bird management, declared as follows:

"Actually the production and maintenance of a suitable habitat in which wild game can flourish demands abatement of pollution in that environment. Thus pollution abatement, conservation of all natural resources, and wild game propagation and management are all parts of the same programme. The persistent man-made poisons are undoubtedly a growing threat to entire ecological systems. Even chemical fertilizers and coated seeds often thought harmless to wildlife are now found to affect adversely the song and game bird populations. Both indigenous and migratory birds are threatened by the entire milieu of persistent poisons and other chemical agents often used in an apparently unrestrained fashion. One of the great hazards in England to the well being of wild bird life is the spraying of crops which kills insect life essential to the birds for food. This is in addition, of course, to the effect on herbage itself."

But no such statement of ecological awareness was forthcoming from Bowaters' collaborators, consultants, or apologists. To the contrary. In July, when Bowaters held a meeting to consider a second attack of poison on the voles, the question of selective underground poisoning was raised. It was pointed out, according to notes kept by Mr. Streetman, "that underground baiting for pine voles would not be economically practical on a low-value-per-acre crop such as timber." Apparently no one raised the point that wildlife has a value, too.

I wrote a newspaper reporter listed by Mr. Streetman. In response, he conceded he was not well up on the affair, but sent revealing clippings. One quoted the Game and Fish Commission: "There was some neglect by Hiwassee Land Co. in not notifying our people when a treatment was in progress." During the first operation the corn "was not dark enough in color and was being taken by other wildlife for which it was not intended." The treating rate was to be no more than 10 pounds per acre, but it was clearly not monitored or supervised. "There was some neglect in the haphazard manner which they scattered the grain when loading their helicopter, particularly grain left along the roadside." The Commission did not add that zinc phosphide is dangerous to livestock and humans.

Another clipping quoted Louis H. Camisa, an official of the company, admitting that mistakes were made, that poison had been sprayed on land owned by others, that excessive quantities had been spilled where a helicopter had been loaded, that adequate liaison had not been maintained with game and fish technicians. Perhaps most significant was his statement that the project was ended and the company had no plans to repeat the exercise.

I wrote also to Buddy Houts, of the *Chattanooga News-Free Press,* a widely respected reporter, who had dug deeper into the case than any newsman in Tennessee. He replied:

"I was notified of the spreading of the poisoned grain and the absence of birds or wildlife on the mountain by Hoyt Bonds last winter when he returned from the area and said there was nothing living there—an area that was formerly abundant with foxes, opossums, rabbits, and other animals, along with game birds.

"This man [Bonds] is a professional trapper, hunter, fisherman, and one of the most learned outdoorsmen and naturalists in this area. He is also a beekeeper. He is considered by me and a great many others to be this area's authority on nature. He can track an animal through the wildest country and tell you approximately how many of each species of animals are in each section of the forests in this part of East Tennessee.

"Mr. Bonds found a dead rabbit and noticed several other rabbits that were obviously ill or in a drugged condition. He then found two dead dogs. He became concerned about this situation when he found piles of poisoned grain under bushes and out in the loading area that had apparently spilled from trucks, and notified me at the paper.

"I have also interviewed and have been contacted by other hunters in this area who personally investigated the area and they all, to a man, agreed with Mr. Bonds."

Bowaters and friends have tried to discredit Hoyt Bonds and other sportsmen who have criticized the poison operation. Nevertheless, Mr. Bonds provided me with a highly significant letter written to him by Marzine Hudson, of the Bureau of Sport Fisheries and Wildlife, which reads in part:

". . . You were with John Oberheu and myself when this investigation was made. You listened to the conversations that we had with many people in the Signal Mountain area and you know what statements each of them made with reference to the disappearance of quail, rabbits, and song birds. All of these people cannot be wrong in the statements they were making. I realize this and I also realize that I have an obligation to the people of Chattanooga as far as the results of this investigation go. Since I am not at liberty to give you a copy of the report that I made to the Regional Office you might secure one by writing to our Regional Director in Atlanta. I have not had an opportunity to see a copy of Oberheu's report, but I assume he reported about the same thing. These reports submitted included interviews with the different people that we talked to on Signal Mountain so therefore you may draw your own conclusions as to how John and I both feel about the vole problem. I feel we investigated the matter about seven weeks late."

However, when concerned citizens and a member of the press of Tennessee wrote to the Regional Director, he refused to make copies of the Hudson report available to them—clearly a violation of the Freedom of Information Law.

At this point I decided to seek other counsel. I therefore went to three eminent biologists, men of national and international stature, asking them to carefully review the files I had assembled and to give their best judgment. I quote from their reports:

Victor Cahalane, former Chief Biologist, National Park Service; president of the organization called Defenders of Wildlife; author of many books, including the *Imperial Collection of Audubon Animals:*

"At this distance, I am not in a position to judge the merits of the paper company's case. However, it is evident that the poison which was broadcast over some 12,000 acres of land had the capacity for poisoning other wildlife as well as the target species. The green dye which was added should have deterred birds from eating the bait, but it would be quite ineffective in safeguarding mammals. Anything eating the voles or other victims would be affected through secondary poisoning."

Dr. Clarence Cottam, Director, Welder Wildlife Foundation, formerly Assistant Director, U. S. Fish and Wildlife Service:

"From the records and comments given it is evident that some mistakes were made in the control operations. There does seem to be evidence that baited and poisoned cracked corn was placed out by means other than being broadcast from a helicopter. If one can pick up any quantity of this and find it in piles it is perfectly obvious that it hasn't been well put out. When poisoned grain is put out in that fashion it is perfectly obvious that it can't help but do a lot of damage to non-target species. An aerial procedure of spreading poisoned bait, spray or dust, makes it almost a sure fact that non-target species will be killed, and I think there is little doubt that a good many were killed in this instance.

"The fact that Dr. Dimmick recommended a much stronger dye and was not satisfied with the coloring in the grain is further evidence that there was a good chance of a good many birds being adversely affected. This, however, should affect only species that are seed eaters, but there are many of these. It would be surprising indeed if many birds were not killed. From my many years' experience in the Fish and Wildlife Service, may I say emphatically that there isn't any question that a sick animal, bird, or mammal, normally seeks cover when it becomes distressed. Therefore, if any significant number of mammals or birds were found it is quite certain that the loss was infinitely higher than what would appear on the surface."

Dr. E. Raymond Hall, Summerfield Distinguished Professor, University of Kansas; for many years Director, Natural History Museum of Kansas, and of the State Biological Survey; author of the classic two-volume work, *Mammals of North America:*

"Before, after, and during the twenty-five years I was Director of the State Biological Survey here I never recommended zinc phosphide and if asked specifically about it recommended against its use, because of its known disadvantages. It does upset the ecosystem.

"The poisoning certainly increases the chances of greater rodent damage to the plantings in the next few years. There are better ways to manage the plantings. Without having seen them I cannot, of course, be sure of which management practice would be the best. Bowaters SPC had bad advice."

In addition to these contacts, I carefully reviewed literature on zinc phosphide published by the National Communicable Disease Center of the Public Health Service; National Pest Control Association; Northeast Regional Pest Coordinators; California Agriculture Experiment Station at the University of California at Davis; Hanna's Handbook of Agricultural Chemicals; and other sources, including the splendid book *Pesticides and the Living Landscape* by Professor Robert Rudd. Although Bowaters and friends insisted that zinc phosphide kills only voles, virtually every piece of up-to-date literature stresses this to be an intense, extremely dangerous and long-lasting poison.

Warnings such as the following are plain and plentiful:

"Zinc phosphide must be used with care, as it is toxic to all forms of animal life. It has poisoned humans, as well as domestic and wild animals . . ." "Secondary hazards do exist. Dogs, cats, or other animals can die from eating zinc-phosphide-poisoned rodents. Zinc phosphide does remain toxic for as long as several days in the guts of dead rats or mice . . ." "In the presence of moisture, zinc phosphide decomposes slowly, releasing phosphide gas which is very toxic. Dry baits must be considered to be toxic indefinitely. It is poisonous to all animals . . ." "Zinc phosphide is known to be nearly insoluble in water . . ." "The use of such products must be carried out with great care . . . be certain to remove and destroy all uneaten baits at the end of poisoning period . . ." ". . . carnivorous birds will find that poisoned animals are easy targets, and consequently secondary poisoning will be likely."

Now for my visit to Tennessee itself. It began with a dinner given by a group of local outdoorsmen, representing at least half a dozen clubs, from the Chattanooga Trout Association to the Tennessee Beekeepers Association. They were fine citizens—civic leaders, professionals, and businessmen—and devoted sportsmen, desperately concerned and angry about deterioration of the native natural resources. Hoyt Bonds, the trapper and beekeeper, was there, of course, respected by all for his courage, personal sacrifice, and public service.

The next day Mr. Bonds, Hubert Fry—a prominent sportsman and former member of the State Game and Fish Commission—and I took to the hills. We stopped first at the barber shop operated on Signal Mountain by J. J. Hillis, president of the Waldens Ridge Sportsmen's Club. He told me that following the poisoning he had walked the woods and personally found two dead rabbits, two dead squirrels, and one dead great horned owl. He presented me with a bill of particulars endorsed by his club members containing the following charges: "It is absolutely a false statement when Hiwassee Land Co. says that members from only one club visited the area poisoned. We feel poisoning of any type should be completely banned. We have inspected the area and found that voles have not caused enough damage to warrant such poisoning. Hiwassee Land Co. has not left 25 percent of the hardwood as they have stated. They are also continually spraying the area, killing hardwood, all types of insects, bees, butterflies, hummingbirds, etc. We believe these poisons are absolutely a detriment to the health of human beings and all types of wildlife."

The expressions voiced by Mr. Hillis were echoed repeatedly during the day by farmers and other landowners on Signal Mountain and the foothills of the Cumberland Plateau. They told of finding dead and dying quail, doves, rabbits, red birds, etc.—and they were the same people who had been interviewed by the State and Federal investigators. One said poisoned corn was all over his property, which adjoins Bowaters land. "I found poison in the water and was afraid to drink," said another. "People are afraid to hunt and eat game with poison in the system." They told me that Signal Mountain had been a squirrel hunter's paradise, rich also in quail, grouse, rabbits, and raccoons, but that now, with its rows of planted pine soldiers, it was nearly sterile. I saw the gaunt and ghostly hardwoods, including many tall trees, killed by poison other than zinc phosphide, as mute testimony of the diverse forest that had been.

On the day that I arrived in Tennessee, Bowaters announced postponement and possible cancellation of its second poison attack on the voles. This was wise: Total annihilation programs for rodents are rarely successful; declines are followed by greater reproductive success. Instead of searching for panaceas in the bag of trick poisons, one might suggest careful research and serious self-searching concerning forest management practices that may account for high vole populations. For example, I saw huge windrows, bulldozed piles of dead hardwood—an utterly wasted natural resource, incidentally— serving as a clear source of protection for rodents.

Oh yes, about the bees. Soon after I left Tennessee, the State Apiarist issued a statement confirming the reported loss of more than 700 bee colonies. "I am quite sure that many losses have not been reported," he added. "I do not believe that beekeeping in or near areas that are sprayed with chemicals from planes is safe due to drifting of the chemicals which are toxic to bees.": His statement was followed by a resolution adopted by the Tennessee Beekeepers Association condemning Bowaters by name and demanding a cessation of its practices "which have destroyed beekeeping and wildlife resources in many counties of Tennessee."

I should differentiate between the chemicals used in vole eradication and hardwood conversion. Zinc phosphide is the rodenticide. Quite a different chemical called 2,4,5-T (as well as another one, 2,4-D, a relative of DDT) kills the hardwoods through spraying by helicopter or tractor-drawn mist blowers. Streetman assured me that, so far as his company knows, 2,4,5-T has no effect on wildlife. But he did not say anything about the effect on people.

On October 29, the White House in Washington announced steps by the Federal Government to no longer permit application of 2,4,5-T on food crops, based on increasing evidence that it may cause cancer and the malformation of unborn children.

It should be evident to all that in areas like East Tennessee, where Bowaters forest holdings and private farms are intermingled, 2,4,5-T constitutes a threat to human life. The White House action was significant as an opening step but did not go far enough. The use of this chemical must be stopped at once. The Departments of Agriculture and Interior have been ordered to halt any use of 2,4,5-T in their own programs "in populated areas or where the residue from use could otherwise reach man." The same rules must apply to forests, public and private, in the South and the entire nation.

During August, *Field & Stream* requested of John Gottschalk, Director of the Bureau of Sport Fisheries and Wildlife, verification and clarification of statements made by his associates in the field in the Bowaters case. One month later he advised orally that his reply would be forthcoming. As of this writing, no reply has been received.

I have many friends in the Bureau of Sport Fisheries and Wildlife and have high regard for them. In the Bowaters case, however, this agency has distinguished itself by incompetence, dereliction of duty, suppression of information, and playing the servant of industry instead of the champion of the public interest.

The people must protect themselves and the game that is their heritage. A clipping sent to me recently from Winchester, Tennessee, reveals the mysterious death of 75,000 or more fish in Beans Creek, the poisoning of truck patches, stock ponds, the death of dogs and bees.

This kind of environmental annihilation can be stopped, but the people must be determined in their demands for responsibility from industry and responsiveness from government.

Chapter 8

To Save the Southern Highlands

It was in 1901 when the Secretary of Agriculture, James Wilson, transmitted to President Theodore Roosevelt the monumental report on southern Appalachia that had been conceived by the Chief Forester, Gifford Pinchot. Never has there been anything like it, before or since that time, that so comprehensively studied the resources of this highlands region and the steps required to assure its lasting protection and productivity.

Appalachia was already then a cultural and social unit, the "Back of Beyond." Horace Kephart, the writer, who arrived in the mountains early in the century, called it the "housetop of Eastern America." He found it a frontier of time, where old legends were daily realities for the pioneer farmers, herdsmen and hunters, trappers and traders, preachers, outlaws, and Indians. It was almost as though he had been carried back, asleep, and had awakened in the eighteenth century to meet Daniel Boone and his kith in flesh and blood.

That 1901 report, however, viewed the Appalachian scene from southwestern Virginia to Alabama with a broader perspective. The region had been sparsely settled and little visited, it revealed, until it was discovered near the end of the last century by lumbermen and miners. At once they joined the hillside farmers in stripping the mountains of their treasures. Forests that had taken centuries to grow were decimated in less than a decade. From any one of thousands of cleared fields more soil sometimes was removed during a

From *National Parks*, January 1971.

single heavy rain than during the preceding ten centuries of natural forestation.

Where the forest was not invaded, it was a wonder to behold. Flowers and shrubs grew everywhere, in the densest woods, and in open clearings and on the treeless, tangled heath balds of the higher mountaintops. The incredible variety of life-forms still is the most spectacular feature of the southern Appalachian land. Here the Fraser magnolia, or "cucumber tree," of the South thrives on the same mountainside with the red spruce of the Canadian forests. The peaks are green, and their slopes are contoured, in contrast to the stony outcrops of New England and the Rockies. Appalachia had escaped the Pleistocene glacial sheets that flowed down over the continent, becoming instead a haven for northern lifeforms that had been driven south in search of survival.

"It may be added," wrote Secretary Wilson about southern Appalachia, "that it contains the highest and largest mountain masses, and perhaps the wildest and most picturesque scenery, east of the Mississippi River; that it is a region of perfect healthfulness, already largely used as a health resort both summer and winter, and that it lies within a little more than a day's travel of the larger portion of the population of this country."

On this basis, he (and Pinchot) proposed establishment of a vast Appalachian national park or forest reserve, with provision for careful and conservative logging of valuable timber trees such as walnut, cherry, tulip poplar, white oak, white pine, and basswood, and assuring protection of the forest cover for the benefit of valleys below and cities far beyond. The idea was endorsed heartily by the President; by the legislatures of five Southern mountain states; and by a host of scientific, patriotic, business, and civic organizations, including the Appalachian National Park Association, which had been founded specifically to advance the cause of the region.

As a result of such rising public pressure, Congress in 1911 enacted the Weeks Law to establish national forests in the East. The first purchase of land was made in North Carolina, the heart of the highlands, for the new Pisgah National Forest. The full scope of the program, however, never was realized.

The principles set forth in the 1901 report are as valid today as when it was published 70 years ago—and as urgently needed. Appalachia is in trouble. In places where forest cover should be carefully protected, the mountains are being exploited through construction of resorts, second-home subdivisions, condominiums, golf courses, and chair lifts, projects that benefit only a few and shut off access to the many. The Appalachian regional aid program, ostensibly designed to serve the undernourished and overlooked humble of the region, has provided a stimulus to highway and dam builders and industrial polluters, while creating few jobs or other benefits for those who need them most.

It is difficult to assess which federal resource agency is most derelict in its duties or is effecting the most damage to Appalachia. The Forest Service, for example, which received the mantle of responsibility under the Weeks Law, persists in promoting timber production above other uses, certainly with disdain for botanical and biological values.

"The vegetation of this area, as part of the Southern Appalachian Highlands, represents the greatest richness of any forest flora on this planet," Dr. Robert B. Platt, Chairman of the Biology Department at Emory University, declared recently. His statement was made in opposition to tree-cutting on moderate to very steep slopes of the Nantahala National Forest, adjacent to a primitive Girl Scout camp called the Standing Indian Natural Area. "Current usage of much of the irreplaceable resources of the national forest is being evaluated primarily in terms of the needs of those who control society today, whereas the needs of the oncoming generations are not yet known. A vastly increased need for recreational areas of all kinds, including wilderness and semi-wilderness areas, can be predicted with as much substance as the needs of the oncoming generation for lumber."

The Forest Service lately has conducted a series of "Listening sessions" as part of what it calls "a bold new program aimed at getting better coordination and balance in land use and planning on national forests in the Southern Appalachian Mountains." Certainly confession is good for the soul, even of an old-line bureaucracy set in its ways. Although the signs may be hopeful, one must wonder about the ultimate objective when the "listening" is accompanied by a stream of color brochures and other promotions describing the abundant blessings of clearcutting, a thoroughly "efficient and economic" system of placing timber production above all other considerations. As recently as March 6, 1971, before a Tennessee wildlife symposium, a Forest Service wildlife biologist, Jerry McIlwain, extolled the ability of clearcutting to provide food for game. He did not, however, discuss such aspects as the disruption of ecosystems; the use of 2,4,5-T to poison native hardwoods, which are the source of game food; the extensive size of clearcuts, leaving bare ground and dead stumps over large areas; or the effect on aquatic life of streams.

"There is little indication of a genuine desire to bring the people into the decision-making process," declares Dr. Charles S. Prigmore, president of the Alabama Conservancy, which is leading the fight to establish an 11,000-acre wilderness in Bankhead National Forest, despite resistance from the federal agency. "The Forest Service indeed holds hearings at infrequent intervals, particularly when public pressure becomes irresistible. But this is an attitude of patient tolerance of public concern and thinking, rather than any real encouragement of joint decision-making. Forest Service personnel consider themselves to be the experts and the public to be ignorant at best and obstructionist at worst."

The case of the projected road across the Unicoi Mountains between Tellico, Tennessee, and Robbinsville, North Carolina, constitutes an especially sorry chapter. For here the leadership of the Forest Service decided for its own convenience—without considering the public—to sacrifice the Joyce Kilmer Memorial Forest, which lies astride the route.

When this marvelous primeval tract of 3,800 acres in Nantahala National Forest was established in 1934 as a memorial to the author of "Trees," the agency pledged to protect it forever as "a place of inspiration and a treasure of native flora and fauna." So it has been loved and enjoyed by countless thousands. But in 1964 Edward P. Cliff, Chief of the Forest Service, approved the construction of a road on steep terrain in the upper portion of Joyce Kilmer. He told his boss, Secretary of Agriculture Orville L. Freeman, that the highway would improve access. But he failed to mention the inevitable scars in the wilderness from cuts and fills, disruption of the ecosystem due to siltation, or that heavy tourist travel would create pressure on a fragile area protected primarily by lack of access. The Chief carefully avoided open hearings. When finally they were conducted, in June 1970, the Forest Service and Bureau of Public Roads chose Robbinsville, off the beaten path, and gave scant public notice.

The public, nevertheless, has protested with vigor. Last October a group went out to observe destruction already wrought by surveying crews. They carried signs bearing such messages as: "Joyce Kilmer, Shot in 1918—Raped in 1970" and "Roads are made by fools like thee, only God can make a tree." Local residents have been told the road would bring in tourist dollars. But the boomers did not say it would disrupt the quality of outdoors life the people now enjoy, or that it would drive away hunters, fishermen, campers, hikers, and nature lovers. "You can't make a scenic highway for people who want to see a virgin forest," Newt Smith, professor at Western Carolina University, declared before an ecology protest seminar.

The Forest Service now speaks of moving the highway across a ridgetop into the Slickrock drainage. But this concession is not enough, particularly when citizen groups are proposing the establishment of a Slickrock–Joyce Kilmer wilderness area. There is no way to minimize damage or restore ecological balance when a modern highway invades a highland wilderness; the road destroys. The most desirable, and least expensive, alternative is to cease construction altogether, utilizing the two ends of the road as gateways to the wilderness and memorials to common sense regained.

Another wanton and wasteful construction project that needs to be canceled forthwith is the Tellico dam project on the Little Tennessee River in East Tennessee. This boondoggle is promoted by the Tennessee Valley Authority as a "multipurpose river development," but is not justified by navigation or flood control needs, or by demand for manufacturing locations, inasmuch as many industrial sites on nearby reservoirs are going begging for users.

In this valley a dam would wipe out nearly 15,000 acres of fertile bottomland. It also would drown the remains of the ancestral capital of the Cherokee Indians, called Echota, or "Chote the metropolis," and nearby Tuskegee, birthplace of Sequoyah, the Indian scholar, which may be among the most important archaeological sites in eastern America. Another major historic site along the "Little T," Fort Loudoun, the first English fort west of the Appalachians, was reconstructed with loving care over a period of many years by patriotic Tennesseans. Though it would not be totally destroyed, the fort would become accessible only by boat, making a mockery of its historical context.

TVA, unresponsive to the people and exemplifying bureaucracy unleashed, has tried to dismiss its opponents as "a handful of selfish trout fishermen trying to deprive the region of progress." But in fact the Association to Save the Little Tennessee has had the widest support from patriotic, farm, and conservation organizations. It is now fighting through legal means to save the last stretch of the river that remains undammed—a clear, cold stream that provides superb canoeing and miles of the finest trout fishing in America. With its unique qualities it could easily be designated a national or state scenic river and provide an economic resource in its own right. The river could become the core of a real regional plan encompassing the adjacent Great Smoky Mountains National Park, national forests, and TVA reservoirs. Only $4 million involved in construction of the Tellico dam thus far would be lost. The cost of development of a national or state scenic river would be fractional and the return far greater.

TVA's masquerade as an experiment in regional planning is over. TVA has deteriorated into an environmental disaster, a booster of unneeded and unwanted construction for its own self-indulgence and self-perpetuation. In western North Carolina it lately has spawned a nightmarish "water resources development" plan for the Upper French Broad River basin, calling for the eviction of hundreds of rural families and the flooding of more than 10,000 acres, including fine farmland. The Upper French Broad Defense Association is mobilizing political, scientific, and legal support to save the area.

One should not fail to record TVA's contribution to the devastation of Appalachia through strip mining. This agency is the largest purchaser of coal in the world. Its purchasing policies drive the price of coal to a level where it can be mined economically only by stripping. As a result, many countrysides, particularly in Kentucky and

West Virginia, have been rendered desolate. Mountain families have been driven to seek refuge in urban ghettos. Lakes, streams, and rivers have been fouled with acid, silt, and sediment. For years TVA operated without land reclamation requirements in its coal contracts; but even now, though such stipulation appears in the standard contract, there is little reclamation or enforcement. Little wonder that the Environmental Defense Fund and other groups have brought suit against TVA for contracting for coal without filing environmental impact statements as required by the National Environmental Policy Act.

Citizens have the right to expect the quintessence of environmental responsibility from the National Park Service, above all other agencies. But in directing the affairs of the Great Smoky Mountains National Park, chosen years ago by Congress and the people for preservation as the wilderness jewel of southern Appalachia, this has simply not been the case.

In 1966 the National Park Service presented a wilderness plan that was, in fact, a design to carve up and fragment the Smokies with modern highways. Only the intensity of public opposition stayed its hand. Now the agency has issued a new report conceding at last that the Smokies comprise "a natural treasure of plant and animal life living in an ecological balance that once destroyed can never be restored." This document seems to recognize the worst enemy of the parks as the automobile, proposing restrictions on traffic and gradual phasing out of Route 441, a main highway bisecting the park. In addition, the proposal of another wilderness-disrupting highway, which highlighted the plan of 1966, is withdrawn in favor of a scenic loop road around the perimeter of the park, as urged by citizen organizations.

But this is not enough. Along the loop road the Park Service intends to locate no fewer than 12 visitor "clusters," complete with campgrounds and a special breed of highway masqueraded under the label "motor nature trail." Disregarding environmental impact and its mandate by law to preserve the wilderness for the benefit of future generations, the Park Service persists in clinging to a 1943 agreement with Swain County, North Carolina, guaranteeing road access between Bryson City and Fontana, to rationalize overdevelopment. Actually, it is the same old appeal for numbers, or, at best, pragmatic solving of today's problems at the sacrifice of tomorrow's civilization.

"It must be clear that the demand which now looms over us can never be satisfied," once wrote Harvey Broome, the late apostle of the Great Smoky Mountains Hiking Club and president of the Wilderness Society. "Slow attrition follows development. Almost without exception, wherever there is a road or dug trail or shelter facility in the virgin forest, there is slowly spreading damage. The areas contiguous to developments become littered, eroded or threadbare from heavy use and abuse.

"No further development of any character should take place. No more trails; no more shelters; no more roads; no expansions, extensions, or additions to existing facilities. To protect what is left we must learn to live with facilities we now have. The hardest thing will be the decision itself."

Federal administrators obviously lack the commitment of courage to make the hard decision. In all the great natural domain of southern Appalachia, only two areas of North Carolina national forests, Linville Gorge and Shining Rock, totaling but 20,000 acres, are protected in the National Wilderness Preservation System. Yet the desire of the people is abundantly plain. Speaking for fellow Alabamians supporting the proposed Sipsey Wilderness, a remnant of the original forest in the gorges of the Sipsey River, Governor George C. Wallace declared, "I am vitally interested in saving some segment of our wild areas for the enjoyment of future generations."

Unselfish people are advancing the same idea throughout Appalachia. An Asheville businessman, John M. Reynolds, proposed in 1969 establishment of a great new wild park composed of federal, state, and private lands north of Asheville, encompassing Mount Mitchell, the Craggies, and Black Brothers range, some of the most picturesque property in the East. "The time is coming fast," he warned, "when there will be no more wild land to acquire."

"We owe it to the human heritage to rebuild 'old growth' or climax forest ecologies in substantial quantity in all elevations of the country," declared George Hermach, of Marion, Virginia, at one of the public hearings conducted by the Forest Service. His idea is to insure the opportunity of generations unborn to walk again in the Appalachian hardwood forests among trees of 5-foot diameter.

Certainly these matchless mountains and their sparkling streams deserve the same love and care that men for centuries have bestowed upon their finest works of art. The 1901 plan still can provide a valid guide. It should be updated with a comprehensive inventory of the Appalachian environment, its flora and fauna, and the needs of its native people. This mission can be accomplished by those who have abiding faith in themselves, in each other, and in the future of the southern highlands.

Chapter 9

Harvey Broome, My Teacher and Hero

Harvey Broome was a man of the wilderness, for all seasons and all weather. As president of the Wilderness Society, an organization he helped found in 1935, he was an able, inspiring spokesman for a movement that is now penetrating the conscience of America.

On my first hike with him in the Great Smoky Mountains, we ventured to the Chimney Tops, a steep climb, almost vertical for several hundred feet, hand over hand from one rocky perch to the next. It was raining and I dared to complain. Harvey answered with a laugh. "You don't complain about weather in the Smokies. You just learn to accept it!"

In *Faces of the Wilderness* (published following his death by his wife, Anne) Harvey reveals himself exactly as I knew and loved him: a gentle spirit, sensitive to the needs of nature and his fellowman, always with tolerance and good humor. Such individuals are rare, and so are such intimate and appealing books as this one.The reader shares discomforts, discoveries and exhilarations of wilderness travel in various sections of the country, on seashores, in deserts and high in the mountains from Alaska to the Everglades; and, when he puts the book down, he feels (as Justice William O. Douglas comments in the foreword) that he has been in the good company of a man who honored the earth for its mystery and beauty.

Most chapters represent personal accounts of field trips taken by the Council of the Wilderness Society in conjunction with its annual

---

From *Smithsonian*, March 1973.

meetings, starting with the first in 1946 up through 1965. Broome died in 1968.

His book is no preachment, but the lesson to be derived from it is plain: Man must live in reasonable harmony with nature or perish from this earth.

On the western slope of the Olympic Peninsula in Washington, Harvey walked through the beautiful Bogachiel and Hoh watersheds, preserved in their pure, natural state as a part of Olympic National Park, and then into logged-over areas administered by the Forest Service. The latter were "places of grayness, dead limbs, dead boles, washings, and of torn, lifeless soil. . . . The waste was appalling." As Harvey recorded the scene: "Gray log butts eight feet in diameter, twenty-four feet long, cracked in the sun. They had been left to disintegrate presumably because they had an unsightly or inconvenient knot. This waste of wood was spiritually devastating. Men had sought to convert the green life and repose of the forest we were in, to the dead grayness of the forest we had left, because of the 'shortage' of lumber. Why had they not used up what they had abandoned? Some of the stumps were twelve and fifteen feet above the ground."

He saw deficiencies as well in our national parks. "The atmosphere was holidayish but there was no wilderness," he wrote of the scene around Old Faithful in Yellowstone. "People swarmed from their cars to see the buffalo, as though they were starved for the sight of something old and natural and primordial. And yet, so far have we moved from that past, several nearly grown boys referred to the bison as a deer."

Perhaps the solution lies in extensive preservation and wise use of wilderness as part of the national life-style. People need to learn, starting in their tender years, love and reverence for nature, and through nature, for one another. This is Harvey Broome's "optimum goal for all mankind"—a message of hope.

Chapter 10

Any Wilderness in the East?

The wooded, rocky region bordering the Sipsey Fork of the Black
Warrior River first came into public attention in 1969. That was the
year the Alabama Conservancy undertook its research for remaining
natural areas that might contain virgin forest to propose for inclusion
in the National Wilderness Preservation System. The hunt inevitably
led to the Sipsey, embraced within the Bankhead National Forest of
northwest Alabama, a naturally hardwood area, threaded with
streams and waterfalls in deeply eroded valleys that fall away
abruptly into towering perpendicular sandstone cliffs.

The Conservancy had been organized by concerned citizens in
order to cope with Alabama resource issues, including air and water
pollution, strip-mining of coal, and the disruption of many natural
streams through construction of dams and technological channel-
straightening, or "channelization." Then there was the challenge
presented throughout the state by conversion of millions of forested
acres of hardwoods and pines, capable of supporting diverse flora
and fauna, into tree farms of pine only, designed strictly for production of pulp and paper.

The area suggested for wilderness review covers 11,000 acres. It
includes the Bee Branch Scenic Area, a 1,240-acre tract of rough
gorges, which had been protected administratively by the Forest
Service for a number of years. In this region the Forest Service was
engaged in a program of "stand conversion": spreading toxic chemi-

From *Battle for the Wilderness* (New York: Praeger, 1974; Boulder, Colo.:
Westview, 1984).

Any Wilderness in the East?   81

cal herbicides (usually 2,4-D and 2,4,5-T), bulldozing, and clear-cutting to kill the natural hardwood forest in order to replace it with even-aged pine plantations.

Here the southern tip of the Cumberland Plateau meets the ecological influence of the coastal plain. In times past the Chickasaw and Cherokee Indians roamed among the towering trees, in company with mountain lion, bear, and beaver, where the abundant water and sheltering walls now enclose an island of the past.

The hiker descending into the deep gorges finds the rimrock cliff exposed in grayish and yellow hues, while waterfalls tumble over monstrous boulders to the valley floor. Only a remnant of the original forest survives in the 30-mile chain of gorges, but it is a distinctive forest. Deep shade, a constant supply of moisture, and cool summer temperatures provide a southern refuge for plants normally found farther north. Alabama's largest tulip poplar tree, nearly twenty-two feet in circumference, grows in the box canyon of Bee Branch. In the same setting are eastern hemlock and sweet birch, crowned with its gracefully symmetrical round top, ferns, flowering shrubs and plants, and mountain laurel climbing 100 feet on the steep slopes.

The proposed wilderness represents only a small portion of the Bankhead National Forest—only 6 percent—and an even smaller portion of all private and public forest lands in the state, one two-thousandth of 22 million acres. Nevertheless, the Forest Service responded categorically that no forest land meeting wilderness standards could possibly exist in Alabama. The Sipsey area, in particular, was disqualified because portions had been briefly farmed by man and a few wagon roads built.

In November 1969 the agency showed members of the Conservancy its management plans. Only the canyons and the scenic area were to be exempt from clearcutting and stand conversion. The gorges were to be preserved, because it was economically unfeasible to cut them, but the ridges (which provide moisture and protection for the gorges' ecosystem) were to be clear-cut and converted. The Conservancy requested and was granted a year's moratorium in order to conduct a wilderness feasibility study.*

---

*The Forest Service conducted a study of soils in the proposed wilderness, examining the cliff slopes and stream bottoms, and reported them to represent

The Conservancy then undertook to survey the wildlife, plants, geology, speleology, and history, with the foremost authorities in these fields contributing their time and talent. The report on the Sipsey was completed before the moratorium ended. The Conservancy investigators found there are still deer, squirrels, otters, mink, beavers, and raccoons in the area. Many fish driven out of major rivers by pollution, siltation, damming, and ditching are found only in remaining natural rivers like the Sipsey and its tributaries. These include not only popular fishing species, such as bass and sunfish, but two kinds of darters, colorful little minnows, previously unknown and unnamed. There are no less than eighty species of birds, ranging from northern whippoorwill to southern chuck-will's-widow, of which more than half depend upon the hardwood environment to survive. Because birds are so mobile, ecological conditions of the Sipsey may affect populations of birds hundreds or thousands of miles away which depend on the kind of food and cover they find during migration or while wintering down South.

There is not a cranny in such rocks, not a foot of the Appalachian wildwood but harbors something lovable and rare. Turn over any rock or log and something unusual is apt to be exposed. Perhaps a red-backed salamander, its fox-red dorsal strip contrasting with a mixture of dark and light spots on its belly, or a seal salamander, or one of the lungless group, living without gills or lungs under the moist, mossy floors of the mountain forests. Many salamanders are endemic to the Appalachians, found in their own special corners and nowhere else. Of what use are they? Possibly none at all, at least not to man, or not in practical terms to man. They're part of a living community, whose members don't go around destroying their own homeland or poisoning their food and water; they evolve and adapt within a given environment and, to the extent that man learns from them, that becomes a use, too.

The committed citizens of the Alabama Conservancy felt they had located an area providing "outstanding opportunities for

---

"the ultimate in hardwood sites to be found in Alabama." The study also concluded that 65 percent, or 7,000 acres, of the suggested wilderness area was "poorly suited" for intensive forestry management such as clear-cutting and that it would be hazardous to construct roads, due to danger from erosion.

solitude, and the primitive unconfined type of recreation" as prescribed, or required, by the Wilderness Act. Legislation to establish
a Sipsey Wilderness was introduced by both of Alabama's senators,
who obviously concurred. It was endorsed by the governor, the
Alabama Department of Conservation, the Alabama legislature in a
joint resolution, major national conservation organizations, and by a
petition bearing the signatures of 20,000 Alabamians.

Despite this outpouring of public expression, the Forest Service
remained unmoved, insisting in May 1971 that the scars of human
use borne by the Sipsey gravitate overwhelmingly against it. Four
months later Associate Chief (and soon Chief) John R. McGuire
expounded the official position that there was no wilderness left
east of the Rockies to qualify under terms of the Wilderness Act.

Is there any wilderness in the East?

This region of America is pictured throughout the world as a
massive urbanized web, overpopulated and overpolluted. The view
is quite correct, of course—which makes the last wild fragments
worth clinging to: those bits and pieces of original seacoast, estuarine
salt marshes and inland fresh-water swamps, the primeval forests
that have managed, without benefit of "management," somehow
through natural attacks by fire, insects, tornadoes, volcanoes, and
hurricanes for millions of years, and the mountains, including some
of the oldest on earth. Certainly every ridge, crag, and wooded
ravine, such as those in the Sipsey of Alabama, will become more
valuable in the flood tide of civilization around them.

The Forest Service administers approximately 23 million acres
of federal land in the East, extending from the White Mountains of
Maine and New Hampshire down through the southern Appalachians to the Florida plain and across the Ozarks and Ouachita Mountains and the states bordering the Great Lakes. Unlike western
national forests, which were carved out of the public domain, most
of the eastern lands were formerly private holdings acquired
through purchase under the Weeks Law of 1911. They include a
variety of formerly remote and undeveloped areas, as well as many
others that have reverted to natural condition through years of
protection.

Conservationists have nominated scores of potential additions to

the wilderness system, but the Forest Service has turned them all
down. When interested and concerned citizens have inquired about
saving what appears to them as wilderness, the answers uniformly
have been either, "The works of man have marred it" or "It is less
than 5,000 acres in size." As Chief of the Forest Service Edward P.
Cliff declared at the Sierra Club Biennial Wilderness Conference held
at San Francisco in 1967, "Personally, I hope very much that we will
not see a lowering of quality standards to make acceptable some
man-made intrusions or defects of other kinds simply for the sake of
adding acreage." On this basis numerous areas throughout the
National Forest System have been withheld from wilderness protection for purposes of multiple-use management, with foresters
making all the decisions on their own.

The concept and spirit of wilderness are defined in the Act; two
key phrases, "retaining its primeval character and influence" and
"the imprint of man's work [must be] substantially unnoticeable,"
are used to describe wilderness. The Forest Service zeros in on the
word "primeval," closing the options to anything but virgin forest,
but there is no requirement that the forest must be virgin or that all
evidence of man be absent. Conservationists believe that the phrase
"substantially unnoticeable" provides leeway for interpretation, as
U.S. District Judge William E. Doyle expressed it in the landmark
1970 East Meadow Creek case in Colorado, and opens the door to
admissibility of recoverable areas.

This question was discussed in 1970 by the second session of the
Ninety-first Congress. In reporting on H. R. 19007, a bill designating
for addition to the National Wilderness Preservation System portions
of several national wildlife refuges, national parks and monuments,
and national forests, located in twelve states, the House Committee
on Interior and Insular Affairs noted near the outset of its report that
the areas range from over 50,000 acres down to 3 acres. "The areas
have little in common except one very distinctive characteristic," the
committee commented. "Each is an undeveloped tract of Federal
land retaining its natural character and influences without permanent improvements or human habitation. Each can be managed and
protected to preserve its natural conditions for the use and enjoyment of future generations. Each presents outstanding opportunities

for recreation and solitude as well as having value for scientific study."

During consideration of these areas for wilderness designation, testimony had disclosed that some were not entirely free of man-made improvements. In most instances, the Department of the Interior and Department of Agriculture had recommended the exclusion of land immediately surrounding such structures or improvements. In a few other situations where improvements exist, the committee had been assured by departmental witnesses that these were scheduled for removal upon designation of the areas as wilderness. "The committee approves and accepts this position and wishes to emphasize its own conviction that these areas must be kept free of man-made intrusions and of nonconforming uses." But it did not say that it would not accept them into the system because of such intrusions or uses.

To the contrary, the report details the subvirginal qualities of the several areas in question. For instance, the Seney Wilderness, the 25,150-acre northwest section of the Seney National Wildlife Refuge in Upper Michigan, includes a varied mixture of tracts. Some lands, though never cut, in the late nineteenth century had been frequently swept by fires that followed logging nearby. The "string bogs," a subarctic formation rare this far south, with low ridges covered with tamarack, embraces two-thirds of the wilderness. The remainder was once a white pine forest, logged off before the turn of the century, then burned over many times, and now covered with large, charred pine stumps, second-growth aspen and jack pine, and a variety of other species. Likewise, in the Moosehorn Wilderness, within the Moosehorn National Wildlife Refuge in Maine, the Edmonds Unit had been logged over several times. "While not true forested wilderness in the strict sense of the word, the Edmonds Unit, if set aside as wilderness, will eventually become wilderness," the committee commented, in terming the Edmonds a "creative wilderness." Then it added, "There will be high interest in the changing ecology as years pass for the serious student and casual visitor alike."

No such expression has been heard from the Forest Service, only disclaimers of qualifications of *de facto* wilderness with the slightest blemishes and repeated assurances that multiple-use management will take care of everything. Yet one of the major purposes of the

Wilderness Act was to remove the power of absolute discretion from the Secretary of Agriculture and the Forest Service by placing the ultimate decision and responsibility for wilderness classification in Congress.

Based on its policy of purism, or purity, the Forest Service has decreed that no areas in national forests east of the Mississippi River qualify as wilderness. Before passage of the Act in 1964, the Service had cooperated with conservationists and designated as wild areas the 7,655-acre Linville Gorge and 13,400-acre Shining Rock tracts in North Carolina and the 5,400 acre Great Gulf in New Hampshire, even though the first two of these areas had been logged by railroad methods around the turn of the century, much the same as other Appalachian forests. In addition, however, other large areas within the eastern forests have regained their cover of mature trees, with fertile soil and high rainfall encouraging rapid growth. In the southern mountains, in particular, forests have the capacity to regrow and regenerate within thirty to fifty years to the point that trees provide the scenic beauty of wilderness. Railroad grades, too narrow and too temporary for use as more than trails, have reverted to the wild state, with overgrown banks and the few cuts into rock covered with moss, fern, and lichens. Nevertheless, the Forest Service has disclaimed wilderness qualifications of statutory and *de facto* wilderness with the exception of the Great Gulf. As John McGuire of the Forest Service declared before the biennial Wilderness Conference, conducted in Washington, D.C., in September 1971, "The areas with wilderness characteristics as defined in the Wilderness Act are virtually all in the West." McGuire told the conference that his agency recognized the pressing need in the East and South for providing primitive outdoor recreation opportunities and maintaining wildland values but insisted this must be done through alternatives to the Wilderness Act.*

The Forest Service has presumed to answer the desire for protection of primitive eastern forests through a variety of administrative designations, such as scenic areas, pioneer zones, and travel-

*The Forest Service offered to support a concept of "wild areas" specifically designed to meet eastern needs. Under terms of congressional legislation to establish such a system (National Forest Wild Areas bill, S. 3973 in 1972, S. 22 in 1973), a component unit would be one that is "an area of outstanding

influence and water-influence zones, within the multiple-use framework. But these have left much to be desired.

For example, in West Virginia, citizen groups, led by the West Virginia Highlands Conservancy, after studying the Wilderness Act, offered proposals for establishment of three units in the Monongahela National Forest: Dolly Sods, 18,000 acres; Otter Creek, 18,000 acres, and Cranberry Back Country, including two units of 26,300 acres and 10,000 acres. All were very choice locations for eastern America; the state of West Virginia, in fact, recommended that the Forest Service preserve "sizable primitive areas" in their natural condition, with these in mind.

The Otter Creek unit includes the complete bowl-shaped basin drained by Otter Creek and at least two contiguous areas of potential wilderness. Though almost completely stripped of timber during the harsh logging era of 1905–15, the area has remained almost undisturbed with hardwood and hemlock forests nearing maturity and is penetrated only by trails, including some on the old railroad grades. Otter Creek is considered outstanding for hiking and backpacking, while the basin is one of the few remaining West Virginia areas sufficiently remote to serve as breeding grounds for the heavily hunted black bear.

The Dolly Sods, a high, wild section of the Allegheny Plateau, also was logged over, but forests, including hardwoods and spruce, are slowly reclaiming the land. Many of the open, rocky higher ridges, known locally as "huckleberry plains," support a variety of heath shrubs, with blueberries summoning pickers when they ripen. Botanists find the sphagnum bogs, with a flora reminiscent of the Arctic tundra, especially worthy of study, while the diversity of plant communities supports many species of wildlife—bear, beaver, deer,

---

beauty; is primarily primitive and natural in character although man and his works may have been present and wherein the marks of man's activities are subject to restoration to the appearance of a primitive and natural condition; is large enough so that primitive and natural values can be preserved; and the area provides outstanding opportunities for public use and enjoyment in a primitive type setting." Conservationists united to oppose this concept, which appeared to duplicate and undermine the wilderness system and to promote intensive recreation rather than preserve wilderness.

wild turkey, and bobcat among them; the varying hare is quite common, a reminder of the Canada-like climate of the Dolly Sods.

The most attractive, varying, and important features of the Cranberry Back Country are its mountain streams rushing down from pine-capped heights, renowned not only for beauty but for their native trout populations. The tree species vary, too, from northern hardwoods at lower elevations up through hemlocks and pines on the mountain slopes to red spruce completely taking over the highest summits. Wildflowers follow a comparable progression pattern; naturalists, both amateur and professional, have no difficulty in identifying dozens of varieties. Trails offer possibilities for hikers of all degrees of competence, including one fifteen miles long completely crossing the back country atop a high ridge.

The Forest Service responded to the citizen wilderness proposals with something less than enthusiasm. On Otter Creek it countered with a plan whereby one-third of the area would be designated a pioneer study area and thus presumably protected against timber-cutting and road-building. The rest of the area would be called a "Back Country," where logging would go on, but timber access roads would be gated against unauthorized vehicles. When conservationists entered a formal appeal against this management plan, the supervisor of the Monongahela National Forest announced the road-building program was going ahead. Furthermore, he granted access to a coal company to build rough roads for core-drilling to establish quantity and quality of coal underlying the area. On the Dolly Sods proposal, the Forest Service agreed to designate a Dolly Sods Scenic Area, but deleted nearly all commercially valuable timberlands from the boundary.

"The Forest Service has administratively divided the Monongahela National Forest into small timber sales compartments, which eventually will have the effect of destroying the wilderness resource," advised George Langford of the West Virginia Highlands Conservancy in a March 31, 1971, statement. In the Gauley Ranger District, for example, the average size of the seventy-six timber sales compartments is 2,015 acres. The pioneer study units (the Forest Service version of local administrative protection of wild areas) in that district have sizes of 3,168, 1,110, 597, and 525 acres—not much different from the size of the timber sales compartments. For the whole Monongahela National Forest (outside of the Spruce Knob–Seneca Rock National Recreation Area, where three pioneer study areas are planned, totaling 21,300 acres), the average size of the ten pioneer zones is 2,430 acres (if the largest and smallest were omitted, the average size would be 2,030 acres).

"The sizes of these Pioneer Study Units," Langford went on, "are generally barely large enough to encompass the drainage basin of a single perennial stream and are too small to provide a wilderness experience or setting comparable with other *de facto* wildernesses within the same national forest. Because of the extensive system of roads existing or planned with the rest of the timber sales compartments, nearly every point within the Pioneer Study Units would be within an hour's walk of a permanent Forest Service road. This presents little obstacle to a poacher or to most other (legitimate) visitors. Solitude and the opportunity for an unconfined type of recreation are unlikely to be preserved in such small areas. The pressure of many casual visitors would probably soon overload all the primitive facilities and trails, as there would be little distance or challenge to filter and disperse the users. In the general forest (the rest of the timber sales compartments) the timber access roads would leave a patchwork of urbanized woodlots of homogeneous, uninspiring character and even smaller walking distances.

"The Forest Service's Travel- and Water-Influence Zones are mere corridors having only a narrow veneer of wilderness encompassing the immediate sight distance or filter strip provided to prevent visual or particulate pollution. These corridors are confining, both esthetically and physically, as the adjacent timber operations are ugly and nearly impassable for periods measured in decades."

The reply from the Forest Service to citizen groups interested in designation of eastern wilderness has been consistently the same: (1) The area you propose doesn't qualify under terms of the Act; and (2) we can give it better protection anyway. But the latter proviso often doesn't work in practice. To illustrate, for the past several years conservationists in the southern highlands have sought a Joyce Kilmer Wilderness, combining Joyce Kilmer Memorial Forest, which covers 3,800 acres in western North Carolina, and the valley of

Slickrock Creek, a roadless area of 10,700 acres adjoining it astride the Carolina-Tennessee border. The Kilmer unit is one of the few choice examples remaining of the primeval Appalachian hardwood wilderness, an area the loggers somehow overlooked. Among its diverse species of trees are patriarchs five and six centuries old, immense fellows, some measuring 20 feet in circumference and standing 150 feet tall, a rare collection showing what the past was like in sheltered coves throughout the hills.

In 1934 the Veterans of Foreign Wars petitioned the government for a living shrine to Joyce Kilmer, the author of "Trees." After a long study of possible areas throughout the country this portion of the ancient Cherokee hunting ground was chosen—not just a grove but an entire drainage, circled on three sides by steep ridges. It is probably as impressive as any woodland of its size on earth. As for Slickrock Creek, 3,000 acres of the upper slopes are composed of virgin timber, while the rest, logged years ago, has regained much of its wilderness quality. With fertile soil and up to eighty inches of rain a year, the forest has grown up with groves of poplars up to two feet in diameter. The old railroad ties have rotted and the railroad grade is now a hiking trail. It is one of the outstanding areas in the southern mountains for the enjoyment of quality sports, favored by boar, deer, turkey, and bear, and by hunters who follow these species. The creek is noted among fishermen as one of the few choice clear-water streams where trout reproduce naturally, largely because of the stable, unroaded, and unlogged conditions of the watershed.

But all has not been well on the Kilmer-Slickrock front. When the memorial forest was established, the Forest Service pledged to protect it forever "as a place of inspiration and a treasure of native flora and fauna." When the citizens came along with their proposal for wilderness, they were told the area was too small to qualify. The Act, in fact, delineates wilderness as an area of at least 5,000 acres or one of "sufficient size as to make practicable its preservation and use in an unimpaired condition." The Forest Service simply read as far as the words 5,000 acres. Its pledge to protect the area "forever" presently was proven to have its limitations; on June 10, 1964, Chief Edward P. Cliff approved construction of a commercial highway, designed to link Robbinsville, North Carolina, and Tellico Plains,

Tennessee, across steep terrain on the upper portion of Joyce Kilmer. Of several possible routes considered, this undoubtedly was one of the worst.*

The highway was also destined to violate still another "administratively protected" area, Falls Branch Scenic Area on the Tennessee side; nothing was known about this until signs of surveying were evident in late 1971 and could never have happened if the Wilderness Act had been applied to areas of less than 5,000 acres. The validity of Slickrock had, of course, likewise been denied: The trees, except for those at the upper end, were not virgin timber; trees only fifty years old symbolized the mark of man's hand; the old railroad grade was a mark of man's hand. Citizens have fought to save the wilderness, proposing that the highway be routed through another, now roadless, valley and that the virgin forest of Kilmer be joined with the roadless valley of Slickrock to be given permanent protection as a unit of the National Wilderness Preservation System.

Until the Roadless-Area Review and Evaluation (RARE) were announced in early 1973, there had not been a single instance, whether in the East or West, in which the Forest Service had nominated an area for inclusion in the wilderness system or had publicly suggested that any be set aside for future study following completion of work on the primitive areas. With the list of new study areas accompanying the roadless-area review, the agency included two in the East (Joyce Kilmer–Slickrock, North Carolina, and Bradwell Bay, Florida) and one in Puerto Rico (El Cacique). In all other cases, however, the public itself has been obligated to make its interests known, both to the Forest Service and to Congress.

In 1973 the Eastern Wilderness Areas Act was introduced into both houses of Congress. It was intended to establish at once eighteen new wilderness units covering approximately 254,000 acres and

---

*In a memorandum to Secretary of Agriculture Orville Freeman, Chief Cliff said the road would "enhance access to the Joyce Kilmer area," but he overlooked mentioning that it would divide and scar the wilderness, that inevitable siltation would disrupt the ecosystem, that heavy tourist travel would create pressure on fragile areas protected primarily by lack of access, or that it would drive away hunters, fishermen, campers, hikers, and nature lovers.

to designate thirty-seven additional units covering 395,990 acres for interim protection pending further study. The fifty-two units all told are located in twenty states east of the foothills of the Rocky Mountains and Puerto Rico.

The Eastern Wilderness Areas Act, in whatever form it might emerge, is part of the second stage of wilderness protection through law. The total acreage it would set aside covers about 2 percent of eastern national forests. Why, one might demand, settle for 2 percent. Under terms of the Weeks Law these lands were purchased for protection of watersheds rather than production of pulp or timber. The basic function of eastern national forests should not be commercial but rather educational, recreational, and scientific, goals wholly compatible with watershed.

As to the responsiveness of the National Park Service—"Conservationists the world over are looking to our National Park Service for exemplary leadership in the field of safeguarding the beauty and character of natural landscape and sites. It would be most unfortunate if the Park Service were unable to fulfill this role in the Smokies."

These words, heard at the first public hearing on wilderness in the national parks, conducted at Gatlinburg, Tennessee, in June 1966, were spoken by Stewart M. Brandborg, executive director of the Wilderness Society. The subject under immediate consideration was the fate of the Great Smoky Mountains, but this also marked the beginning of scheduled reviews to be held in many national parks, monuments, and additional units of the National Park System, preceding congressional action on each one. The expression of concern seemed to touch the heart of the historic issue with simplicity and directness. It made the listener conscious of the greatness of moment before the audience in the hall and before the vaster unseen audience. For as someone said during the flood tide of feeling and eloquence, "A wrong decision will be severely judged by untold millions still unborn."

Considering the interest of the Wilderness Society in the Wilderness Act and in making it work, Brandborg's comments were fitting. They might have been more fitting as part of a keynote delivered by a representative of the National Park Service, pleading for public support for a program designed to protect and enhance the Great Smoky Mountains, the largest mountain wilderness remaining east of the Great Plains.

Instead, a regional director of the Service opened the program, reading carefully and without digression from an uninspired statement. He read it once in the auditorium at Gatlinburg, as the hearings began on the Tennessee side of the Smokies, and again two days later as they resumed in Bryson City, on the North Carolina side. The statement offered nothing new or consequential in wilderness philosophy or protection. It was, rather, more of a road plan intended to solve seasonal traffic jams, a plan outlining the location of a proposed transmountain highway plus corridors for additional inner loops. What was left over, 247,000 acres, or less than half the park, was offered for inclusion in the National Wilderness Preservation System—not in one contiguous unit, nor even in two, but in six broken blocks, ranging in size from 5,000 acres to 110,000 acres.

Congressmen and local office holders spoke first at both Gatlinburg and Bryson City and, after hearing representatives of chambers of commerce and local promoters extol the Park Service plan, departed. Neither they nor officials in Washington could possibly have felt the pulse of those who followed, including schoolteachers, scholars, scientists, scouts and scout leaders, the hikers, trout fishermen, botanists, and bird-watchers, speaking up to defend the integrity of national parks. Over 300 witnesses presented oral statements; 6,000 letters from all over the country were later received for the hearing record.

Not one single national conservation leader, nor scientist, nor representative of a significant outdoors organization spoke out in support of the Park Service proposal. Leaders of the Appalachian Trail Conference, National Audubon Society, Izaak Walton League, National Parks Association, Nature Conservancy, and Sierra Club, as well as the Wilderness Society, endorsed a larger plan of at least 350,000 acres of the park safeguarded as wilderness, with the remaining 150,000 acres for reasonable development and traffic arteries. Scientists pleaded with passion for large expansion of primeval land for biological, botanical, and ecological studies. "No road on earth," warned one, "is important enough to destroy the values inherent in these mountains."

The finest hours of the hearings were derived from the enthusiasm of people. "I love the wilderness so much that I must oppose the transmountain road," said one. "As much as I like and admire the National Park Service, I just can't approve this plan," said another. They looked into the future, beyond the perspective offered by the Park Service, expressing hope for their children and grandchildren. "Wilderness is never idle land," reminded a young mother from Georgia. "Saving the wilderness may be one of the few worthwhile accomplishments of this generation." People spoke of the joys of wilderness, the spiritual exhilaration, the threats of a multimillion dollar political road-building boondoggle. They identified themselves with love of land, with idealism, representing the qualitative experience that must be the essence of our national parks.

The government plan for the Smokies clearly was a weak and poorly drawn document, designed only to solve short-range pragmatic and political problems. The justification was based on a 1943 legal agreement. In that year the Tennessee Valley Authority had decided to construct Fontana Dam on the Little Tennessee River as a source of power for the atomic energy plant then being built at Oak Ridge. This involved flooding a narrow mountain road and evacuating the residents of several towns between the south boundary of the national park and the high-water line of the future lake. Parties to the agreement included TVA, the National Park Service, the state of North Carolina, and Swain County, which held outstanding bonds in payment for the original state road. It provided for acquisition by TVA of 44,000 acres of land above the shoreline, which it turned over to the national park, thus filling in a logical topographical boundary, and the payment by TVA of $400,000 to the North Carolina Highway Department to be applied toward retirement of the county bonds. The Park Service, as its share of the agreement, pledged to provide a new road, a rural transportation artery linking the towns of Bryson City and Fontana, when funds became available after World War II. The state in fulfillment of its part of the bargain constructed the road upon the agreed route from Bryson City to the park boundary.

For a number of years following the war the Park Service sought to convince Swain County to accept improvement of Route 129, along the south shore of Fontana Lake, pleading that a road on the north shore would disturb large parcels of wilderness with choice trout streams. This proved unacceptable: After all, it was not transportation for local citizens at stake but rather the opening of a new tourist route for the commercial benefit of little Bryson City.

Thus, finally during 1963-64 the bulldozers were brought into the back country. Construction proceeded 2.5 miles into the park, at a cost of nearly $2 million. The result was disaster: Mountains were slashed, natural beauty destroyed, the landscape scarred with cuts and fills and with erosion that will require many years for nature to heal. A halt was called to the project.

At this point an observer might conclude the Park Service had endeavored to fulfill the bargain and thus discharged its obligation. Competent lawyers, in fact, have questioned the validity of the 1943 agreement, although the Park Service has never put it to the test. In September 1965, to the contrary, at a meeting in Bryson City George B. Hartzog, Jr., director of the Park Service, offered officials of Swain County still another alternative: a major, multimillion-dollar transmountain route across the Smokies wilderness into Tennessee. There had been no advance notice of this proposal to citizen conservationists, no public hearings at which national conservation organizations might have been represented. And when they complained, the parks director and associates explained that hikers on the Appalachian Trail had been well considered; they were to be spared by the construction of a tunnel just below the mountaintop. Pollution of the environment and disruption of the ecosystem were not discussed.

By the end of 1965 the new agreement, providing for the transmountain road, had been signed by the parties in North Carolina and was only awaiting confirmation by Secretary of the Interior Stewart L. Udall. But he was having second thoughts, his mood reflecting, perhaps, the strong tide of protest, including editorials in major newspapers, against the road. "The proposed new transmountain highway is being offered as a 'substitute.' The wonder is why," commented the *Milwaukee Journal*. "It won't link the two communities. It will be enormously expensive. The sensible course is to scrap plans for both highways. Surely, an alternate route can be found *outside* the park." And from the *New York Times*: "The Park Service has put forward a road-building project that transgresses the spirit of the Wilderness Act and that would bring heavy automobile traffic streaming through the very area that needs to be protected. The proposal for this transmountain road reflects weariness rather than foresight and clear thinking."

The agreement had arrived on Secretary Udall's desk at a time when wilderness hearings were soon to be held for the Great Smokies. The proposed road would slice through one of the two areas in the Park waiting to be delineated as wilderness zones under terms of the Act.

A review of events after 1965 raises the question as to whether the 1943 agreement was anything more than a device employed by the Park Service leadership to avoid fulfillment of the wilderness opportunities in the Great Smokies, whether its intent throughout *all* the parks was to keep wilderness small and unprotected by the Act. Director Hartzog gave strong evidence this might be the case when he addressed the Sierra Club Biennial Wilderness Conference on April 7, 1967, in San Francisco. "To assume that the Wilderness Act establishes new standards and new criteria for national park wilderness, replacing the old and time-tested wilderness standards and criteria, would jeopardize the whole national park concept," he declared. But exactly what standards and criteria did he mean?

"It is obvious that Congress could only have intended that wilderness designation of national park system lands should, if anything, result in a higher, rather than a lower, standard of unimpaired preservation," he explained. In other words, as with the Forest Service, the Park Service standard was the essence of purity itself; even though very few areas would pass the test of absolute purity and though the Wilderness Act's criteria insist only that wilderness appear to be affected primarily by the forces of nature with the imprint of man's work unnoticeable.

Hartzog defined three land zones within national parks: (1) the enclaves of development "for the accommodation of visitors" connected with roads, bridle paths, and foot trails; (2) transition zones between these developed sites; and (3) the untrammeled, primeval wilderness. This was one manner of possibly subdividing the parks into small wilderness areas and large facility areas.

Though pledging there would be no lowering of park values on the remaining park lands not designated as wilderness, Hartzog then revealed still another system for zoning or land classification (based on a formula prescribed for application to federal lands by the Bureau of Outdoor Recreation), with the following six separate classes: Class I—high–density recreational areas; Class II—general outdoor recreation areas; Class III—natural-environment areas; Class IV—outstanding natural areas; Class V—primitive areas, including, but not limited to, those recommended for designation under the Wilderness Act; and Class VI—historical and cultural areas.

"Often, Class III and Class V lands both represent significant natural values," Hartzog conceded. Still, he said, the former are not considered lands that meet criteria for wilderness. "If we are to preserve the integrity of national park wilderness, we dare not lower its standard or compromise its integrity by the inclusion of areas that express in less than the highest terms the definition of national park wilderness."

Then he announced that Class III lands would be managed to provide the "transition" or "setting" or "environment" or "buffer" between intensively developed areas and higher classifications and "wilderness threshold" when they abut or surround wilderness. "The wilderness-threshold lands afford the newcomer an opportunity to explore the mood and the temper of the wild country before venturing into the wilderness beyond. Herein the wilderness-threshold is an unequaled opportunity for interpretation of the meaning of wilderness."

While Hartzog insisted Class III lands were not "intentionally reserved for future intensive developments," he then spelled out the first steps in the process of inevitable development, including "one-way motor nature trails," small overlooks, and informal picnic sites. He pledged that, "Such limited facilities must be in complete harmony with the natural environment," but the relevancy or compatibility of roads and cars with a natural environment is certainly subject to challenge. So is the entire outlook. "We must come to grips with the use of the automobile," he asserted. "Shall we explore the possibilities of the monorail, the funicular, the shuttle bus or other means of mechanical transport, in an effort to separate the visitor from his car while he enjoys his parks?" Shall it be cars, trams, or trains? But no question is raised about the essentiality of enjoying the parks without mechanical transport, of exploration and enjoyment on foot as the basic element of "harmony with the natural environment."

Conservation leaders on the program of the conference criticized Hartzog's program on the very day it was presented. Stewart Brandborg rejected the large Class III exclusions. Although peripheral to larger wilderness tracts, he said, they themselves are essentially wild in character and would qualify under the Wilderness Act definition. He raised the question as to whether any lands in the national parks should be designated for high-density, mass recreation purposes. Anthony W. Smith, of the National Parks Association, expressed a parallel idea. Warning later at the same conference that "threshold zones" could easily be used to accommodate increasing crowds in years ahead, he said there was little value in denying that Class III areas would not be used for development of facilities: "If they are not to be used for that purpose, then let them be protected as wilderness."

By the end of 1970 the National Park Service had fallen far behind in its schedule of wilderness reviews. Six years after passage of the Act, a total of only two areas (within Craters of the Moon National Monument in Idaho and Petrified Forest National Park in Arizona) with a combined acreage of 93,503, had been designated by Congress for inclusion in the wilderness system. Various reasons were given by the agency. One was the need to prepare and maintain a "master plan" to guide the use, development, interpretation, and preservation of each particular park. But the same need applied also to national forests and national wildlife refuges, whose administrative agencies had kept their schedules up to date and secured statutory protection of their areas while planning proceeded.

Another reason given was the lack of funds to conduct wilderness reviews, but even this might be questioned; in 1971, apparently, funds were available for publication of a booklet entitled "Back Country Travel in the National Park System," with scant mention of "wilderness" and no reference at all to the wilderness system or its benefits. Park Service wilderness proposals have continually recommended exclusion of large acreages from wilderness for threshold or buffer purposes. Then followed another concept of excluding "enclaves" within wilderness for purposes of development. In advance of the wilderness hearing on Bandelier National Monument, scheduled for December 18, 1971, in Los Alamos, New Mexico, the Park Service announced a recommendation for zero wilderness out of a total of 30,000 acres, on grounds that it would detract from study and preservation of archeological sites, but citizen groups pledged to fight for setting aside 25,000 acres.

And what happened, meanwhile, to the Great Smokies, the meeting ground of northern and southern forests, with an incredibly varied vegetation that has ever charmed naturalists, and where the Appalachian Trail follows the mountain crest for over seventy miles, the full length of the park? On June 23, 1969, a delegation of almost 100 conservationists, representing groups in Tennessee and North Carolina, came to present their case to Secretary of the Interior Walter J. Hickel.

He gave the group a serious reception—much more serious and straightforward than anything conservationists had received from officials of the Park Service. "I am impressed by your numbers and sincerity of your purpose," the Secretary declared. Then he assigned the Park Service to develop a new plan, with an 18-month deadline.

The new report, issued by the agency in January 1971, conceded that the Smokies comprise "a natural treasure of plant and animal life living in an ecological balance that once destroyed can never be restored." This document seemed to recognize the worst enemy of the parks as the automobile, proposing restrictions on traffic and gradual phasing out of Route 441, a main highway bisecting the park. In addition, the proposal of another transmountain highway, which had highlighted the plan of 1966, was withdrawn in favor of a scenic loop road around the perimeter of the park, as urged by citizen organizations.

Still, along the loop road the Park Service said it would locate no fewer than twelve visitor "clusters," complete with large camp-grounds and "motor nature trails." It appeared to be the same old appeal for numbers, or, at best, a pragmatic solving of today's problems at the sacrifice of tomorrow's civilization.

Arno B. Cammerer, director of the Park Service in an earlier day, delivered a speech in Washington in 1938, in which he spoke of establishing a national park that might not measure up to all that everybody thinks of it at the present time, but that, 50 or 100 years from now, with all the protection we would give it, would then have attained a natural condition comparable to primitive condition. He reflected on how such an area might look 1,000 or 2,000 or 5,000 years hence. Cammerer had the Great Smoky Mountains specifically in mind. Even under the most destructive type of lumbering, the flowers, shrubs, and trees had grown back as if nothing of that kind had occurred. In another 20 to 50 years even the stumps would have rotted to furnish humus for the plant life to come, so that it would be difficult, even for the ecologist, to ascertain whether a certain area was cut over or not or that a certain mine had been worked years ago in a given location to the detriment of the park.

Such vision among administrators is rare, particularly in our time. The focus today is centered on expediency and immediacy, survivability in office, political realities, rather than on fundamental principles and issues of the long range. Under terms of the Wilderness Act the administrators are directed to gather and disseminate information regarding use and enjoyment of wilderness, but this has not been done, or has been done feebly at most, certainly not with enthusiasm or commitment. If it had been, there would be much better understanding, both inside and outside of government, of what the law means, of all its rich potential.

Insofar as devotion to "purity" of wilderness and unwillingness to lower lofty standards are concerned, the Wilderness Act delineates more than a procedure; it outlines a point of view, a philosophy of land management. Considering the declared intention and uses it specifies—to provide outstanding opportunities for solitude and for a primitive, unconfined kind of recreation—there should be no doubt that areas where the human imprint is only slightly noticeable, with capability for restoration are fully acceptable. Certainly they would have been to Arno Cammerer. Had they not, there would be no such areas as the Great Smoky Mountains National Park today.

Public enthusiasts have had to pick up the burden. Citizen study teams have made significant contributions by determining the adequacy of agency proposals. These teams have included local experts in conservation matters or professionals trained in biology, archaeology, botany, and related fields. There have also been strong representations in support of wilderness proposals from specialized national groups. The Ecological Society of America, for example, provided important information on the probable ecological impact of the transmountain road proposal in the Great Smokies. Recommendations of the National Speleological Society for the protection of cave wilderness in Mammoth Cave National Park in Kentucky resulted in restudy and revision of master plans. Agency personnel may be fully qualified for the wilderness studies they are paid to undertake, but their freedom of judgment is circumscribed, whereas the external experts are able to apply their talents with independence and enthusiasm. In a number of cases citizens have agreed with boundary proposals of the agencies. In some, the citizen proposals have been larger; they have never been smaller.

Now is the time to act. If wild lands under federal administration are not placed in the wilderness system and protected by statute, the odds are they will disappear. The only parts of today's living wilderness that will remain alive are those designated specifically as such, and under the Wilderness Act these designations can be made. The process challenges the public will.

Chapter 11

Protecting the Public Options

I appreciate the warm and generous introduction by Mr. Towell. Thank you, Bill. It is always a pleasure to come to the Smokies and the surrounding Appalachians in order to review the scene of *Strangers in High Places* and to be reminded of how glorious these Southern mountains really are.

I can't help but pay tribute to two men who helped shape my appreciation of this region and who inspired me to interpret and to defend its natural values to the fullest of my ability. One was Garth Cate, of Tryon, the founder of the Fontana Roundup. When Garth died, Mrs. Cate (who is here today) wrote me that he had felt as a father to me. I was obliged to reply that I never felt as a son to him for the simple reason that Garth's outlook was ever young. He may have been much older in years, but certainly not in spirit. Garth was over ninety when he died, but thinking and pointing to the future, rather than ruminating over the past. Harvey Broome, of Knoxville, the other source of inspiration to whom I refer, was much the same way. He was a gentle, selfless and thoroughly determined man. Harvey was president of the Wilderness Society at the time of his death, with far-reaching interests and activities, but his heart was in the Smoky Mountains. I daresay that the security of the wilderness within the national park at our doorstep is due to the diligence and devotion of Harvey Broome more than to any other man.

Before heading down from Washington, I thought I should go to

Paper presented at Fontana Conservation Roundup, Fontana, North Carolina, June 1975.

the Capitol and obtain clearance from Representative Roy Taylor to come into his district. Mr. Taylor examined and did indeed find my papers in order and extended freedom of passage in Western North Carolina. We have had our serious differences, but I have always respected the Congressman as a competent legislator of integrity and principle. I recall once, several years ago, Luther Shaw, his administrative assistant, said to me: "Now listen, Mike, you and the environmentalists have us blocked at almost every turn: You have stopped construction of the trans-mountain road in the Smokies, the Tellico Plains–Robbinsville Road through the national forests, the TVA dams on the Upper French Broad River, and Beaucatcher Mountain tunnel in Asheville. Why don't you be reasonable and let us have something?"

Actually, I haven't been involved in the Beaucatcher project at all and feel unqualified to comment. On the other three, however, I can speak with some knowledge and experience of involvement. In all cases it seemed hopeless to resist because they had been planned by powerful forces and their completion seemed inevitable. Nonetheless, when there's something worth saving one must never give up, certainly never give up hope. Because enough people cared and refused to quit, these programs for land desecration have either been scrapped completely or remain unfulfilled to this day.

There is always hope as long as there is a cadre of people, or even a single individual, with commitment and a willingness to fight. There is hope at this very moment that we may still save the beautiful New River in northwestern North Carolina and southwestern Virginia. It hasn't been easy to overcome the power of the utility companies and of the Federal Power Commission. Congress in the last session might have given the New River protection of the Wild and Scenic Rivers Act, but surrendered to the iniquitous nationwide lobbying of the utility companies and their allies in the high command of the construction unions. At that point all seemed lost. But the leaders in the government of North Carolina, responding to the wishes of the people of this state, have consistently pursued their legal appeals to save the New River. Moreover, the North Carolina legislature has voted to designate 26.5 miles of the river as part of its Natural and Scenic Rivers System. This in itself does not save the

New River, but the Secretary of the Interior can designate state-administered components of the National Wild and Scenic Rivers System. Governor Holshouser has made application that this be done. North Carolina environmentalists have done their share. Now it is up to the rest of us to encourage the new Secretary of the Interior, Stan Hathaway, to respond positively—to recognize an opportunity to get off on the right foot, following the abundant criticism and mistrust surrounding his nomination.

North Carolina is moving on several fronts to achieve protection and sound management of its land and water resources in ways that other states could afford to study and follow. The legislature has passed an act barring billboards within 1,000 feet of the Blue Ridge Parkway, an action urgently needed to preserve the most scenic corridor in America from commercial blight. Now the legislature is considering a Mountain Area Management Act (following passage of the Coastal Management Act of last year). Maybe action hasn't come as fast as it should, but anyone can see that the upland meadows, fields, forests and farms are gradually being supplanted by subdivisions, tourist attractions of varying quality, and assorted other commercial enterprises. People of the mountain areas, not only in North Carolina but everywhere, will have to come to grips with some form of regional land planning. Local and state bodies must give serious attention to cooperative planning relating to land use and economic development. Strong citizen support must be solicited and encouraged to prevent further exploitation and unplanned growth from seriously damaging the highlands environment and from destroying its natural and recreational integrity.

We citizens will need all the hope and determination we can muster. We are now being robbed of our land-use options. At a time of critical resource shortages, big industries are pressing to maximize immediate profits without regard for long-term consequences to the land. They are being given all possible encouragement and assistance by President Ford and his administration. No other President has made as many wrong moves and continues to do so as Gerald Ford. He has given absolutely no recognition to the truism that proper management of limited natural resources and protection and enhancement of the quality of life are investments of economic value for the future of America and the world. When he became President, Mr. Ford spoke of establishing a mood of "communication, conciliation, compromise and cooperation." His appointment of Stan Hathaway, a hardlining anti-environmentalist if ever there was one, showed that Mr. Ford has no desire for meaningful communication or cooperation with citizens who care.

The President has given no leadership to meeting the desperate need for energy conservation, no answer to unrestrained growth mania which is plaguing the earth. At our present rate, the shrinking resources of our land are doomed. All sections of the country are under attack—Appalachia, the western plains, the Four Corners, the outer continental shelves, and the Arctic slope of Alaska. The public's land-use options are being rapidly preempted for the benefit of private profit. Clearly, we must begin at once to alter the life-style that makes us enemies of ourselves. We must reassess the value system by which we confuse superconsumption for the quality of life.

Land-use regulations are critically needed to protect what options remain. The nation can move toward sensible regulations through passage of H. R. 3510, now pending before the House of Representatives in Washington. This legislation does not: create Federal zoning, threaten private property, remove decisions, or provide sanctions. It does: furnish grants to states to help them in their own planning process, based on simple requirements for preparing and administering plans. It does provide protection of "areas of critical environmental concern," but even this is left to the states' discretion.

H. R. 3510 has been the subject of heavy lobbying by the agents of the timber trust and the U. S. Chamber of Commerce, who have distorted the issues. The fact is that federal policies already have a major impact on land use; legislation such as H. R. 3510 would actually restore power to state and local governments by helping them to solve major land-use problems themselves.

As an environmental activist, I share the apprehension manifest at grass-roots America over the spreading influence of federal agencies. I can't think of one single agency that is tuned into the desires and needs of the people and truly responsive to them. Assorted land management agencies may be represented at this

Conservation Roundup, but they are here to tell us all the good things they are doing, not to find out what we really want them to do. I speak specifically of the Tennessee Valley Authority, Corps of Engineers, Forest Service, National Park Service, and Fish and Wildlife Service. Fortunately, we have means of restraining these agencies from abusive land-use practices—other than the pending H. R. 3510—such as legal action in the courts; the pressure of public exposure through the media; the education of the people as to the damage to the public estate being conducted with our own funds; the passage of new laws (such as the Wilderness Act, National Environmental Policy Act and the Endangered Species Act), and Congressional transfer of land from one jurisdiction to another (as in the case of the North Cascades).

The Forest Service, in particular, is doing intensive damage to the resource while conducting a charade of public involvement. In past years there were the "show-me trips" and the "listening sessions." The "listening" was accompanied by a stream of color brochures and other promotions extolling clearcutting, a thoroughly "efficient and economic system" of placing timber production above all other values. Cutting soared, tripling in volume over a period of twenty years; the resource, in turn, suffered and wildlife habitat deteriorated.

"Public comments are invited but the consultant atmosphere appears to be lacking," complained Senator Jennings Randolph, of West Virginia, in early 1972, after an investigation at the behest of his constituents. "The prevailing feeling expressed by those after attending the hearings is that decisions have already been made and their expressed concerns have only been accepted as an empty polite gesture."

In the same year, Charles Prigmore, president of the Alabama Conservancy, charged much the same: "The Forest Service indeed holds hearings at infrequent intervals, particularly when public pressure becomes irresistible. But this is an attitude of patient tolerance of public concern and thinking, rather than any real encouragement of joint decision-making. Forest Service personnel consider themselves to be the experts, and the public to be ignorant at best and obstructionist at worst."

Public involvement, understanding and support are essential to any land management agency genuinely consecrated to leadership and service in behalf of the people. On this foundation the Forest Service was born and blossomed many years ago. The alternative to involvement and alertness of the public is surrender to the special interests, the exploiters who never sleep and are unrelenting in their political pressures. This was perfectly plain during the fight over the National Timber Supply Act of 1969. "Believe me, we have waste of great magnitude in our national forests, parks and wilderness areas," Jim Bronson declared in behalf of the National Forest Products Association in the midst of that fight. If the people had not risen to defeat that act, Mr. Bronson and his crowd would now be devouring the whole domain of public lands.

In 1970, the Regional Forester in the South, then Ted Schlapfer, sent me a letter enunciating his principles of public involvement. He wrote: "We are hired as professionals and paid by the taxpayers to make and act on decisions based on our education, training and experiences. While the public must be involved if we make changes in management practices, we still have the managerial responsibility of making the final decision."

Those days are done. No agency can be allowed any longer to make the final decision. Personnel in charge are too narrow in their training and experience to be considered sufficiently competent. And in innumerable cases they have shown a lack of forthrightness worthy of trust. This is not my own idea alone, I assure you, but an increasingly widespread feeling among concerned citizens everywhere. According to a recent issue of the Georgia Conservancy Newsletter, the Conservancy's Executive Committee has voted to challenge Forest Service planning and management of timber operations. The Conservancy won't even trust the foresters as timbermen.

The Forest Service is so driven by its timber-first policy that it lacks the breadth to appreciate or properly manage the rest of the resources. Let me cite my experience in trying to get straight answers from Forest Service leaders over two issues in this very area: sacrifice of the Bemis tract in the Snowbirds and Little Buffalo drainage of Graham County, here in western North Carolina, and construction of a portion of the Robbinsville–Tellico Road across the Falls Branch Scenic Area in the Cherokee National Forest, in Tennessee.

The former Bemis tract consisted of 15,000 acres of high mountain land privately held within the authorized boundaries of the Nantahala National Forest. I understood that when the lands became available for sale in 1971 the Forest Service made no serious effort to acquire them. This was astonishing, particularly in light of a statement made to me by Chief Ed Cliff stressing the need of large scale acquisitions in the Appalachians because of encroaching land-use conflicts. Moreover, the area embraced choice trout streams and a connecting link on the migration route of the last and largest bear country in North Carolina outside the Smokies.

When I inquired of the Forest Service for the facts about its delinquency and disinterest, I received the most curious replies. For instance, the Forest Supervisor in North Carolina, Del W. Thorsen, wrote me a letter which included the following: "As to foreseeable watershed impacts from impending developments, we can only surmise. We do know that the soils in Little Buffalo and Snowbird are relatively stable and are not highly erodible." Now how did the foresters know this about the soils, since no detailed soils study had been completed or was available to them? But such language flows easily in the typically bureaucratic brush-off given to concerned citizens. To continue: "Since most of the tracts were sold to individuals who presumably intend to build vacation cottages in a forest setting, we believe they will want to protect the environment and not damage the watershed. Construction of access roads possibly will expose more soil to the elements than any other anticipated use. However, this damage need not be long lasting if the roads are properly designed and maintained." No need for a Mountain Area Management Act there!

Then there was another letter from Deputy Chief E. W. Schultz, which I also found unsatisfactory. He wrote: "With respect to the auction, the Forest Service is without authority to participate in a sale procedure of this sort where payment is required prior to examination and approval of title by the United States. The matter was discussed at some length with the Nature Conservancy prior to the sale. It is our understanding that their decision not to participate in bidding for the property was reached after they had evaluated the situation." This statment was an untruth, plainly and simply. I can say this on personal knowledge. On the day before the auction I was contacted in Washington by a Tennessee Congressman, Lamar Baker. He was responding to pleas from sportsmen constituents hoping to prevent the Bemis tract from being cut into a thousand pieces. I urged him to call Patrick F. Noonan at the Nature Conservancy. Mr. Noonan, in turn, telephoned the Forest Service—it was the first contact on this issue—and was willing to make an effort to save the tract, even at this late hour; he was furious at the Forest Service disinterest, as he advised me later in the day. I recall in particular his grave concern over the potential precedent of the sale for owners of other large blocks of land in the Appalachian national forest boundaries. The Forest Service is not concerned, however, over the loss of bear habitat or trout streams, or rare flora, or the inevitable watershed damage, or pollution caused by roading and building in the high mountains.

In 1971 I wrote John R. McGuire, then Associate Chief, concerning the intrusion by road builders into the Falls Branch Scenic Area, with sanction by the Forest Service. Of course, this is the kind of thing that made the Wilderness Act imperative; administrative protective designations are not strong enough. Mr. McGuire in reply said the determination of the road location had been made in consultation wih the late Harvey Broome and that Harvey had concurred on running it through the Scenic Area. I challenged Mr. McGuire for substantiation. On November 24, 1971, he responded: "The discussions with Mr. Broome and the Wilderness Society concerning the impact of this road on the Falls Branch Scenic Area were for the most part of an informal nature." Now that vague informality strikes me as a thoroughly inadequate, irresponsible and unacceptable basis for a statement presumed to be factual—especially when the quoted source is no longer among the living.*

Is it any wonder that citizens fought so hard for the Eastern Wilderness Act in order to take the basic decision-making in land-use

---

*Following my presentation at the Roundup, I was approached by Edward G. Ellenberg, a Forest Service official, who declared he was present at the scene when Harvey Broome approved construction of the road within the Scenic Area. Ernest Dickerman, of the Wilderness Society, a close associate of Mr. Broome for many years in Knoxville, has no such recollection. "Conservationists have been opposing the closeness of this new highway to

away from the foresters? This process is still underway. Citizens are looking forward to hearings on S. 520, which would establish three additional wilderness areas and twenty-three study areas in the Eastern National Forests, and hopefully to passage in 1975.

I'm not especially satisfied with the process of decision-making or the policies governing land-use within the Great Smoky Mountains National Park either. The prevailing official policies are designed to cater to crowds of unlimited numbers, rather than to preserve the natural resource for fitting use and enjoyment based on the carrying capacity of the land. To quote from an article by Sam Venable in the *Knoxville News-Sentinel* of approximately four years ago:

"Down below the Chimney Tops, work crews are busy with bulldozers, dynamite, chain saws and boom trucks. They're cutting trees, shooting rock, moving earth and hauling away river stones in order to carve a new trail up the mountain. Civilization is getting a stronger grip on the Chimneys."

Apparently it never occurred to the park management to make its plans known in advance and to seek public opinion or comment. In fact, the way this came out was that someone on the park staff sent me a confidential message, I telephoned my friend Venable, and he proceeded to investigate on the ground. The assistant superintendent, Merrill Dave Beal, gave him this dubious explanation:

"So many people are using the present trail, it's become necessary to improve it. In many places, the old trail is slippery because of seepage. In others, tree roots have become exposed due to heavy pedestrian traffic and erosion is taking place."

If a preservationist on the public payroll would examine the same problem he might say: "It's time to reduce the impact of heavy use, or even to close the trail." After all, if the tree roots are exposed what's the point in blasting them out with dynamite or in trying to solve the erosion with a bulldozer?

---

the falls since the days of Harvey Broome when he was fighting it," wrote Mr. Dickerman in a bulletin to environmental leaders dated March 1, 1972. "The Forest Service and the Federal Highway Administration need increased public pressure applied to induce them to locate the highway an adequate distance away from the Falls Branch Scenic Area."

But Mr. Beal, alas, explained it this way: "There are many people who simply can't get out and scramble over rocks to enjoy the park, but they still have a right to enjoy the Smokies. After all, it's their park, too." What an ingeniously dangerous statement! If the value of parks is to be measured on the basis of use by the greatest number of people, with the value of the implicit wild, natural resource, and the use of it by bears, birds, insects and plants, to be secondary, then all of our parks are doomed, one after the other.

It takes agencies repeated lessons before they learn. In 1974 the Park Service decided to proceed with the access road into Cataloochee Valley. In order to short-cut the requirements of the National Environmental Policy Act, officials prepared an "Environmental Assessment" instead, based on their intent to proceed with construction within thirty days. They tried to keep it as quiet as possible. They never notified anyone on the Tennessee side, let alone any national publication, national organization, or any concerned citizens. Someone in Haywood County appealed to me out of desperation, and I did what I could to spread the alarm. It frightens me that this is how our public officials are doing business on our public land.

The Environmental Assessment arrayed valid reasons why the access road should not be built: a potential increase in use from 250 to 8,000 persons per day, a volume which the fragile valley cannot stand; potential for strong temperature inversions; inevitable soil erosion and stream siltation, inevitable destruction of wildlife habitat. Nonetheless, the agency decided to proceed. When I raised the question with the park superintendent of the potential for a temperature inversion to trap and concentrate auto emissions, as mentioned in the assessment, his response was: "That's just a potential. It doesn't say it's going to happen." If this is the kind of principle guiding our national parks, we are in deep trouble.

Nevertheless, the citizens were forced to take legal action in order to protect Cataloochee. Or perhaps I should say to protect the options in land-use decisions. How, indeed, could the citizens give any credence to the regional planning about to begin in the Smokies if the important options are foreclosed to them by road construction?

Lately the Park Service has conducted a planning session on the Smoky Mountains region in conjunction with other federal, state and local agencies. I was interested to read a report by John Parris in the

Asheville Citizen where the multi-agency task force of planners recommended that a comprehensive environmental impact statement be prepared by the Park Service on the proposed Cataloochee access road. That's not only a vindication of the citizen position, but a clear sign for more heavy internal training by the National Park Service.

The guidelines of the task force also recommended that consideration be given to charging an entrance fee into the Great Smokies as an attempt to reduce congestion. Personally, I'm opposed to it. In the first place, it's illegal under the terms of the grant of land from the State of North Carolina to the Federal Government. In the second place, it tends to benefit those who can afford to pay while penalizing or discriminating against those less fortunate who cannot.

Most important of all, however, popularity and congestion are clear signs that the Great Smoky Mountains National Park needs to be enlarged. The national park should be doubled in size, to at least one million acres, in order to meet the needs of the people in Appalachia and of the nation. One new section should include Mt. Mitchell, which deserves national park status in its own right as the highest peak east of the Rocky Mountains. The enlarged park should include the Nantahalas, which compare in magnificence to the Smokies themselves. Another section should include the unflooded Little Tennessee River, which TVA will have to surrender in order to comply with the Endangered Species Act, and the bordering historic lands that embrace Echota, the capital of the Cherokee nation, and the birthplace of Sequoyah. It should include the Tellico uplands as a national recreation area open to hunting, in the same relationship to the Smokies as the Ross Lake and Lake Chelan National Recreation Areas hold to the North Cascades National Park in the State of Washington.

Most of the lands needed for expansion of the park already are in public ownership, principally in the Pisgah, Nantahala and Cherokee National Forests. The summit of Mt. Mitchell is in a state park. The additional high elevation lands should be acquired by purchase, in order to insure protection of the watersheds, of wildlife and fisheries habitat, and of the rare Appalachian flora. All these are implicit park purposes.

Soils in the highlands aren't sufficiently deep or fertile over large enough areas to justify intensive timber management. But the qualities that make the area a liability for production make it a natural for human enjoyment: a variety of species virtually unequalled anywhere in the country; high ridges affording breathtaking views; high elevation affording cool climates and escape from congested cities and sweltering lowlands; streams for fishing and enough protective cover and food for wildlife. The land developers recognize these values and their marketability to those few who can afford it. Now, while the real estate market is down, marks the ideal time to acquire the land for the benefit of all people, of this generation and generations hence.

The multi-agency task force has proposed establishment of a 13-county Great Smokies Recreation Region. This proposal is good, but not as bold or positive as the enlargement of our great national park. The purposes of the Forest Service and TVA are incompatible with the protection of unique natural systems in the region. The proposal in South Carolina to establish a Southern Appalachian Slope National Recreation Area, in order to protect a significant area of the Blue Ridge Front, which Representative James Mann is sponsoring in Congress, demonstrates the widespread citizen interest in natural area preservation. And there is little time to lose.

TVA represents an extremely serious challenge to sound land use. This agency, which began with great promise, has come to play a destructive role in the region with a negative impact on the land, its people and its healthy development. TVA is presently unaccountable to the public, the public service commissions, or the states it is designed to serve. Public opposition is growing to TVA's huge electric rate increases, its promotion of strip mining and tall stacks, its proliferation of radioactive nuclear facilities, dams designed to wipe out beautiful natural streams like the Duck and Little T, and to self-authorized projects like the pumped storage development at Raccoon Mountain. TVA is the personification of bureaucratic arrogance. It is an agency that, like CIA, has grown bigger than the law. Fortunately, the tide is turning. The Senate Public Works Committee recently held oversight hearings in Washington on TVA activities. It was the first time in TVA's 41-year history that such hearings have been held—and they can hardly be the last. Further, before leaving Washington, I learned that either this week or early next week the Department of the Interior will list the snail darter, a small fish found only in the Little Tennessee River, on the endangered species list. The Department will declare the completion of Tellico Dam would "totally destroy the habitat of the darter." Since TVA has pledged compliance with the Endangered Species Act of 1974, it must voluntarily stop the dam project, and stop it now, before any further damage is done.

Determinations of land use belong to everyone, but above all to the little people. To quote a guest editorial appearing in the *Asheville Citizen-Times*, April 9, 1972, written by Merrimon R. Doster, executive secretary of the Franklin Area Chamber of Commerce:

"We cannot let ourselves be lured into swapping our quality of life for any quantity that could possibly result in any deterioration of our environment. If a new industry wil increase incomes, raise living standards, strengthen our institutions, enhance the quality of life in general, then we want it and need it, but if it pollutes a stream—we can't afford it. If it dirties our air—we don't need it. If it defaces a mountain—we cannot tolerate it. If it reduces the dignity of our citizenry—we must fight it to its end.

"All our resources are natural—majestic mountains—pure water–clean air—grand scenery, and, above all, decent, intelligent people. Our people are the grandest resource we have, for it is within their power and choice to either conserve or destroy all the rest . . .

"If we are to plan for the development of a tourist industry, we must first build the tools with which to work. The last tool to be used must be the first one developed. That is a method to stop when growth has reached that point of maximum efficiency, where resources are used but not abused. The cold hard fact is ever before us that when our resources are expended they cannot be replaced.

"That all-important tool is called 'Land Use Planning.'

"'Land Use Planning' is a difficult and ofttimes painful program to formulate and implement. But never have the penalties been as devastatingly tragic as those experienced in areas of unplanned growth. We must not make the mistakes that some of our neighboring states have made. We cannot afford to."

I view the future with a sense of great hope and patriotism. The

Society of Colonial Dames has just given my new book, *Battle for the Wilderness*, an award of merit. I really didn't know they cared, but it makes me feel particularly patriotic. On the eve of the nation's Bicentennial, we should commit ourselves at this Roundup to protect and perpetuate our most precious heritage, the American earth. Environmentalism, after all, is not concerned with solving problems of the present, but rather problems of the future. I can't think of a better legacy to hand down to the future than open options of land use.

Someone said to me here this morning that it's futile to fight the battle of the Little T because TVA has too much power and has foreclosed all opposition. Our forefathers of 1776 faced even greater odds. They were the masters of grass-roots activism. And now, all across America, the fight for a better environment has begun. Let us make the most of it.

Chapter 12

Panthers Wanted—Alive, Back East, Where They Belong

On a July evening in 1975, five Great Smoky Mountains National Park maintenance workers were lounging on their bunkhouse porch watching a doe and two yearlings. Suddenly the deer fled into the forest and a large, grayish cat with a long tail emerged from the woods and bounded after them. The five men followed quickly, but found nothing more than tracks along a creek. They were convinced, however, that they had seen a panther hunting its traditional prey.

The report they filed in late September 1975 triggered a new sense of awareness of the largest, rarest and most secretive of the wild American cats. The Eastern panther was thought long ago to have followed the trail into oblivion of the great auk, Labrador duck, heath hen, passenger pigeon and sea mink. Recent sightings by some professional biologists, wildlife personnel, and forest and park rangers show this may not be the case. The Eastern panther may be coming back from the brink of extinction for a second chance.

For me the news was especially exciting. For years I've been an aficionado of the Great Smokies, the half-million-acre mountain sanctuary astride the North Carolina-Tennessee border. More than 15 years ago I had asked the then park naturalist about reintroducing the panther into the Smokies. After all, national parks are supposed to be wildlife sanctuaries and I can't think of any better suited for such a role than the Great Smoky Mountains. Fifty years ago, or less, it was not uncommon for mountaineers to catch sight of the sleek panther (or "painter" in the vernacular) three or four times a year, or

From *Smithsonian*, June 1979.

to hear its shrill song pierce the wilderness night, and the animal's hams and shoulders were the source of "painter bacon." Even now Panther Creek, Panther Mountain, Cat Run, Painter Branch and Painter Creek are familiar place names in the Smokies and neighboring Nantahalas across the Little Tennessee River.

The biologist to whom I had posed the question responded flatly that the big cat requires too much room even to be considered for reintroduction, and that its day in these mountains was definitely done.

Now we know better. "It appears that nature has succeeded where the National Park Service feared to tread," Boyd Evison, who was the park superintendent (and who has personally seen panther tracks), conceded quite willingly when I was last in the park. "There seems no reasonable doubt that there *are* cougars in the park; and it seems likely that they have been here for some time. Very little seems to be known about their habits and needs in this kind of country, but the park, if kept free of excessive development, offers the best sanctuary for cougars north of the Everglades and east of the Rockies."

The 1975 observation in the park and concurrent reports of panthers along the Blue Ridge Parkway in North Carolina stimulated me to investigate the whereabouts of the big cat, one of the least known of North American mammals today, not only in the Southern mountains but throughout its range. I found these lonely wanderers of our mountains and forests far more widespread than I could possibly have dreamed. The numbers of animals must be dangerously low, but they apparently are breeding and the long thread of life, though tenuous, remains unbroken.

Felis concolor, "cat all of the same color," varies from light brown or gray to soft reddish brown, or tawny, possibly changing with the season. In the United States and Canada there are 15 subspecies, all essentially the same animal. Many names have been given, including catamount (for cat of the mountain) in the Northeast, cougar in Canada, panther in the Southeast, mountain lion in the West, "el leon" in the Southwest (to contrast with "el tigre," the jaguar), puma in South America, as well as red tiger, silver lion, mountain devil, mountain screamer, deer killer and king cat. Now it is known mostly as panther, puma, cougar, mountain lion or long-tail cat.

That unmistakable tail is as long as an African lion's, though the panther is only half the size of the king of cats. The average male weighs about 150 pounds, the female about 100, though a large animal may weigh 200 pounds and measure eight feet in length. Our American lion is lean and lithe, endowed with tough skin, sharp claws and sharp teeth.

Though panthers are expert hunters, worthy of a sportsman's admiration, sport hunters long despised them as competitors for deer and played a key role in doing them in. "For the sake of the deer supply," argued *Forest and Stream Magazine* in 1885, "the panthers should be systematically pursued and destroyed, and the bounty should be such as to encourage this." Likewise, when the nation's leading sportsman, Theodore Roosevelt, became President, he denounced the panther as "the big horse-killing cat, the destroyer of the deer, the lord of stealthy murder, facing his doom with a heart both craven and cruel."

Though deer are the main prey, a panther will eat almost anything. It does humans a good turn by devouring rabbits and rodents, but earns the wrath of stockmen by taking an occasional sheep or calf. Its diet includes porcupine, fox, skunk, badger, frogs, slugs, grasshoppers and even its little cousin, the wildcat.

In the late 1940s a Canadian biologist, Dr. Bruce S. Wright, equated the relationship between panther and deer and came up with a surprisingly hopeful forecast. Wright had observed new forests and abandoned farms developing into first-class deer habitat and hunters encouraging the increase in deer. He predicted that panthers would follow the deer back into new habitats in the east.

The Eastern panther in 1972, according to Wright, had passed the immediate danger of extinction, but only by "the merest fraction." He estimated the total number surviving in eastern North America, exclusive of Florida, at not more than 100 (with the largest number, 25 to 50, in New Brunswick) and possibly fewer, yet he foresaw the animal making a slow comeback in both the Southeast and North, from Florida to the Laurentians, providing it was given protection.

Despite reports of sightings up and down the Eastern seaboard during the 1960s, many government agencies and scientists remained dubious. Reports of panthers often turned out to be cats, dogs or spooks in the night. Even today some biologists concede only that the panther *may* exist and refuse to grant anything further in the absence of an acceptable photograph of the animal in the wild, a freshly killed specimen or a confirmed sighting by a scientifically trained observer. Ten years ago the official view of the National Park Service was simply stated: "There are no panthers in the Great Smoky Mountains." Anyone suggesting otherwise was subject to ridicule. Pranksters made things worse here and there by dropping the remains of a panther that had died in captivity, or by creating a trail with a dismembered limb. One or two footprints may be faked realistically, but not a whole trail complete with natural signs, . . . and a competent tracker can spot a fraud in a short time. But the pranks made the whole idea of living panthers seem like a fraud or joke.

Until recently, seeing one was a little like seeing the Loch Ness monster, a vision best kept to oneself. But not any longer. Reports of sightings are solicited rather than ridiculed. And instead of being a despised predator, the panther is increasingly viewed as a prized species that must be rescued from extinction.

Field Biologist Robert L. Downing has begun a five-year project, funded jointly by the Forest Service and Fish and Wildlife Service, to search for panthers and panther signs in the Southern mountains. From his headquarters at Clemson University, South Carolina, Downing has established a network of contacts among state and federal resource agencies to help screen, and validate, sighting reports.

One of the first submitted to him, a photograph of a panther track, came from West Virginia early this year. "It's the first I've seen personally and I'm pretty positive it's authentic," he told me.

The three national park units in the Appalachians—Great Smokies, Shenandoah and the Blue Ridge Parkway—are cooperating with Downing in the search for cats, tracks and scats. A young Virginia outdoorsman and expert tracker, Champlin Carney, has been hired to search Shenandoah for tracks and to attempt to obtain photographs using a self-tripping camera.

So goes the search in southern Appalachia, but it's not the only area of interest and activity. New Hampshire officials are cautious believers: "Although none has been authenticated, enough sightings have been reported by people of good judgment that our department now considers there is a distinct possibility that the mountain lion is making a comeback in our state," says a spokesman for the New Hampshire department of game management.

Reports have been made continually in Massachusetts. West Virginia has stronger evidence. In April 1976 a young 100-pound male was shot by a farmer near Droop Mountain State Park after he saw it attacking his sheep. Though several sightings have been reported in the rugged high forests of Pocahontas County, this was believed to be the first panther killed in West Virginia in at least 50 years. One week later a second mountain lion was located on another Pocahontas County farm. The cats may have been wild or released by someone; yet sightings in relatively undeveloped areas, particularly in national forests, argue against the oft-expressed idea that all such animals must be "escapees from captivity." Besides, there aren't that many zoos or keepers of pet panthers in the Appalachians.

Blue Ridge Parkway rangers reported seeing a mother panther and two cubs near the Pisgah campground on at least two occasions as recently as 1977, a single panther near Frying Pan Tower Lookout, one of the wildest sections of the Blue Ridge, and another single panther at Gales Mine Falls, at the edge of the Asheville watershed.

In the Great Smokies, Ray DeHart, a retired trails foreman of the national park, within the past five years has seen three panthers on hiking trails—including one chasing a wild boar along the Appalachian Trail.

Lions clearly have learned to avoid men. They are shy but inquisitive about humans and sometimes like to be around them, sometimes seen, sometimes unseen, like phantoms. The panther seems to be a puzzling combination of what humans call courage and cowardice. Smaller cousins, the wildcat and lynx, are much more ferocious when cornered or trapped. The panther might attack a bear one day and run from a small dog the next. Complaints of depredation are surprisingly few, and so are unprovoked attacks.

At present the Eastern panther either survives, or may possibly survive, in south central Canada and northern Maine, the White Mountains, isolated areas in Massachusetts, the Adirondacks, the

Appalachian Mountains from western Pennsylvania down through Alabama, lowlands of South Carolina and Georgia, southern and central Florida, hardwood bottomlands of northern Louisiana, and the Ozarks of southern Missouri, Arkansas and eastern Oklahoma.

Firm, conclusive data are very difficult to come by. The Eastern panther has been photographed alive only in Florida, with one possible exception. While tramping in the Adirondacks in 1972, Alex McKay, a New Yorker, saw a huge cat stalking silently about 20 feet ahead of him. The cat, seeming to sense him simultaneously, crouched low in the grass and stared with yellow-almond eyes. McKay raised his camera, snapped the shutter . . . and looked down briefly to wind the film. When he looked up again the big cat had vanished.

The single picture he had taken revealed only a feline head with dark cheek patches, a clear muzzle, those glaring almond eyes, and the faint outline of the body crouched in the grass. The State Museum in Albany advised him that a photo is not acceptable documentary evidence; only the fresh skin of a specimen could be considered authentication of the animal's occurrence—yet it's against the law to collect the skin of an endangered species.

Many biologists and wildlife officials shun discussion of the Eastern panther. They seem to fear that recognizing the animal's existence would encourage hunting, regardless of its status as an endangered and protected species. They could be right. "The greatest danger to the panthers today," wrote Bruce Wright, "is from the 'shoot it to prove I saw it' philosophy." And Aldo Leopold's first response 30 years ago on learning that panthers survived in New Brunswick was: "We must not tell anybody."

In a recent study undertaken for the United States Forest Service, biologist George Lowman urged complete protection as "the most necessary step" for management of the panther in the East.

National forests in the White Mountains, Green Mountains, Southern Appalachians, Florida and the Ozarks all are designed to serve many purposes, including wildlife preservation. In places national forests border national parks, including Shenandoah, the Blue Ridge Parkway and Great Smoky Mountains, and are like extensions of them.

"As much of each national forest as possible should be maintained in unbroken undisturbed tracts," urged Dr. Lowman. "Certainly any type of habitat reduction should be avoided."

Among the states, North Carolina has moved with particular zeal. In 1971 it granted complete protection. Two years later Dr. Frederick S. Barkalow Jr., professor of zoology at North Carolina State University, began to solicit photographs or casts of tracks. Most recently the North Carolina State Museum of Natural History issued 1,000 posters as part of the first statewide effort to obtain reports.

With passage of the Endangered Species Act of 1973, federal agencies are obligated to give priority to saving the panther and its habitat. The Blue Ridge Parkway and Great Smoky Mountains National Park top the list because evidence of the panthers' presence there is so strong.

As Boyd Evison (who later would become assistant director of the National Park Service, then regional director in Alaska) puts it: "The cats' only real enemy is Man and we will do what we can both to prevent poaching and minimize 'people activities.' You and I may not see one of these lions, but knowing they are there means a lot to us."

Chapter 13

If the Panther Can Make It,
So Will We

In the summer of 1975, five maintenance workers were startled to see a large grayish colored cat with long tail bound across the trail near their bunkhouse in the Great Smoky Mountains National Park. The men scrambled from the porch to follow its path. They found only tracks in the mud along a creek bottom, but these native mountaineers were convinced they had observed a panther, and so they reported to park headquarters.

This took a modicum of courage since sighting a panther in Appalachia till then had been largely regarded like sighting the Loch Ness monster, a vision best kept to oneself. Naturalists and biologists had long denied the panther's existence, or capability of existing in the national park. Anyone suggesting otherwise was subject to ridicule. Once when a ranger called in and said, "I think I just saw a mountain lion," the park dispatcher retorted, "Have another drink and you might see its mate."

Fifty years ago it was not uncommon for mountaineers to catch sight of a panther (or "painter" in the vernacular) three or four times a year. The Cherokee called it Klandaghi, "Lord of the forest." More recently, however, the Eastern panther was assumed to be gone forever, even moreso than the American chestnut, rare specimens of which are still found here and there. The panther sighting was not the first (nor the last) reported, but it was advanced as the collective experience of five individuals. It triggered a new sense of awareness of the largest, rarest, and most secretive of wild American cats.

From *National Parks*, June 1980.

Throughout Appalachia resource managers became conscious of their opportunity and responsibility. In a study undertaken for the Forest Service, George Lowman, a consulting biologist, urged complete protection as "the most necessary step." He wrote as follows: "As much of each national forest as possible should be maintained in unbroken undisturbed tracts. Certainly any type of habitat reduction should be avoided."

The panther was taken seriously in the park as well. In December 1976 Superintendent Boyd Evison reported that a deer had been killed by a panther. "The pattern of this kill left no doubt in our minds that it was performed by a mountain lion. It is the first material sighting of the animal of this nature." In a subsequent statement the superintendent went further: "There is no reasonable doubt that there *are* cougars in the park; and it seems likely they have been here for some time. Very little is known about their habits and needs in this kind of country, but the park, if kept free of excessive development, offers the best sanctuary for cougars north of the Everglades and east of the Rockies."

Because most of the Great Smokies have been protected in undisturbed tracts, our generation is free to determine whether the panther should be sacrificed to progress, or saved, or how best it should be saved. The options are open. But in Cataloochee, the very scene of the key sighting, that option was nearly lost. As the *Quarterly News Bulletin* of the Carolina Mountain Club reported in the third quarter of 1974:

> Again, a lovely mountain area is threatened. Land developers, motel operators, politicians, highway builders, some chambers of commerce, and senior citizens interested more in dollars than in the out-of-doors are pushing for construction of a paved highway from Interstate 40 into Cataloochee Valley in the Great Smoky Mountains National Park. The National Park Service is also recommending the road.
>
> This fragile valley cannot stand any more visitors than it is now getting. It would be ruined by the ravages of litter, stream pollution, game poaching, land development, drug abuses, etc., that always come with crowds in primitive areas. This would be a catastrophe.

The National Park Service recognized the same threats. In an "environmental assessment," the bureau forecast that if the road were built this little valley would be subject to noise pollution, air pollution, soil erosion, stream siltation, temperature inversion (by trapping and concentrating auto emissions), loss of primitive character, destruction of natural vegetation and of wildlife habitat, and then, for reasons of its own, said it had decided to let a construction contract virtually forthwith. The Department of Natural Resources of North Carolina commented critically that this precipitous decision made a mockery of the Park Service program of master planning and regional planning then underway. But it took a law suit by a group of citizens of Haywood County, North Carolina, to block construction of the access road. It may indeed one day be built, but the option to save the habitat of the panther still remains open.

The Great Smokies and their surroundings in Southern Appalachia are abundant in treasures of flora and fauna, still little known or understood. The Smokies themselves are the best catalogued because they have been set aside for preservation purposes. Here have been found insects and spiders new to science; twenty-seven or twenty-eight indigenous types of gastropods, the lowly slugs; the unique spider of Cades Cove, found only here and across the world in China; a large number of distinctive salamanders, reptiles, and amphibians—the whole chain of life from the lowest of living things up to the bear and panther. But in other areas, still unprotected and uncatalogued, prospects are different. Once defaced or disrupted, their values are lost.

The future will be able only to speculate over what species might have been found at Copper Hill, Tennessee, a manmade badlands south of the Smokies, where fumes from the copper works early in this century killed everything as far as the eye could see; now Copper Hill is a monument to man's ability to eliminate with chemical waste every vestige of life from earthworms to trees.

In 1969 the Duke Power Company preempted the Keowee-Toxaway area, a wild region in southwestern North Carolina. Ten years later the power company would have had a much more difficult time, considering the beauty of the region, with its deep river gorges and diverse flowers, ferns, and shrubs.

The Keowee-Toxaway region was visited and described by William Bartram and, a few years after him, by André Michaux. Oconee bells or *Shortia galacifolia*, one of the rarest known wilderness plants in North America, was found by Michaux in 1787, probably at the juncture of the Horsepasture and Toxaway rivers, which join to form the Keowee. The attractive little plant was given its scientific name by Asa Gray, while inspecting Michaux's collection in Paris in 1839. Gray and others searched for it in the wild, but not until one hundred years later was it rediscovered, growing in the most restricted acid humus settings along shaded mountain streams.

The power company generously catalogued such resources, but then proceeded to obliterate the entire scene to make way for a network of generating plants and reservoirs. In clearing and preparing the basins, loggers removed 32 million board feet of mixed hardwoods and softwoods. Yellow poplars, some measuring 7 feet in diameter, 200 feet in height, and over 200 years in age, tumbled before the chain saws. The presumed discovery site of the Oconee bells in due time was flooded by the backwaters of Lake Jocassee. Nevertheless, Duke Power announced with pride that one section of the ancient forest would be saved "for naturalists and lovers of the untouched outdoors," a considerate gesture, but mostly in public relations, since it covers all of fifteen acres.

The world might never have known a species of fish called the snail darter nor have probed and pondered its special role in nature had the Tennessee Valley Authority not delayed completion of the Tellico Dam in the shadow of the Smoky Mountains. Initiated in the 1960s this project is intended to open new industrial sites and create jobs, although within a 50-mile radius almost two dozen impoundments already surround the Little Tennessee River and many industrial sites are not being used. Federal agencies seem determined to build or underwrite factories and then to find something for them to make, whether the specific product is needed or not, and all the while factories elsewhere may be idle—the factories employ machines more than people anyway.

Tellico will flood fertile bottomland, farms, a major tree nursery, and some of the most important archaeological sites in the Eastern United States—the Overhill Cherokee homeland, including the ancient capital of Echota, or "Chote the metropolis," and nearby Tuskegee, birthplace of Sequoyah. TVA tried to dismiss its opponents as "a handful of selfish trout fishermen trying to deprive the region of progress," but the Association to Save the Little Tennessee was fighting to save a fragment of natural heritage, the last stretch of the river that remained undammed, in free-flowing condition.

The snail darter is part of that heritage, though no one knew it existed at all until a University of Tennessee biologist discovered the three-inch-long species in 1974. This may not have been the most earth-shaking scientific discovery, but the snail darter was destined for fame in preservation and politics. In 1975 the Department of the Interior declared that completion of Tellico Dam would "totally destroy the habitat of the darter" and that protection must be accorded priority under terms of the Endangered Species Act of 1973. The validity of the act to save a seemingly obscure fish was sustained in the Supreme Court and against attacks in Congress; TVA in the late 1970s backed off and opened consideration of broader options than completion of the dam.

Whatever the ultimate outcome, the lesson of the snail darter transcends the case itself: that species and their surroundings are inseparable, that the seemingly undistinguished are as worthy and essential as the "desirable" or more visible. A snail or a clam or a snail darter is plainly an implicit piece of a river in the same way that a moonrock is a piece of the moon. The survival of the snail darter in the Little Tennessee—and only the Little Tennessee—enables the curious to investigate the darter's place and purpose there in the clean, gravelly shoals with cool, swift, low-turbidity water.

Through the 1970s various parcels of the Southern Appalachians were set aside for the future under terms of one law or another. The Chatooga River, a classic whitewater stream which forms in the mountains of North Carolina and then flows between Georgia and South Carolina into Georgia, became part of the National Wild and Scenic Rivers System. So did the ancient New River in northwestern North Carolina and southwestern Virginia, even after it had seemed lost to commercial hydropower development. The Obed River, a deep-gorge river in a true wilderness setting, and the Big South Fork of the Cumberland River (where the Army Corps of Engineers had planned to build the highest dam in the East), both on the Cumberland Plateau of Tennessee, were added to the National Park System. In an age where most rivers are crossed by highways, fenced in by farms and fields, fouled with effluent of cities and factories, or dammed by concrete, these streams still flow through wild country; where unaffected by logging or mining, their waters are clean and clear.

The Wilderness Act of 1964 and the Eastern Wilderness Act of 1974 served as the vehicles to identify and protect additional areas, large and small. Among these are the Cohutta Wilderness, astride the Tennessee-Georgia border, a composition of rugged, steep-sloped mountains, laced with deep gorges, waterfalls, and the Conasauga and Jacks rivers, covering 34,500 acres (which makes it the largest protected mountain wilderness outside the Smokies), and the Joyce Kilmer-Slickrock Wilderness, astride the North Carolina–Tennessee border, embracing within its 15,000 acres one of the most impressive remnants of the nation's virgin forests and the deeply sculptured valley of Slickrock Creek; but then there are natural gems of smaller size, like the Gee Creek Wilderness in Tennessee, about midway between Knoxville and Chattanooga, covering 2,570 acres.

Other areas need attention, too. Mount Mitchell, 65 miles north of Asheville, is the highest peak east of the Rockies, rising 6,684 feet above sparkling streams and waterfalls and forests that shelter rare plants and wildlife. "I've looked at a lot of areas and none was more majestic and beautiful than the Mount Mitchell area," observed Representative Roy A. Taylor (a life-long resident of nearby Black Mountain), when he, before retiring from Congress in 1976, successfully sponsored legislation authorizing a study of a proposed new national park.

The Nantahalas, which compare to the Smokies themselves, may also be worthy of such attention, as should Roan Mountain, north along the North Carolina-Tennessee border, one of the most distinctive mountains in the entire Appalachian chain. Roan embraces grassy balds, natural rhododendron gardens, and hillsides covered with flame azalea in the spring and mountain ash in the fall.

Once these areas were protected by their own remoteness; now they must be saved by desire and design. Most of these lands already are in public ownership, the summit of Mount Mitchell as a small state park and the bulk of the remainder in the Pisgah, Nantahala, and Cherokee national forests, where pressures for logging and other commercial uses chronically preempt preservation.

Soils in the highlands are not sufficiently deep or fertile over large enough areas to justify intensive timber management, nor subdivision development on available pockets of private land. But qualities that make these high places a liability for production make them a natural for preservation and compatible human enjoyment.

In 1978 and early 1979 a substantial number of citizens of Yancey County, in the environs of Mount Mitchell, voiced disapproval of the proposed park. "Residents feared future development might have been hampered. The best reason for approval of the Mount Mitchell Park would have been to limit development," editorialized the *Hendersonville Times-News* (on March 24, 1979). "The idea that land should be kept forever wild presents a hard decision to those accustomed to making a living off the land, but the present is not as important as the future and that calls for resources not only to be conserved, but preserved."

In the final analysis, it is impossible to decouple a natural treasure, such as Great Smoky Mountains National Park, from the technological society around it. The accelerated development of the world should give pause and inspire a deeper exploration of the meaning of preservation.

The esthetic experience of release from cares is highly dependent on the context of the outdoors. But a changing context can radically alter, if not destroy, the total experience. There is, of course, more at stake than enjoyment or esthetics.

To save the resources—the plants, panthers, soil, scenery, and the rest—through conscious intent constitutes an unselfish act of a generation in keeping faith with itself. It insures a legacy worth passing down, a choice of open options the future has the right to expect.

Part 2

Conscience of a Conservationist

Chapter 14

America the Beautiful—
Heritage or Honkytonk?

What are they really like today, the places your kids read about in school and which you hope to show them sometime as the finest representations of the American spirit? In case you haven't looked lately, a shock is in store. Marvels like Yellowstone National Park and Gettysburg battlefield are infested, often within their borders and almost always around the edges, by a spreading disease of our time—tourist blight.

It's more than a sickness of an era marked by mobility and leisure; the manufacture of tourist blight is also a lucrative business. Competition is keen among those who cater to and exploit the simplest expressions of public taste.

Now Coney Island is one thing. It serves a delightful purpose, aflutter with pennants and sideshows and mistaken for nothing else but itself. So does Atlantic City, for those who like to walk the Boardwalk and Steel Pier, feeling content in company of loud signs, loud noises and throngs of people. But this is hardly the atmosphere to spread from one coast to another, hardly an appropriate symbol to find at the gateway to, or within, a national shrine.

Of course, everyone is entitled to his own taste and should pursue it freely. But the public landscape, which all of us must live with, deserves farsighted care. And our national monuments should be more than an opportunity for promoters to make a fast buck.

Perhaps the surge of the last decade to lay waste to large sections of the countryside owes its inspiration to the success of Disneyland.

From *Changing Times*, November 1962.

Walt Disney built a synthetic thing, ballyhooed it on television and proved that millions of families would come running. Enterprising hopefuls copied some of the Disney image, playing up to public interest in history, the American West, nature, patriotism and religion. In almost every part of the country—often adjacent to a National Park or Monument drawing millions of visitors—are places bearing such names as Fantasyland, Six Gun City and even Bibleland.

But they lack Disney's greatest promotional advantage, the handy access to network television, and have to compensate in other ways. They resort to mammoth roadside billboards unashamedly representing their attractions as the "most outstanding," "foremost," "most historic," "most scenic" single spot in the state or nation. They harass with their signs, they demand attention, they cajole through appeals to children and parents until the poor family can hardly pass the place by without a guilty conscience.

Some resort to the lowest form of attention-getters, the display of caged animals at souvenir stands, gas stations and other tourist places.

Is this really what the public deserves? Some of those who profit from blight say, "Yes, most people have poor taste and we give them what they want." Yet there is the pitiful example of the Civil War Centennial to show how little opportunity the public is accorded to express its taste freely.

Long before the Centennial began, it was marked as a target of exploitation by all manner of commercial interests hoping to capitalize on the instincts of patriotism. Manufacturers of toys and gimcrack souvenirs advanced from one direction. Tourist operators attacked from another, establishing paid attractions close to the gateways of sacred battlefields.

When Allan Nevins, the distinguished historian, became chairman of the Commission in late 1961, he pledged that the sufferings and sacrifices of a century ago would not be memorialized with a carnival and that commercialism would be "muted and disciplined." The hopeful objectives became "to save a neglected battlefield, commission a symphony, raise a monument, get important books written." The scholar, very clearly, expresses a different concept than does the self-serving tourist promoter.

Dr. Nevins and others like him, the garden clubs, historical societies, the advocates of planning and zoning, endeavor to preserve and protect the characteristics that made them natural wonders and historic shrines in the first place.

What can you do to help, besides let your blood boil? We'll get to that later, but for now come aboard the calliope and tour the country for a look at blight on the landscape. The following are choice examples:

Gettysburg, Pennsylvania. No matter how you approach this hallowed ground, the route is lined with signs leading to extraneous commercial attractions. On the west, the Chambersburg Road, which Lee followed en route to the fateful battle, there is an Indian village, complete with totem poles and tepees; it's labeled "authentic," although Indians have not been in this area since 1750, and never did use totem poles or tepees when they were here. On the north, the road from Harrisburg, near the place where General Jubal Early's force smashed Union defenses the first day of battle, there is a Horse 'N' Buggy Museum, variously and modestly advertised as "America's largest" and the "World's largest" collection.

But to be *near* is not enough. The new Howard Johnson motel advertises happily that it is "practically in the center of the Battlefield," inviting guests to experience the art of pleasant living only a few hundred yards from the field of Pickett's Charge and the scene of Lincoln's Gettysburg Address. Then there is "America's most beautiful land of make-believe," a place called Fantasyland, with monkeys and Mother Goose, "right in the center of things" facing General Meade's headquarters just below the National Cemetery. And Stuckey's garish red and yellow roadside emporium, accompanied by Texaco's Fire Chief, astride the line of Longstreet's daring and bloody attack of the second day, where you can purchase mementoes of the battlefield, including ceramic birds, dogs, horses, alligator bags and ash trays with such inscriptions as "Gasoline and alcohol don't mix—but gasoline straight ain't bad!"

Then there is another group of attractions at Gettysburg—the "inspirational and educational." One is the Hall of Presidents, an array of wax figures that constitute an "exciting and patriotic exhibit" and a "must' for every American." Next, the National Civil

War Wax Museum, with more than 150 figures in "stirring" tableaux. If you find them not sufficiently stirring, proceed to the "newest and finest attraction," the Gettysburg Battlefield Diorama and Museum, which features sound effects of smoking rifles, burning wagons and blazing cannon fire.

These places are determined to leave absolutely nothing to the visitor's imagination. The Battlefield Tour provides "moments of emotion-drenched history" in stereophonic sound. You travel by bus and listen to the "voices" of Lincoln and Pickett, with cannons thrown in as "chills run up and down your spine."

Lincoln, in his utterance that brave men consecrated these fields far above our poor power to add or detract, proved a poor prophet.

Natural Bridge, Virginia. Thomas Jefferson would hardly recognize the towering limestone arch that he once owned. He treasured the great bridge, carved by rushing mountain streams over the centuries, and described it as "the most sublime of Nature's works." He resisted suggestions for man-made changes and said the bridge should remain as nature left it.

Today the wide Bridge, 215 feet above Cedar Creek, supports Route 11, the main road down the Shenandoah Valley. But the view is blocked by a wooden fence, as though protecting the inside of a baseball park. Jefferson would be required, before gaining admission, to pay his fee of $1.50. But there would be no extra charge if he elected to visit during the evening to see the "soul stirring" performance of the "Drama of Creation," when the Bridge is illuminated with colored lights and voice recordings evoke various religious images. And after coming through the entrance, he could also stop at the swimming pool, skating rink and an enormous souvenir counter vending a multitude of trinkets and doodads.

A recent addition at Natural Bridge is the antique car collection known as the "Museum of Motoring Memories"; this kind of companion piece is now widely found together with money-making commercial tourist attractions. Natural Bridge is perhaps the pacesetter for Route 11, a once-beautiful route, now adorned from Winchester to Roanoke with unrestrained advertisements for motels, commercial caverns, a place called "Zoorama" (it failed after a short, unhappy life, but the signs remain) and some ill-maintained state roadside rests.

The Great Smokies, North Carolina. The lowest form of tourist blight involves the exploitation of wild animals, and some of the most distressing examples are found in the highlands of western North Carolina. Gracing the foreground of the historic gateway to Pisgah National Forest is a roadside souvenir and refreshment stand. Here you can buy a Coke, hand it to a bear through the bars of his cage and watch him drink it. The purpose of his presence is to attract your interest and trade. Western North Carolina has a variety of such crude attractions. One is the "reptile garden," which everyone who loves wild creatures should see, not because it is good, but to observe how the animals, assorted scraggly deer, a bear and snakes, are cared for. There are the "Twin Yona" (*yona* is Cherokee for bear) caged on the roadside in the Indian Reservation between the National Forest and Great Smoky Mountains National Park. And like displays of wildlife before gift shops and gasoline stations in Maggie Valley.

How are these creatures captured? And how are they cared for? The North Carolina Wildlife Resources Commission endeavors to place the full blame on the Cherokee Indians—although bear-displaying souvenir stands invariably are just as likely to be operated by white Carolinians. Officials of the Wildlife Commission concede the bears are kept in "deplorable, unsanitary and inhumane conditions" but have so far failed to protect the animals from their roadside exploiters.

The Tennessee side of the Great Smokies provides hardly a better foreground setting for the most popular of America's National Parks. The town of Gatlinburg, an obscure mountain crossroads until chosen as the site of park headquarters, offers all manner of neon-lit commercial diversions, plus a chair-lift ride over the town and a biblical garden with dioramas of the life of Christ. There are some fine craft shops, in the best Smokies tradition, but far more prominent are those inevitable trinket stands—where the price is cheap but the markup is high. "Sure, I'm in the craft business," said one souvenir dealer with a laugh. "Get some of my best merchandise over the mountain—in Jay-pan!"

Lookout Mountain, Tennessee. From top to bottom, four commercial tourist attractions decorate the landscape of Lookout Mountain. But their influence does not end there. The city of Chattanooga, with signs of all sizes and shapes advertising attractions, motels and restaurants, is a difficult maze to pass through unscarred. And for hundreds of miles around, barn tops, billboards and birdhouses exhort the motorist and his family to "See Rock City."

Many visitors actually find Rock City, atop Lookout Mountain, an attractive place, with sandstone formations and trails over suspension bridges, through tunnels and "fairyland caverns." Admission may be high-priced at $2.75 cents for children (plus extras for "special" displays), but 30% percent of the revenue is poured back into highway advertising. Then there is Ruby Falls, reached by elevator, located in a cave below the surface. This attraction considers itself "the most spectacular of the world's wonders," and if this slogan is not sufficient enticement, there is another: "worthy of the Master's hand alone."

To go up and down the mountain, there is the Incline Railway, which spans "America's Most Amazing Mile." To visitors the cost of being "breathlessly suspended above the city" is $1 round trip, while to commuters it is 36 cents. At the base of Lookout the new Confederama, "the world's largest battlefield display of its kind," is guaranteed to tug at the heartstrings of every red-blooded son of Dixie.

If you persevere in ascending the mountain, and successfully penetrate this glowing ring of commercial superlatives, you will ultimately reach Point Park. Maintained by the federal government to commemorate the Civil War "Battle Above the Clouds," it overlooks the city of Chattanooga and the sweeping Moccasin Bend of the Tennessee River. And, without binoculars, there's not a billboard in sight.

Silver Springs, Florida. The jungle waters and swamp growth of the Springs have been a tourist attraction ever since a paddle-wheel steamer carried passengers up the Oklawaha River a century ago. Today this is big business, even by booming Florida standards. The traditional one-hour electrically operated boat trip is only the beginning. From there you're invited to the adjacent reptile farm, or "institute"; the Prince Of Peace Memorial (depicting the life of Christ in diorama); the deer ranch, and, of course, the inevitable collection of antique automobiles. Each of these components charges a separate admission, and the average family is likely to spend $10 or more.

Big business requires big promotion, and Silver Springs is a master of the art. Billboards are located all over the state, tracking the visitor from the instant he crosses the line; what is more, boards change frequently to keep timely and topical. Door mats at motels are not inscribed with the usual word of "welcome," but with "See Silver Springs." Bath mats are apt to say the same. So are place mats at restaurant tables. Any child traveling with his family to a vacation in Florida who doesn't say, "I want to see Silver Springs, Daddy," has clearly had his head buried in a comic book the entire way.

Customers leaving the Springs are also enlisted in the campaign, voluntarily or otherwise. One autumn a Florida newspaper editor thought he would take a presidential poll by assigning a reporter to tally Republican and Democratic bumper strips. "Sorry, chief, neither party can win," his man advised after spending a day on the street. "It's 'See Silver Springs' way out front."

Ocala, Silver Springs' neighbor in central Florida, bears the heaviest saturation. Advertising assumes urgent, imperative qualities, with such expressions as "Don't Miss" and "You Must." This basically attractive town appears despoiled and mesmerized, with its beautiful live oaks and subtropical foliage on the verge of obliteration by the unending message of "See Silver Springs."

Curiously, almost adjacent to the Springs lies Ocala National Forest, where no pennants flutter, a welcome reminder of Florida's natural glories; yet its recreation areas receive scant attention from tourist promoters in Ocala or the state government. Little wonder, perhaps, considering the overwhelming emphasis on real estate, industrial development, hotels, motels and man-made tourist attractions. Places like the Ocala National Forest and Everglades National Park are hard put by many pressures. Yet they are the pattern for the synthetic—like the tourist place in southern Florida that offers the convenience of "A Little Bit of the Everglades in the Heart of Miami."

Black Hills, South Dakota. "Yes, it is amazing to see the long line of commercial attractions on the road out here," a prominent and responsible citizen of the Black Hills area told a visitor from the East last summer. "The number is growing each year, too. Of course, we receive many complaints from visitors that this sort of thing destroys the feeling for Rushmore. But it seems somebody is bent on trying a new gimmick on every piece of private land from Rapid City to Mount Rushmore."

The gimmicks are multifarious indeed. The 25-mile road to Rushmore is an obstacle course of commercial attractions, all seeking to divert a million visitors, heading for a famous shrine, into their little crannies. The Reptile Gardens leads the way with the largest number of signs. There are four separate self-professed natural phenomena: Gravity Hill, Gravity Spot, Dizzyland, U.S.A. (Mysteries of Gravity) and the Cosmos (the *Real* Nature's Mystery Area). Then assorted caves and gold mines, and the usual Horseless Carriage Museum and Fairyland's Bewitched Village.

At one point the tragic contrast between the shrine and the commercial surroundings becomes most evident. A neat, small green and white sign reads "Mount Rushmore Memorial, 3 miles," but this can hardly be seen for the much larger, garish signs above and around it advertising mines, motels, caves and bars.

There is a novel little stunt in the Black Hills not seen elsewhere, a seal of approval at the entrance to many of these places. This sign reads "Family Approved Attraction." Approved by *Parents' Magazine?* The Automobile Club? No, nothing as objective as that. These tourist operators have their own organization, the Black Hills, Badlands and Lakes Association, and simply approve each other.

The picture within the Memorial grounds has its dim side, too. One would think the National Park Service maintains the vantage points facing the four presidential heads carved high on the granite mountain. But one of the best spots is operated by a commercial concessionaire as a kind of carnival.

The mammoth souvenir shop carries the feeblest assortment of native handicrafts made by the Sioux Indians. The emphasis is on merchandising such items as nylon flags of all nations, Japanese-made plates bearing pictures of President and Mrs. Kennedy and figurines of Jesus Christ.

Yellowstone National Park. The sorry truth is that federal officials sometimes contribute to tourist blight, too. Despite the proud tradition and generally high standards of the National Park Service, the core of Yellowstone, the nation's oldest and largest National Park, has deteriorated into a scandalous slum, the consequence of poor commercial management over a period of years and of soft and sloppy administration by Park officials.

Park people concede this privately, often with grim humor. "I heard my neighbor brushing his teeth this morning," says one visiting park man to another after spending a night at Canyon Village Motor Lodge, the first new overnight accommodation in the park in 30 years. "That's nothing," his friend replies. "I heard my neighbor *thinking* about brushing his teeth. When do we leave?"

In short, 512-room Canyon Village, intended as a model in commercially developed lodgings for the entire Park System, has turned out to be a failure, faulty in design, faulty in construction, with poor heating, flimsy soundproofing and a multitude of other shortcomings. Rooms are horribly overpriced ($13.50 for two, $18.50 for four), and the entire setting is incongruous with the great park, landscaped largely with black asphalt and blinking lights over the cocktail lounge. The gift shop offers one of the worst assortments of trinkets in America, 8,000 separate items, principally cheap (but profitable) importations from the Far East, including imitation English Wedgwood, Spanish toreador figurines in several colors, bells of Sarna and bongo drums.

The tragic debacle of Yellowstone illustrates the power exercised by private concessionaires. The three firms at Yellowstone appear to have more authority than the park superintendent. The Yellowstone Park Company, which operates lodgings and restaurants, made profits over the years while its plant became outmoded, overused and ill maintained. Finally goaded into construction of Canyon Village, the company paid $5,500,000 for a project originally estimated at $3,500,000. In an effort to recoup its losses, the firm last summer cut the number of college boys and girls on its payroll, then cut the wages of those it hired (to the barest minimum of compliance with wage-hour laws).

Yet for all the failings of the concessionaires, it remains for the park staff to answer the many complaints. The principal ones last summer were poor housekeeping, antiquated facilities, poor service, poor food.

Avoid the blight of Yellowstone? It is possible to a certain extent. You can find decent, clean and modern cabin and motel-type accommodations at the Grand Tetons, or well-kept campgrounds in surrounding areas. Look only at the thermal wonders, the wildlife and the marvels of a vast wilderness, shutting your eyes to all else.

But this is exactly the trouble: thinking Americans have shut their eyes for too long while blight and mass vulgarization have swept over the landscape. The amusement parks, the souvenir stands, the roadside animals won't go away by themselves. But neither must they be accepted as being here forever.

The point isn't that such places are not interesting or entertaining, or even, in some cases, in good taste. But, rather, do they belong where they are? What does Mother Goose have to do with the commemoration of a Civil War battlefield? What are commercial biblical dioramas doing in the Great Smokies?

It's Never Too Late

"Honky-tonk, cheap-facade joints in the mountain areas are a disgrace to the state" declared a recent editorial in the *Greensboro* (N.C.) *Daily News*, which pointed out what should be done. "Agitation in the public prints will do something to tidy up these roadside monstrosities. A little local or community pride might jolt the owners into at least partial recognition that an attractive, neatly kept roadside establishment is the best advertisement in the world for business."

Look over your own community. Demonstrate pride in its appearance and your desire to protect its inherent values. Sure, there's money in the tourist industry, but beauty is a far better advertisement for any town than a billboard. Certainly accommodations and commercial attractions are entitled to directional signs, but unrestrained coercive advertising to a captive audience is quite another thing.

Support the type of beautification work undertaken by the garden clubs, the true historic restoration urged by preservation groups, the strict zoning proposals. They will do far more to create a favorable image that visitors will remember—and that you can live with—than gimcrack attractions, high prices and unrestrained signboards.

In going places with your family, be selective. Visit places of reputation and stature because they really interest you, not because of their repetitive advertising along the roadside. If you want to see animals, there are zoological gardens in major cities. For souvenirs, purchase craft items indigenous to the area, not some cheap trinket that will scarcely survive the trip home. Cultivate an appreciation of the best of America in your children.

When you're good and mad, write letters. To the President, about the tragedy of Gettysburg. To the governor of the state where you feel any shrine is marred. To the director of the National Park Service, about the shabbiness of Yellowstone or of National Park souvenir counters. Letters to the editor of your daily newspaper are useful because other people see them, too. Tell about places you are not going back to visit a second time.

Such words will find their way around, and nothing will shake a tourist community more than realizing it may lose business. Perhaps nothing will do more to encourage it to enhance—instead of exploit—its endowment of history or natural wonders.

Chapter 15

Let's Rescue Our Roadsides— Now!

I shudder to think of how old Walt Whitman, my favorite poet, would respond to the American roadside of this day. Would he find the strength to sing the "Song of the Open Road"? That is, if he were inclined to sing at all. I doubt it. One look at the morass of eyesores and ugliness bordering the modern highway and he'd be through, finished, his last lyric line behind him. Walt was built of stern and sturdy stuff, but this he could never take.

The old wanderer was spared. He made his last journey sixty-odd years ago, just about the time our marvelous monster, the automobile, made its first. For the American public today, however, motorized to the hilt, there is no escape from endless thousands of miles of roadside delirium. The highway border is carved, cut and littered, reflecting neither forethought, plan nor pattern—except for one overriding theme, which is the inalienable, incontestable God–given right of any free-enterprising Twentieth Century businessman, large or small, to set up shop and collect his pound of profit.

As for responsibility beyond protecting and promoting his own interest, any such question is immaterial, irrelevant, impertinent and indecent. Let anarchy reign and each man have his way. Tomorrow the road may become unsafe, unsightly and obsolete, and therefore uneconomical. The public can be counted on to buy a new road. Today, business is good.

Sadly—tragically, I should say—the National System of Inter-

From *American Forests*, November 1963.

state Highways appears to be no exception. The public thought it was paying forty billion dollars–plus for a blue ribbon thoroughfare. Something new and different. Accident-proof. Uncluttered. Opening a wonderland of scenic beauty to traveling Americans. The late Senator Richard Neuberger led a valiant fight to keep it free of billboards: a seeming victory that cheered the hearts of motorists. But the signs are widespread that cheering was premature.

From one direction comes the report of Secretary of Commerce Luther Hodges pleading with Congress to extend the right to control advertising on vast portions which had previously been exempted, in order, as he said, "to end the heedless and needless desecration of our countryside." From another direction, a warning from the American Automobile Association that billboards are "sprouting like dandelions along the Interstate in states which have not acted to eliminate them." And it furnishes the evidence of 200 signs along a single 15-mile stretch. From coast to coast, highway officials express their grave concern over uncontrolled developments at Interstate approaches and intersections, which are causing the same conditions that ruined older roads. As if all these were not enough, add the serious proposal before Congress to prohibit the Interstate from swinging around a community without its express consent. Every curio shop, cafe, filling station and motel is entitled to a crack at the trade—isn't that what roads are for?

It's not just the Interstate that matters, however. Nor only the billboards that offend. They may disfigure scenery and open spaces. They may invade privacy and thrust themselves upon a captive audience. They may contribute to highway accidents and deaths. They may owe their very survival to the nation's most intensive band of lobbyists, who know every trick in the book. But billboards and the Interstate constitute only a fraction of the picture. It's the whole conglomerate of road and roadside, covering millions of acres, a tremendous segment of American soil, mostly owned by the public and the rest of which the public must look at and live with.

It's the automobile junkyards, of lifeless and unwanted machinery with no place to go except the convenient dumping ground of the roadside. It's the mass of garish, pennant-flying automobile filling stations, outdoing each other for attention. It's the motels, plush places crowding and competing to have first turn at the motorist. It's the hot dog stands, tar paper shacks, the curio stands, most of whose curios are made in Hong Kong and Japan. It's the animal farms, so-called, which usually are the poorest possible places to introduce children to wildlife. It's the abuse of God-given beauty along the roads of the Adirondacks, the Poconos, the Shenandoah Valley, the Great Smokies, the Black Hills, the Sangre de Cristo of New Mexico, some of the finest parts of Arizona, and along the shore of Lake Superior in Minnesota. It's the intrusion of roads themselves into cherished scenic and wildlife areas, whether for the benefit of land developers or to help a zealous highway engineer keep his alignment straight. Likewise, it's the invasion of fishing streams by dredge and bulldozer without regard for habitat and spawning ground of fish. It's the indiscriminate blanket spraying of the roadside with herbicides and pesticides that turn the hopeful slogan of "Keep Our State Green" into the awful truth of "We Have Now Browned It."

Add all these together. You have seen these places, or their types. Everyone has. A charming representation of an enlightened, advanced, soulful civilization. Walt Whitman would die a thousand deaths.

But the ludicrous part is that it barely represents our civilization at all. Take away the problems presented by the highway engineers. The commercial interests that have claimed the roadside as their very own, to do with as they wish, comprise a very small percentage of the American body. Extremely willful but small.

The irrepressible billboard boys, for example, never rest. When Congress set up the Interstate highway program in 1956 it prohibited service stations, but the lobbyists' devotion to duty forced it to back away from billboard control. Two years later a billboard item was included in the form of added money for states willing to accept a code of rigid standards on roadside signs—since then the billboard boys have blocked thirty states from acting. "Illinois is on the outside looking in," as the *Waukegan News-Sun* reported, "because the state senate highway committee succumbed to the blandishments of the billboard lobby." When hearings were held recently in Tennessee, the general counsel of the Outdoor Advertising Association of the state was privileged to sit beside the floor leader of the Senate and cross-examine witnesses; he also happens to be the former law partner of Governor Frank Clement.

Even where laws have been passed by state legislatures, the lobbyists return to sponsor crippling amendments, pleading not their own cause but the hardship of the poor farmer deprived of rental fees, and of the poor workingman—though it has never been anybody's doctrine that an enterprise is socially desirable solely because it pays wages. They enlist the support of tourist groups, which too often join in the argument that signs are necessary to guide people where they are going and show them where to eat and sleep. This might have a degree of validity were it not for the prevalence of so many other kinds of signs. Beer. Whiskey. Cigarettes. Washing machines. Nevada's largest gambling house, directing traffic from Florida. These are pertinent forms of travel guidance? But above all, there is always the anguished cry of individual "freedom," though courts have ruled repeatedly that roadside advertising is an unwarranted intrusion upon the freedom of the motorist, that there is no inherent right to exploit the highway for commercial purposes.

They never quit trying for the roadside is too precious, too valuable. A modern highway built at a cost of half a million or a million dollars a mile embodies a substantial investment. It may be the expenditure of *all* taxpayers, but this is purely incidental. Purely incidental to the giants of the automotive industry, General Motors, Ford and Chrysler, who truthfully should be the first to encourage safe, pleasant motoring, instead of undermining it with thousands of distracting billboards. Purely incidental to the humble—and far more defensible—owner of a jerry-built tar paper shack. What they all see is the mass market, America on wheels, attracted at a very cheap rate, at little expense to them.

The roadside spoilers don't score victories every time. If one wanted to be hopeful, and the marvel of America is that there is *always* hope, he could say their zenith is behind them. Despite their expenditure of money and nervous energy in Washington, they still came off second best in Congress, where Senators Maurine Neuberger and John Sherman Cooper have led the hard heroic fight to safeguard the Interstate System—or portions of it, at any rate. It was still possible recently for Secretary Hodges to present to Kentucky the first payment for complying with the federal anti-billboard provision and tell Governor Bert Combs of Kentucky, "Your people have given concrete evidence they want to be free from signs which mar the beautiful countryside—and an example to encourage other states."

There are courageous governors like Combs, who not only fight off the increasing forest of signs and billboards but, as in his case, banish the auto junkyards from public view.

In New York State, the Thruway Authority furnished a further demonstration of hope when it tore down and destroyed 53 offensive billboards after the owners had ignored warnings to comply with the law banning them within 600 feet of the right-of-way. California has probably provided the finest example of all by adopting a comprehensive program for a "scenic highway system," which incorporates not only safety, utility and economy, but also beauty, and by requiring that local governments take necessary action to protect the appearance of "scenic corridors" adjacent to the right-of-way.

"Beauty" is a word that is loosely used by tourist promoters, even after the beautiful has been dissipated and despoiled. But tourist groups are at last awakening to recognize that unless they help protect the roadside their areas must pay the penalty—both in loss of trade and in reputation. One example of an alert group is the Route 100 Association of Vermont. Having witnessed the spread of "Indian" trading posts, chinchilla ranches and animal "parks" on nearby roads, it called for saving the lovely pastoral west flank of the Green Mountains "before it is spoiled by cheap roadside stands, auto junkyards and other foreign-to-Vermont commercial developments." But I believe the prime example of how the defense of natural beauty pays tourist dividends is the experience of the Blue Ridge Parkway, in Virginia and North Carolina. Superintendent Sam P. Weems, a stalwart, stubborn public servant, resisted pressures from operators in adjacent mountain towns to "place a sign here and there so people can know about our attractions and where to find a night's lodging." Instead, he offered the opportunity to place community literature at the regular stopping places along the parkway. At first some of his neighbors took to it unkindly. But how has it worked out? Business in the valleys and coves is better than ever. The tourist interests are prospering.

More important is the record of traffic volume on the parkway itself. This marvelous recreational route attracts 5,000,000 visitors yearly. There is no road like it anywhere in America, or in the world, and none more loved. It demonstrates the desire of the motoring public to express pride in the good land, to explore forested mountainsides and clean valleys, to feel the nearness of wildflowers and shrubs in bloom at the road's edge. It's the kind of experience that reminds me roads and motoring can be fun. But when you take away such natural, attractive qualities inherent in the roadside, or cover them with blight, then you leave the face of America as the frontispiece of a selfish, unhappy, frustrated place.

Maybe not every road can be a Blue Ridge Parkway. I don't suggest that it should be. But there's no reason why roads and their environs can't be pleasant—particularly since we spend so much time of our lives in their midst. Certainly intelligent landscaping has its place, as highway officials have learned, not only in beautifying the roadside but in varying the mental tempo of the man behind the wheel.

Highway builders and maintenance officials, however, are not above criticism themselves. Have you ever seen the anomalous presence of a "Keep America Green" sign in a stretch of dead and dying vegetation, after an over generous dosage of spraying? Consider the knowing testimony of Rachel Carson: "Blanket spraying of chemical herbicides to control roadside vegetation is turning our roads into barren, unsightly wastes. The wildflowers, the ferns, the shrubs bright with flowers or berries are rapidly being replaced with nearly lifeless strips." But, as Miss Carson points out, when the roadside is maintained as a community of shrubs and flowers it provides food and shelter for birds and many small animals, and for the bees, an incredible number of species which are the wild pollinators important in maintaining crops and other plants.

Is blanket spraying really necessary? The Audubon Society of Western Pennsylvania asked Dr. Frank E. Egler to observe the roadsides in its area, which had been laced with "brown out" from indiscriminate spray. In order to control scrubby hardwood trees and tall shrubs, he reported after study, long stretches had been sprayed unnecessarily and wastefully, utilizing techniques which were not only outmoded but "reflected professional incompetence or a failure to utilize professional competence." Such vegetation, this prominent ecologist said, demands either mowing or selective spraying with herbicides known to be non-poisonous to man or wildlife, and in ways which appear unobtrusive from the road. After two or three seasons of such treatment, a stable plant community is established, low growing shrubs, ferns and wildflowers, which need not require another spraying for twenty or twenty-five years. Pennsylvania, obviously heeding his words, has put mowers to work in many sections, and shows an improved roadside for it.

Then there is the damage done to fishing streams, through planless dredging for gravel required in highway building and reshaping the streams whenever they stood in the way of new roads. The dangers have been well known. For a decade or longer the Sport Fishing Institute, Izaak Walton League and other conservation groups warned highway officials that dredging smothers food supplies, eliminates cover and spawning sites, that poorly designed culverts would take their toll. In Montana, a biological study showed where a trout stream that one year had yielded twenty pounds of fish was reduced to 1-1/2 pounds after being dredged, cleared and straightened for 350 feet. In the West, spawning areas of the salmon and steelhead were threatened; in the South, the smallmouth bass, and in the North and East, some of the finest local trout streams. But it proved difficult to convince state highway engineers that recreational resources might be as important as moving people from Point A to Point B in the shortest time.

It took numberless protests from the conservation groups, conferences between the Bureau of Sport Fisheries and Wildlife and the Bureau of Public Roads, and finally the introduction of legislation by Senator Lee Metcalf and Representative John Dingell. At last it paid off, in August 1963, when the Bureau of Public Roads agreed to recognize protection of fish and wildlife as part of its problem, too, and directed its engineers to reckon with these resources in planning all federal aid projects.

The experiences of spraying in Pennsylvania and of the fishing streams prove the broad interest and knowledge required to make the cosmos of the road and roadside a part of America that can be lived with and loved. They prove how much can be accomplished by the expressions of people who care. Everyone cares, of course. But too few have found the means to show it. It is almost laughable, if it were funny, to picture the band of devoted women, the "garden club gals," holding the forefront of public concern against batteries of billboard lawyers, roadside businessmen and legislators afflicted with conflict of interest. They have been aided and abetted by men like Robert Moses, the late Richard Westwood, president of the American Nature Association, and Arthur N. Pack, who participated in the National Roadside Council, an organization which has not existed since 1955. But in some states the women's groups have stood virtually alone. The American Automobile Association has rendered valued assistance, though some of its affiliated clubs restrain themselves to the encouragement of school safety patrols and driver training. Or, as Raymond Mostek, president of the Illinois Audubon Society wrote recently, "It is discouraging to find that the powerful Chicago Motor Club has never taken a stand against billboard blight in Illinois though the equally powerful American Automobile Association has always supported highway billboard control on the national level."

Roy Carroll, Jr., president of the American Institute of Architects, stated the need very clearly in addressing the convention of his professional organization. It is: acceptance of the sense of responsibility as well as the concern for one's own affairs. Said he, "We would blame the doctors if our people were covered with running sores. If crookedness ruled the courts, we would blame the lawyers. So the 15,000 architects in America must take the blame for ugliness in their own communities. If each architect gave one day a year to the fight for zoning and planning, and against the blight of signs, billboards and gas stations, it would be a much better country."

Verily, it's the "better" side of America that is involved. It is not a question of being against something that is wrong, as being for something that is right. Or, as Architect Carroll said, "Few profit from ugliness and these are seldom related to the community."

The sound approach to the American roadside is known. In the score of states where Roadside Councils are functioning, the landscape shows the result of their efforts. There should be roadside councils in fifty states, coordinated by a National Roadside Council, to make the public's viewpoint known, understood and felt in the legislative councils. They should be led not only by the garden clubs and women's groups, but by the automobile clubs, considering their primary responsibility in saving lives, in the sound highway investment and in encouraging tourist travel. Roadside Councils should represent the whole broad spectrum of public interest from architects and landscape architects to conservation organizations and tourist groups.

For who can say that wayside plantings do anything but make a state more livable and lovable, the kind of place that visitors will remember and recommend? Who can say that landscaping of highways does anything less than highlight fundamental scenic values? Who can say that dignified marking of historic points of interest does less than stir learning and pride in the American experience? Who can say that the orderly development of attractive roadside service districts, with service stations, motels, craft shops and information centers, will not benefit the community as well as serve the traveler?

Such developments must come. They are in the best public interest, the interest of the nation. The question is, When? How long will it take the mechanized society to show it can save and enhance the landscape that Whitman found in the natural state?

But there is no time like the present. Let's rescue the roadside—now!

Chapter 16

On Such Foundations—
The National Park Service at Fifty

The National Park Service was born one half century ago this year, in an age of courage and strong convictions. The President of that day, Woodrow Wilson, was not unlike Theodore Roosevelt, his predecessor once removed, a scholar and pioneering conservationist. Both men insisted on fighting issues of principle openly, before the public, rather than dealing with back room politicians on a basis of expediency.

The Congress voted to establish the Park Service in 1916. By so doing it recognized that not even imminent commitment to a World War must stop a nation from conserving its treasures of nature, which are the essence of democracy.

The Secretary of the Interior, Franklin K. Lane, understood his proper role. It was not to dominate the Park Service, nor to use it for political purposes, but to buttress the agency. If an assistant secretary had publicly ridiculed the entire personnel of the Service, and derided its esprit de corps, as did one assistant secretary in 1963, Lane would have given that man thirty days' notice, regardless of his political sponsorship.

As for the director, Stephen T. Mather, when a lumber company disregarded his order to dismantle its mill and depart the bounds of Glacier National Park, Mather personally headed a brigade that exploded the mill with thirteen charges of TNT. When it was suggested to him that park superintendents be appointed under the

From *American Forests*, November 1966.

same political terms as postmasters, Mather replied that he was going to pick his own people according to capability alone.

On such foundations the National Park Service has built its traditions of the past fifty years. In commemorating the historic golden jubilee of the Park Service in 1966, the American public can express no fonder hope than that principles of renewed courage and strong conviction will guide the agency's destiny for the next fifty years.

The administration of national parks, monuments and allied areas at the half-century mark can hardly be called flawless. But let us record in appreciative tribute that there is far more right than wrong.

The National Park Service is a vigorous, capable, aggressive and loyal organization, devoted to public service.

It has safeguarded wilderness values, and often enhanced them, despite powerful opposition, in areas like Big Bend, Sequoia, Yosemite, Glacier and the Great Smokies, all subject in years past to uses such as logging, grazing, mining and settlement.

It has been the single most important influence in cultivating the art of intelligent travel in America. And not solely because of laws. The men of the Service, superintendents, rangers, historians and naturalists, have given meaning to the areas in their charge, enabling visitors not only to see the U.S.A., but to understand it, to derive inspiration from the national heritage.

The National Park System symbolizes the nation itself. It affords an opportunity for all persons to enjoy and appreciate the richest resources of this land; it invites all to share the sense of pride required to assure that these resources will endure. The national parks afford a "window" to all that is best and wholesome in America.

The popularity of our national parks is not enough to guarantee their survival for the next thirty years. What is most needed, to quote the venerable Horace Albright, who links the day the Park Service was born with our day, is "wider support from more citizens who will take the trouble to inform themselves of new needs and weak spots in our conservation program."

Thus, an informed public must ask many questions. It must ask for bolder efforts at regional planning and development, in which each national park is considered not an island in itself, but the heart of a large recreation area in which tourist slum villages are uplifted into attractive park foregrounds. It must ask for wider experimentation with minibus transportation, in parks like the Grand Canyon, Great Smokies and Yellowstone, for better ways of doing things for more people without impairing wilderness values. It must ask the director of the Park Service and the Secretary of the Interior to raise the level of park concessions. It must ask the Secretary to press for elimination of the Schedule C classification, which reduces career officials to the dangers of political dependence. It must ask the President and Congress to respect and protect the pride and non-partisan integrity of the National Park Service.

The National Park Service needs public understanding and support. It needs stimulation in order to perpetuate the legacy of courageous action. It deserves the best the public can give in return for all that it has given.

Chapter 17

The Politics of Conservation

Last spring I observed at close range two of the principal performers in the great contemporary game called the politics of conservation, in which we all are players, one way or another. The first was the little old lady in sneakers. I met her, filled with emotion and idealism, at the rim of the Grand Canyon, where she had come to join a protest against damming the Colorado River flowing through the gorge below. The second was the master politician himself, Lyndon B. Johnson. At the White House I watched him sign a bill, proclaim his desire to be recorded in history as a "conservationist President," and proceed to mix conservation generously into politics.

Conservation wears a thousand faces at a thousand places; the game is played by a thousand different sets of rules. They are all trying, it seems to me—the little old ladies in sneakers, the President, the politicians, their friends and foes—to determine what conservation really means in our age and how to apply it within the framework of their own interests. Is it natural beauty? Is it the construction of more dams to provide more hydroelectric power? The development of more outdoor recreation areas for play and pleasure? The promotion of parks and wilderness? The cultivation of forests for timber and wildlife? Or is it perhaps some part of all of these, and something larger besides?

For most Americans, conservation's present and future are both a riddle. The concept is still young and searching for its own maturity. The word itself, conservation, was unknown in its present usage

From *Holiday*, February 1967.

until the early years of this century. The man who discovered and defined its meaning, Gifford Pinchot, pioneer forester and practicing conservationist, based his creed on the proposition that "no generation can be allowed needlessly to damage or reduce the future general wealth and welfare by the way it uses or misuses any natural resource." Thus, said he, "Conservation means the wise use of the earth and its resources for the lasting good of men. Conservation is the foresighted utilization, preservation and/or renewal of forests, waters, lands and minerals, for the greatest good of the greatest number for the longest time."

The definition is as valid now as in the age of Pinchot and his ally, Theodore Roosevelt. The critical need for its application must be self–evident. The United States, having thoroughly despoiled its seemingly limitless natural treasures in the process of growth, has been reduced to husbanding its diminishing reserves. Yet even within the outline of agreement that such must be done, there is vast disagreement of how to do it, and diversions to prevent it from being done. The premise that conservation cannot be wrapped in a neat package acceptable to all, however, has more good than evil to it, for needs change and views change as times change. Besides, the public deserves alternatives from which to choose. For myself, I try to listen to articulate advocates of all sides, to weigh their arguments in searching for the truth, and always reserve the right to be wrong.

The lady at the Grand Canyon represents one particular school of thought. She wasn't little, really, or very old, and wasn't wearing her sneakers at the time, but was clearly a member of the generic type of preservers, composed of tree lovers, flower lovers, bird lovers and wildlife lovers. Her kind is pure anathema to spokesmen for commercial interests that serve society's immediate needs by exploiting the land and water: loggers, miners, sheep and cattle raisers, paper and pulp manufacturers, land subdividers, road builders and dam builders—all old masters at playing the politics of conservation, from the level of the county commissioners to Congress and the Cabinet.

A highway lobbyist showed his resentment last year at the breed of little old ladies by suggesting they be renamed "beautniks." But eventually he recanted, conceding that beauty and highways should indeed go together. In the same context belongs the effort of the Consolidated Edison Company to convince the opponents of its proposed power plant at Storm King Mountain on the Hudson River that "You can have scenery and electricity, too." Likewise, the campaign of timber companies in Northern California to convince a public clamoring for a Redwood National Park that "You can have scenery and timber, too."

These old professionals have changed their pitch. They recognize that, whether they like it or not, the ladies in sneakers are on the march everywhere, and are a political force to reckon with. For conservation today begins in everybody's neighborhood, where a little old lady may be a he, or even me; where all people are feeling the pinch for parks, playgrounds, public gardens, and appreciate the right of a little stand of trees to live and the right of children to watch those trees grow. The lady at the Grand Canyon hailed from Colorado, where she was a leading light in the Ornithological Society of Colorado Springs. Her group had been looking for some place close to home for bird watching, but with all the rampant construction and urban sprawl they could not find a single handy bird sanctuary. "That was how I became a conservationist," she told me.

The smart politicians have also learned to appreciate the needs and growing role of the little old ladies. In 1959, California enacted an open–space law. Then, in 1961, the voters of New York State surprised everyone by voting three to one for a $75,000,000 open space bond issue designed to halt planless chaos and sprawl. They were followed by voters of Connecticut, New Jersey, Massachusetts and Wisconsin. As Governor of Wisconsin, Gaylord Nelson found wide support when he fought for acquisition of recreation lands and wildlife habitat, for billboard control, and for the principle of scenic casements. His conservation activity, by his own reckoning, earned more public support than any other program. It helped him become the first Democrat in the 20th Century to be re-elected as Governor of Wisconsin, later helped him to be elected to the United States Senate.

In Kentucky, Gov. Edward T. Breathitt built an enviable record with a comprehensive program embracing stimulation of better farm practices; protection of small watersheds and establishment of a pioneering statewide water authority to assure clean water for all communities; development of new state parks and historic areas; and natural-beauty laws that safeguard streams and lakes, as well as roadsides, from litter. Breathitt risked his political future, too, by sponsoring the best strip-mine control law on the books of any state, and insisting on its enforcement.

Enforcement is no small task in Kentucky, where mining interests have always made the politics of conservation a rough and rugged game. So Harry Caudill, Appalachian lawyer and author, learned when he was a member of the Kentucky legislature in 1954. That year Gov. Lawrence Wetherby had proposed a mild control bill for strip mining in the coal industry. "Lobbyists for the mining companies descended on the state capitol by the score," writes Caudill, "and a diluted version of an initially weak bill was passed." Moreover, successive governors failed to enforce its mild provisions and the bill became meaningless. But Breathitt and Caudill stood up to fight, placing principle above expediency.

They learned that the tougher the fight, the stronger the support from the army of little old ladies.

The timid, the hesitant, the compromisers often have failed. The bigger and bolder the program, the greater the chance of success. So I found myself thinking while at the White House watching the President play the role of the master conservationist. The occasion was a ceremony at which he signed the bill establishing Cape Lookout National Seashore in North Carolina. "I want to be judged as we judge the great conservationists of yesterday as benefactors of our people and as builders of a more beautiful America," the President told the assemblage. Then he passed out 200 pens. The politicians stood first in line, smiling for the benefit of any photographers present; they were followed by civic boosters from Carolina, leaders of conservation organizations, and the press. When my turn came, I introduced myself. The President looked me in the eye and said, "I'm doing everything I can," as though he really meant it.

I believe the President does mean it, in his own way, but it does not necessarily follow that he is doing everything he can. Mr. Johnson has made major contributions to conservation in his "little old two years," as he said at the ceremony (which came out as "little over two years" in the official transcript). But he and the people around him have a long, long road to travel, and much to learn, before they can be judged in the same historic class with the Theodore Roosevelts, Gifford Pinchots and Stephen T. Mathers.

Theodore Roosevelt was distrusted by politicians and championed unpopular causes; he fought the barons of American industry, the railroads, meat packers, power companies and lumbermen. In our day, by contrast, Lyndon Johnson pursues in practice a course of halfway measures and "consensus conservation" designed to gain support from everyone and to please all. Secretary of the Interior Stewart L. Udall, during a recent interview, was asked about his mistakes or regrets. "All of us," he conceded, "overcompromise and therefore fall short of our ideals." Such overcompromise results from mixing conservation so deeply with political considerations that principle becomes a matter of secondary concern. This is why appointments of key officials at the Interior Department are dictated by the White House, the Democratic National Committee and the Senate Interior Committee on the basis of patronage and nepotism. This is why Secretary Udall fails to support his bureau chiefs when the going gets rough; why he endorses construction of dams across the Colorado River in his native Arizona, and why he backs away, under pressure of a powerful special interest, the sheepmen's lobby, from curbing the sheer brutality practiced by one of his own department's divisions in the pursuit of predatory animals.

Yet on the other hand, Mr. Udall makes much of a program to save "endangered species." This is part of the word game in the design to woo little old ladies in sneakers without losing support of the special interests. As in the case of the President, the Secretary wants everything to be right, and wants to be praised and publicized for his own meritorious deeds—which are considerable. His efforts in promoting passage of the Land and Water Conservation Fund Act, assuring Federal expenditures for recreation land by all levels of government, represent one of his memorable achievements. Still, some words are empty, such as the Interior Department report that details noble efforts to make certain that "the chirp of the prairie dog and honk of a Canada goose are not to become oddities heard only on archive tape recorders," while 600 Government hunters are scattered over the Western states spreading poison like the all-destructive "1080" compound, setting steel traps, hunting dens, shooting from planes, and claiming an annual toll of at least 200,000 coyotes, foxes, bobcats, mountain lions, wolves, prairie dogs and pocket gophers.

Congress has been singularly lacking in conservation vision. Except for Senators Clinton Anderson, Lee Metcalf, Gaylord Nelson, Rep. John Dingell and a handful of others, few members are in fact knowledgeable in the field. The recent advances, such as passage of the Wilderness Act, Water Quality Act, Water Resources Planning Act, Food and Agriculture Act, Land and Water Conservation Act, and the meager program to improve highways as part of the landscape have been part of the backlog of inaction piled up by former Congresses, Democratic and Republican. Rep. Wayne Aspinall, the powerful chairman of the House Interior Committee, does not support the President's program. He represents the provincial mining and grazing interests of the western slope of Colorado, and measures conservation in traditional terms of resource utilization, to the neglect of the crying new need for open space.

The most important conservation eras have resulted only from strong Presidential leadership, exercised by Theodore Roosevelt, Franklin D. Roosevelt, and now, hopefully, by Lyndon B. Johnson.

Consider the record of recent years in dealing with the National Parks. During the Eisenhower days, even while the volume of visitors was soaring as part of the postwar recreation surge, the National Park Service was kept weak and poor by Congress. In the Democratic days that followed, Rep. Michael Kirwan distinguished himself as chairman of the House Interior Appropriations Subcommittee by blocking the expenditure of money for acquisition of park land, while such shrines as the Gettysburg battlefield were being despoiled with tawdry commercial developments on pockets of private land. Thanks to Mr. Kirwan's sense of expedient economy, some of the choicest areas in the nation were lost to public access forever.

Today the President speaks proudly of enlarging the Park System, but he fails to mention that some of the new historical areas come under the heading of political pork and plums, and could as well be administered by states, or in some cases, even by counties.

He fails to mention that while new areas are being established, older areas are undernourished and understaffed; they don't get enough funds for protection of bears, wolves and other key animal resources from poachers or to carry on improvements that are thirty years overdue.

One problem faced by the President in building a conservation legacy is the lassitude of large segments of the bureaucracy. Old thinkers in all agencies find it hard to think new thoughts about the immense, shattering changes facing the nation. The words appearing in attractive reports, brochures, press releases, and the lip service in public speeches are easy to come by; they seek to create an illusion among the little old ladies that all is going well. But a stomach for fighting and martyrdom, and a thirst for testing new ideas, are rare. Many Federal officials are either timid or have been intimidated by political pressure to the point of losing imagination and zeal.

Instead of providing a model of water conservation techniques, Federal agencies have been found to be among the worst sinners in pollution. In the offices of the Bureau of Indian Affairs, I have met officials in key spots who neither understand nor like Indians. At the Cherokee reservation in North Carolina, this agency did everything it could to encourage development of a tasteless tourist fake called Frontier Land, which scars the Smoky Mountain landscape with atrocious billboards. On the other hand, it discouraged, and contributed to the demise of, the time-honored Cherokee Indian Fair, long a point of pride for the Cherokee people.

Then we have the case of the Tennessee Valley Authority, the largest purchaser of coal in the country (to feed its steam plants) and the largest single customer of strip-mining firms in Appalachia. It could have heeded the advice of the U.S. Forest Service that contracts be written with a built-in plan for land restoration in advance of mining, and by so doing set a shining example for other buyers. Instead, TVA buying practices contributed directly to the fantastic havoc wreaked on the mountain slopes of the Southeast. Ironically, the Government is spending $36,000,000 under the Appalachian Development Act for strip-mine reclamation.

The Federal Highway Administrator has assured us that people who build highways hope to "serve the spiritual as well as physical needs of the nation," but in fact the engineering mind conceives a road and not a roadside; the highway builder heeds the highway lobby far more than he heeds the little old ladies worrying about the landscape. My friends of the Forest Service espouse the broad principle of "multiple use," which they generally practice well, except in portions of the Pacific Northwest and Montana, where multiple use is likely to mean logging and bulldozing areas of unique scenic beauty, in the manner prescribed years ago by industry-oriented professors of forestry.

These Federal officials have a lot to learn. So do we all, from the President to the littlest little old lady; and perhaps the greatest lesson is not only an appreciation of conservation in its broadest sense, but the discovery that everyone has a part to play in shaping the future.

This can be a difficult lesson. For instance, at the Grand Canyon, I listened to Representative Morris Udall, the younger brother of the Secretary, present his views on the proposed dams across the Colorado River. Here was one of the finest conservation figures in Congress, who fought sincerely for the Wilderness Act and the Land and Water Conservation Fund Act when they brought him little political mileage in Arizona. But on this day he was supporting the dam proposal before an audience composed of the little old lady from Colorado Springs and over a hundred others who had answered the call from the Sierra Club, an ardent, creative, uncompromising conservation organization. And for his efforts Mr. Udall was rewarded with catcalls.

It is hardly possible that he deserved such hostile treatment from his friends. Neither the Sierra Club nor any other group possesses all the answers to the problems of conservation, and today's answers may be invalid tomorrow.

The President himself is an example of one who has come a long way. It was only a few years ago when he, as majority leader, observed without dissent his good friend, the late Robert S. Kerr of Oklahoma, flailing his arms on the Senate floor and warning his colleagues pointedly to stop wasting time on "asz-thetics." Since taking his place in the White House, however, Mr. Johnson has enunciated a thoroughly comprehensive conservation program.

Likewise, in retrospect, Representative Aspinall has played a particularly constructive role for little old ladies. As chairman of the Interior Committee, he bottled up the Wilderness Bill for eight years until public pressure expressed through other members of Congress became hard to resist and sufficient changes were made in the legislation to mollify the opposition of logging, grazing and mining interests. When the Act became law in 1964, a total of 9,000,000 acres administered by the Forest Service was protected at once as part of the National Wilderness Preservation System. In addition, the Act provided for public hearings in the next eight years on the feasibility of including approximately 160 other areas of National Forests, National Parks and Wildlife Refuges in the System. These include all roadless areas of more than 5,000 acres, which would henceforth be protected from development except when authorized by an Act of Congress (though mining and prospecting are permitted in National Forest wilderness units until 1983). This complicated procedure was not what the conservation organizations sponsoring the bill had originally hoped for and the mining provision seriously weakens the wilderness concept. Yet now the issues must be debated, area by area, before the public and not in the back rooms. And if the ultimate decisions are based on the active participation of more people clamoring for understanding, refusing to settle for platitudes or lip service, this in itself represents a signal victory.

I saw this demonstrated last summer in the Great Smoky Mountains, at the first wilderness hearing conducted by the Interior Department. Although the National Park Service has carefully defended its role as guardian of wild places, in this instance instead of presenting a bold, courageous program to embrace the heart of the park in the National Wilderness Preservation System, it offered a weak, unimaginative plan for solving the problem of congestion the easiest possible way—by crisscrossing the park with roads and other developments that render wilderness meaningless. The Service was supported at the hearing by sixty-some local politicians and tourist promoters. But three times as many college professors, hikers, ministers and, above all, little old ladies—trim, thoughtful and eloquent—came from all over the country to speak up and to remind Secretary Udall & Company that wilderness is a vanishing national treasure not to be tampered with lightly. Moreover, they offered ingenious alternatives to accommodate more visitors without intruding in the wilderness. They provided a lesson to politicians and bureaucrats on the temper and talent of little people and their feeling for the American earth.

Among the national conservation issues of 1967 will be the proposals for the Wilderness System to be considered at thirty more hearings, including those involving Shenandoah, Everglades, Mammoth Cave and Sequoia national parks. The hearings themselves settle nothing; they provide a record for review by the Secretary of Interior or the Secretary of Agriculture (in the case of the National Forests), and a basis for recommendations to the President and by him to Congress. The legislators have the last word in adopting a separate law on each wilderness unit. But certainly the flood of 6,000 letters and statements accompanying the hearings in the Smokies can hardly miss making an impression.

A related key issue this year will be the proposal to establish a Wild Rivers System, aimed at saving a few choice streams from commercial use and dams. The Senate passed a weak bill last January, well watered with permissive, ambiguous amendments, including one that would actually encourage road building along the banks of a wilderness stream, but there is hope for more constructive action this year.

One objective of the Wilderness and Wild Rivers Systems is to block the dam builders of the Bureau of Reclamation, the Army Corps of Engineers and the Tennessee Valley Authority from civilizing the entire face of the land. Wherever streams flow free, from Alaska's Yukon River to the Grand Canyon of the Colorado, the Little Tennessee and the Everglades in the South, the engineering minds propose dams for flood control, hydro power, irrigation and recreation, asserting that improving on nature is the test of conservation. In some cases this may be true and "reclamation" of public lands in the West was a keystone of Theodore Roosevelt's pioneering program.

However, in Arizona today, and to a lesser extent in Alaska and elsewhere, everybody wants dams, or thinks he wants dams, like a panacea, or religion—to guarantee a better life, thus inducing increased bank deposits, freeway construction, congestion and sprawl. Where there should be fundamental research into problems of water storage and comprehensive long-range planning, political hysterics prevail. Harnessing natural features and improving upon rivers represent man's splendid ingenuity, beyond a doubt. But the greater ingenuity is to show that man can survive while leaving some few features of the earth to their own devices. This is the true test of our mechanical, intellectual and moral skills.

This same principle applies to the redwoods area of California. It is perfectly true, as the lumber industry points out, that rapidly growing coast redwoods are capable of attaining 240 feet of height in the first century of their lives, and that areas containing second-growth timber from twenty years of age up are ideal for recreation. I believe the large redwood companies have every right to practice scientific forestry in woodlands already cut over, and that they deserve encouragement for opening their private lands for hunters, hikers, fishermen and campers. However, the second-growth products of a timber company can never match the 50,000 acres of virgin stands preserved in California state parks and over 200,000 acres remaining in private ownership—all that remains of a mighty forest that once spread over 2,000,000 acres.

Congress missed the opportunity last year to vote the establishment of a Redwood National Park because of its own hesitancy and political pressure against the proposal by the lumber industry. In the key area of Mill Creek, lumbermen have agreed to a one-year moratorium on cutting, which makes 1967 the year of decision, and the time for President Johnson, who has recommended establishment of the park covering approximately 40,000 acres in this area (including 16,000 acres already in state parks), to press earnestly.

There is also strong support for establishing a larger park centering on the Redwood Creek Valley between Eureka and Klamath. Discovery in 1965 of the tallest known tree on earth, a 385-foot-high coast redwood, in this area brings it into sharp focus. The discoverer of the tree, Dr. Rudolph W. Becking, exploring on a research grant from the National Science Foundation, has proposed a 73,900-acre Redwood Creek National Park, embracing "nine of the most magnificent river flat redwood groves," plus giant specimens of grand fir, western hemlock, Douglas fir and red alder. This area, included in the first set of National Park Service plans for the redwoods, has been dropped from current administration proposals.

The big issues of 1967 are close to home as well as in the far-off places. Counties and states must develop comprehensive plans for matching money under the Land and Water Fund. This means far more than recreation, but examination of all land uses. In addition, the majority of legislatures will consider action on the Federal Highway Beautification Act of 1965. The President had proposed a weak bill to begin with, a consensus measure designed to allay opposition from the outdoor advertising lobby; it was then watered down by Congress (almost all of whose members employ campaign billboards) before tossing a bone to the little old ladies in sneakers. Under the 1965 law, the Secretary of Commerce was directed to withhold 10 percent of Federal Highway funds from any state which fails to provide effective control of advertising within 660 feet of interstate and primary highways. Generously exempted, however, were areas zoned by state law as industrial or commercial and unzoned areas for which the Secretary was empowered to set advertising standards after holding public hearings. While the Bureau of Public Roads assembled 60,000 pages of material at fifty-two hearings across the country, it is clear that the superior lobbying power of the billboard industry prevailed over the spokesmen for beauty; for the standards proposed by the Bureau to the Secretary comprise virtually a complete surrender—the billboard-control act would now apply to only a small percentage of the nation's road network.

Still, the President can say that the law covers junkyards and roadside landscaping, as well as billboards. He can say that it supersedes a 1958 law that was almost a complete failure; that twelve states have already acted favorably, and almost all the rest are likely to follow suit this year. He could say that it represents a beginning, albeit meager and far from fulfillment of public desire, and he would be right.

The little old ladies have not lost all battles for conservation of the roadside. In Colorado, their Open Space Action Committee mounted an offensive in the 1965 legislature, after the lobbyists had bottled up their billboard-control proposal. Arguing that scenic highways and removal of roadside clutter are paramount in building a healthy tourist economy, they snatched victory from defeat and achieved a moratorium on billboards pending the Federal Highway beauty standards.

In my opinion the little old ladies in sneakers, working through such groups, are the force that holds the key to the future. But they will be at their best, and so will the organizations speaking for them, with a mature, realistic attitude toward conservation in its broadest sense and toward industry's effect on natural resources.

Preservation and natural beauty are vital in American life, but are only components of the total pattern. "From birth to death, natural resources, transformed for human use, feed, clothe, shelter and transport us," wrote Gifford Pinchot. "Upon them we depend for every material necessity, comfort, convenience and protection in our lives. Without abundant resources prosperity is out of reach. Therefore the conservation of natural resources is the fundamental material problem."

Conservation is the planned, orderly development of the earth and all that it contains, accepted as a public responsibility. In the protection of the priceless water supply, it begins at the head of every stream in America and embraces every watershed and major drainage. It embraces the needs of neglected small ranchers and farmers out where the earth is raw, unable to obtain adequate technical help from the unheralded, under-staffed Bureau of Land Management and Soil Conservation Service.

In this age, conservation should put behind it the ancient inbred antagonism to industry. There is little to gain by continually whipping big corporations like a tired horse; the practice is almost in the same class with the old saw that controls are immoral because they are "bad for business" and interfere with free trade. In facing the monumental task of purifying and protecting the nation's water, the correction of industrial pollution will cost billions of dollars, which the public must pay one way or another, either through taxes or in the cost of manufactured products. It may prove best in the long run, as Senator Nelson has suggested, for Government to help pay industry a portion of this cost through tax writeoffs or direct grants to construct treatment facilities. In this way, the ultra-conservationists and ultra-polluters can find themselves lobbying for a goal desirable to both.

In the politics of conservation, it strikes me that it is best to find areas of agreement wherever possible, and to build from that point. When a major timber company, Georgia-Pacific, contributes funds for ecological studies of eagle nesting areas, for whatever reason, this is worth cheering. So is the action of Humble Oil in curbing oil seepage into the sea from refinery and tankers. As a conservationist, I can only hope they feel the inducement and encouragement to do more.

We are all in this together, for better or worse. Conservation is the fulfillment of many needs. This is why wilderness enthusiasts should support the motorcyclists in their desire for specialized recreation areas, for they safeguard their own cherished places by so doing, and why the grazers should support the wildlife people, and why the residential subdividers should meet the planners and park people at least halfway in courthouse politics.

The truth is that everybody conserves—the little lady with flowers in her window box, the deer hunter, boater, birdwatcher, family camper, cattleman, farmer, forester, hiker and Sunday driver. The day of maturity will dawn when all recognize the common interest within conservation's wide scope, and when government faces the natural resource problems with wisdom, conviction and courage.

Chapter 18

A Conservation Ethic

The controlling force in the lives of the ancient Cherokee was a natural religion. Every animal, stone and tree was believed to have its own spirit and a particular reason for being. Ceremonials were devoted to fulfillment of man's role in the grand design of the universe. The Green Corn Dance, for instance, was a two-week-long thanksgiving celebration held in the seventh moon, when the first corn ripened and became fit to eat. Enemies were forgiven, fires extinguished, and new fire kindled by the shaman, or priest, then fires were lit on each family hearth. The first fruits were deposited in the council house for the poor, who might otherwise have no corn for winter. On the main day no voices were heard until nightfall, when the whole town assembled to watch the shaman sacrifice the new fruit, express thanks for the sweet beneficence of earth, and pray for the spirits to bless the corn and meat during the year.

Searching farther back into the history of man on this continent, one finds the people known as Wandering Hunters, who crossed the dry land passage of the Bering Strait, had few impersonal, artificial instruments to cloud their views of natural forces. Their movements were intimately related to the Pleistocene climatic swings—vast natural pulsations, like the beating of a pump, the heaving of a sea, the throbbing of a heart, stirring life within thousands of miles of shifting ice fronts, driving life southward with icy winds, drawing it north as cold and dampness were replaced by warmth and drought.

From *George Washington University Magazine*, July 1967.

Those people could feel the rhythms, the cycles, the continuum between the hours of their lives and centuries of time. Their early rituals, dances, lustrations, ceremonial hunts—these natural expressions bound the generations with the stars and seas and all living things.

In contrast, within the past century, even the past half-century, Americans have moved rapidly into a shell of artificial, mechanical insulation. We have lost touch with our surroundings and the essence of creation. We ascribe to science and engineering the highest of all talents. We are conditioned to accepting the generator and computer as the source of blessings, and, it is assumed, whatever problems one devises the other will resolve. As for nature, it must be harnessed, managed, improved upon, reshaped, never left to its own.

Thus we are welcome to overexploit and pollute the environment, to invade without discipline, to construct buildings and cities along known earthquake fault lines and in flood plains, to unleash immense mining machinery with foreknowledge that it will destroy mountains and rivers. In the event of damage to our civilization, we are geared to anticipate that engineers and limitless public funds will put the pieces together—to be knocked askew once more.

What we are trying to do is to replace a natural environment with a synthetic one. Pesticides have reached the polar regions and the deepest part of the ocean, altering the ecological balance in the remotest corners; but why not, when we are presently preparing to devour the riches of the sea as we already have those of the land?

Why not, indeed, when Federal agencies, which are supposed to express the public conscience, are outdoing each other with programs to advance the synthetic? I will cite the energetic aspiration of a branch of the Fish and Wildlife Service in the Department of Interior to poison the population of coyotes and other predators into extinction in behalf of the sheep industry and its own self-perpetuation. Where the predators are virtually gone and rodents have spread, this agency is now promoting artificial rodent control. When the rodents are gone, it is safe to say that it will be something else, with the controllers employing a new laboratory creation, a new machine, a new management approach intended to render the atmosphere more antiseptic and sterile. Along the way they are certain to place into use the insecticide heralded in *National Wildlife* as the kind that destroys only the "bad" bugs while leaving the "good" bugs unscathed.

In the meantime, we are robbing the earth of much of its interest and attractiveness. We are robbing man unborn of the spiritual re-creation derived solely from nature's own resources and handi-work—but, alas, unlike the primitives, who felt themselves as part of the design of eternity, we are unable to project beyond our own fleeting period.

Emerson defined the true conservation ethic as a concept of morality and the integrity of the human spirit. "To the poet, to the philosopher, to the saint, all things are friendly and sacred, all days holy, all men divine," he wrote. "For the eye is fastened on the life, and slights the circumstance. Every chemical substance, every animal in its growth, teaches the unity of cause, the variety of appearance."

Conservation is both a science and a philosophy, but the latter is essential to the former. It is true that conservation in its modern technical application represents the means of protecting and renew-ing ample natural resources for the material needs of humankind. Without it, the unlimited survival of the species can hardly be assured. But there is the older form of conservation, more compre-hensive, patient and intellectual. As Professor Arnold Henry Guyot of Princeton wrote one century ago, the natural scientist must be a philosopher as well, and the source of his philosophy the unity of earth, with all its "living tribes of the waters and the land" fulfilling their purposes and preparing for other developments beyond them.

Lacking this rounded approach, conservation falls short of serving its full obligation. Consider the scientific aspect alone as discovered and defined early in the century by Gifford Pinchot. "Conservation," he wrote, "is the foresighted utilization, preserva-tion and/or renewal of forests, waters, lands and minerals, for the greatest good of the greatest number for the longest time." This is valid as far as it goes. Pinchot in his chosen field of forestry insti-tuted a system of planning and management where only planless-ness had prevailed and his constructive influence was felt in much broader spheres of land use. But the tragedy is that he unknowingly sired a school of conservation engineers who have too little grasp of philosophy or appreciation of the humanities. Impelled by their training they must forever demonstrate man's conquest of nature; they despair at vestiges of primeval land left "idle," when such land can be managed.

Thus at times the poorest performers in conservation are not necessarily the free enterprise profiteers, but the management-minded agencies of the Federal Government. The Bureau of Reclamation, for one, is convinced that the waters of the Colorado River, already harnessed on most of its course, are being utterly wasted because they flow freely and untamed through the Grand Canyon. Pinchot's own agency, the United States Forest Service, cannot stand to have a scrawny forest of virgin lodgepole pine survive in the Selway-Bitterroot Wilderness of Montana without the blessing of sustained-yield harvest. The National Park Service has joined a senseless political scheme to gut the Great Smoky Mountains with roads and over-sized campgrounds and transform this finest wilderness of Eastern America into—by the word of one of its own officials—a "playground." The Tennessee Valley Authority, which has the kind of power for comprehensive regional design which Pinchot envisioned, feels obsessed with the need to pour one concrete dam after another, whether needed or not, destroying beautiful mountain streams and thrusting smokestacks and factories on pastoral valleys.

The ultimate effects on the land and its inhabitants are fearful to anticipate. Without a more firmly established conservation ethic, we are not equipped to undertake development of the resources of the sea or exploration of the lunar surface. Mechanically and technically, we have the skills to move in any direction, but the intellectual, moral and spiritual levels lag behind. We need to reach the point where the immense mining machines are controlled and scaled down, and so too the ship-borne machines used in hunting whales—perhaps I should say mining of whales—on the high seas; and so too pesticides must be controlled in order to sustain the cycle of all life on earth. We need to take serious stock through ecological research of where we have been, what changes have been wrought in the natural balance, and what measures must be taken to assure our future.

The fact is that we now have the power to effect changes in the total environment of man. It is also possible that, before we learn the full extent of this power, we may commit blunders that injure the entire human race.

For example, more than half the fuel ever burned by man has been burned in this century. Consequently, it appears likely that the carbon dioxide content of the atmosphere has increased by at least 10 percent in this period and that the gas is being released into the atmosphere more rapidly than it can be absorbed by green plants or dissolved in the oceans and eventually precipitated. Now, the only reason the earth's atmosphere contains oxygen for us to breathe (and oxygen to burn fossil fuels) is that it is constantly given off by green plants. Should we reach a point at which the rate of combustion exceeds the rate of photosynthesis, the oxygen content of the atmosphere must start to decrease.

We cannot afford to surrender endless millions of acres of photosynthesizing vegetation by building concrete highways and factories that consume more oxygen. Nevertheless, our government insists upon thrusting industry on the people of Africa and South America, and on those of Appalachia and the Indian reservations. This country may be well established as the global fountainhead of science and technology, but in such moves there is not the slightest consideration of the science of ecology. Nor is there any application of human engineering, considering that we are dealing with a rare and dwindling species of humankind, the free-spirited people, whose ways we should conserve and study, rather than destroy.

In summary, we have always been governed, and continue to be governed, by the natural laws that controlled the lives of primitive peoples, and that still control the lives of wild animals and wild plants. We need to replenish air and water. We need to maintain the soil nutrient cycles that are basic to food production. In this age, we now need to fathom controls of population size and rate of growth. We need to recognize that, despite the ingenuity of automation and electronics, whether applied to agriculture, transportation or communication, when the generator fails, man must revert to the day-and-night cycle and we need to appreciate and understand it more.

But these are material questions. Man, above all, is a creature of intellect and a spiritual being. The further we move from the natural ways of our ancestors, the more we should safeguard the slender primeval places as fountains of sustenance and renewal to the soul.

Chapter 19

On the Day
Martin Luther King Died

On the day Martin Luther King was martyred in behalf of the human race I was at Yale University, where I had been invited to speak at the School of Forestry, a longtime fountainhead of conservation ideology.

At the seminar of students and faculty I cited the words of a man of common stock who had but four grades of book learning, but who, nevertheless, had been called to Yale to receive an honorary degree of arts. And when he accepted the award Mark Twain did so in behalf of the guild of American funny men and in vindication of their techniques of combating stuffiness. Their purpose, he said, was "the deriding of shams, the exposure of pretentious falsities, the laughing of stupid superstitions out of existence; and whosoever is by instinct engaged in this sort of warfare is the natural enemy of royalties, nobilities, privileges and all kindred swindles, and the natural friend of human rights and human liberties."

I quoted Twain's commencement address at Yale for two reasons.

First, I believe that we too live in an age of shams and falsities and stupid superstitions and awful swindles that must somehow be driven out of existence, whether by laughter, courage or some other means of stirring the public conscience and the responsible exercise of power.

Second, the task confronts those of us concerned with conservation of natural resources as much as any part of the national population. The challenge is inescapable and we must be up to it by purging ourselves of stuffiness and shams. Gifford Pinchot, the founder

From *American Forests*, May 1968.

of modern conservation, who as a student heard Mark Twain at Yale, understood full well his role in promoting human rights and human liberties. What we must do is catch up with him and Twain before time runs out.

"The rightful use and purpose of our natural resources," Pinchot wrote, "is to make all the people strong and well, able and wise, well taught, well fed, well clothed, well housed, full of knowledge and initiative, with equal opportunity for all and special privilege for none."

Dr. Paul Sears, the eminent ecologist of Yale, said it another way: "Conservation is a point of view, involved with the concept of freedom, human dignity and the American spirit."

Because I agree with Pinchot and Sears, I feel that we are engaged in a great social movement and thus, as I told the Yale class on land use, the place where we must begin to conserve and restore is in the dark slums of the cities.

The same message I gave the week before when speaking at a National Park Service seminar at Harpers Ferry, West Virginia, on "Goals." It does our social movement no good at all to save the large wildlands if we fail to bring air, space and a community of growing things, other than rats, to the poor people in the ghetto prisons where they live. I recalled to the park superintendents and naturalists how two years ago I had gone to the opening of the new baseball stadium in Atlanta, a city that now confuses the affluence of its economic power structure with progress for its people. Before the game began a party was given, with plenty of booze and food, by the ball park management for the in-crowd and the hangers-on. However, I saw something of greater importance outside the stadium: picketers eight or nine years of age, dark of skin, carrying placards reading, "Where are the Parks we were Promised?" These are our most important clients. If we fail to appreciate their true needs, and to provide for them, success is impossible in any form.

And the same message I delivered the week before that when speaking at the Supervisors Conference of the Eastern Region of the Forest Service. I tried to impress on these forest managers the notion that the day of idealism is not done, it must not be done, although idealism is hard pressed by technological overkill, short-sightedness, self-interest and political venality. Idealism is sustained in the land. It must be husbanded by managers of the land who have imagination, boldness, passion and devotion to public service, and the wisdom to reach out and touch the thoughtful public for ideas, cooperation and support.

Men like Gifford Pinchot and Martin Luther King, who speak with purpose, clarity and courage, who give unflinching leadership and hope, cross our paths one at a time, one to a lifetime, at most. The former was permitted to live out his age and make his full contribution, just as Mark Twain did. The premature death of Dr. King fills our generation with a sense of pain, of being cheated, for now the world can never know the total gift of his genius and compassion for us all.

Our generation, alas, knows violence too well. We live with a national psychosis of destruction and violence, which absolves the assassin of personal guilt. By our standards, peace, ethics, morality and intellectuality rank low in the scale of values. Resources come cheap, and so do human lives. The destroyer, despoiler, the exploiter of land, water and people, the political fixer and political faker all fare quite well. They are the people who count in the shape of society.

That Memphis served as the assassination scene is not surprising. The political leadership of the city and of the State of Tennessee is sterile. The mayor of Memphis, Henry Loeb, serves the land speculators, merchants, and moneyed class, and not common people. The Scripps-Howard chain controls the news media of Memphis. Its management in that city is morally bankrupt, as it clearly demonstrated in its ruthless campaign to destroy Overton Park in behalf of the profiteers, creating a reign of hysteria and terror, even among its own Scripps-Howard employees. What model there for behavior?

But it could have happened anywhere, I suppose. It could have happened in the cool of the Middle West, where I recently visited a friend, a Catholic priest, who is interested in both civil rights and conservation. The preceding Sunday the good father had delivered a sermon on the brotherhood of man—of all men, and all women, of all origins—and for his reward he was treated to a week of anonymous calls filled with profanity and threats of his life.

The assassination could also have happened in Washington, D.C., the national city, run by the President and Congress. The poor people have been thrown by the Government to the mercy of the landlords, known in the newspaper headlines as "slum lords," who show no mercy. I can recall when the heralded Southwest Washington urban renewal program began, supposedly designed to aid the poor. Today one part of the face-lifted Southwest is most attractive, dominated by high-rise apartments providing accommodations for attractive people—like the Vice President of the United States, and others in his economic and social class. Another part of the Southwest has emerged with the most monstrous, poorly planned conglomeration of Government and private office buildings. "Oh, I know I have been criticized," said the head of the Redevelopment Land Agency, an old-time politician from Kentucky, in a recent newspaper interview. "I know I've evicted Negroes instead of helping them. But think of what I've done for the tax base."

In the land use class at Yale we discussed taxability and values. Someone commented on the high standard of living prevalent in the United States; but another countered that our standard is measured mostly in material wealth and that if we used other judgment values, of culture and morality, our living standard would be found wanting. One or two students pressed the idea that land in and around cities may have become too valuable to be conserved as open space, whether in the form of forests, farms or parks. To at least one the concept of government subsidy to conserve open space seemed improper.

The propriety or impropriety of such things relates to one's concept of ethics and morality. In this age of shams and falsities, of destruction and violence, the Nation accepts the subsidization of germ warfare and tests that cause the death of sheep in Utah; it accepts the subsidization of nuclear warfare and senseless multi-billion dollar tests in the Aleutians, destroying the flora and fauna of a national wildlife refuge; it accepts the subsidization of all kinds of "sophisticated" warfare techniques, which can only lead to the ultimate destruction of mankind.

I agree that we must press the cause of liberty throughout the world, but by example and not the waste of youthful blood and muscle; the defoliation of forests, and the destruction of an ancient Asian culture. We can set examples for the world by subsidizing the rebuilding of our cities in behalf of the poor, in promoting useful programs like the Job Corps, in controlling pollution of air and water, in protecting the soils, managing the forests, and safeguarding wilderness, all of which are related in assuring a fuller life and enjoyment of democracy's fruit.

We are, I fear, racing away from our national destiny of freedom and brotherhood. It is still not too late to recapture the cause if we can transcend stupid superstitions and awful swindles. Respect for the land is part of the challenge, for respect for all men is implicit therein.

Chapter 20

Welcome Back to School from the Old Professor

It was in the last year of his life that I was singularly blessed with the opportunity to visit and interview Robert Frost. He impressed me as a thoroughly country-type person, with shaggy white hair, large head, simple dress, gruff good humor, and strong voice. The setting was the plainest of places, his farm cottage in the foothills of the Green Mountains, where he dwelled in company with two spunky cairn terriers, and surrounded by all outdoors. He was 88 years of age.

"You are too young," he counseled at one point in our conversation, "to understand the young."

Eight years or so have passed since then. I have matured to the point of appreciating the wisdom of his words. Nevertheless, as I travel over the country, with the chance to listen to young people and to look them in the eye, and as I read many of the letters which they write to us at *Field & Stream,* it strikes me that youth needs, and craves, a certain kind of guidance, companionship, direction, reassurance, and criticism which it may not now be fully receiving. The opening of the fall term seems an especially appropriate occasion to discuss a few of the problems and prospects of young people who yearn for the chance to protect and enhance the natural environment.

"There is plenty of talk about conservation and ecology, much of it coming from the President and other high governmental officials," writes a wildlife biology senior at Utah State. "The problem is that almost all of the people who have spent the last four years or more in

From *Field & Stream*, September 1970.

college, majoring in various fields of natural resource management, cannot get jobs when they graduate. The government is simply not hiring people, not even to fill jobs where employed persons have quit or retired."

Some of the students thus affected, he continues, are wildlife biologists, foresters, range ecologists, and watershed managers. He then adds: "Each time one of these trained people has to find a job in unrelated fields, conservation suffers a loss. When I graduate I would work for practically nothing if someone would give me the chance. All the people I know in natural resources management are equally eager to work, but all are finding there are no jobs."

No, it is not easy these days to hook on to a professional conservation career. But management, per se, is not the only means of fulfilling one's aspirations, and certainly it is not the total solution. Far from it. Government recruiting is often on a formula basis, which may or may not have bearing on the things that count.

A graduate going into soil conservation or watershed management, for example, may become involved in channelization projects, turning streams into concrete drainage ditches while wiping out fish and game habitat. Foresters, of course, are fundamentally timber-oriented by their training, more inclined to economics than to the environment. In fact, if you want to become a Federal forester, Civil Service standards demand that 75 percent of your studies be in tree forestry and logging, plus 25 percent in range, recreation, and wildlife. There is neither credit, nor requirement, for sociology, government, range ecology, or law, let alone the humanities.

Both technicians and scientists tend to be so specialized in their experience and studies they seldom comprehend clearly what others are doing and often are removed from the actual conditions and problems of life. This even applies to the ecologists, some of whom worry so much about the complexity of things they can't get anything done. They speak broadly about the total interrelation of all things, but they do so objectively and bookishly, lacking subjective personal involvement. Scientific ecology verges at times on becoming just another way to manipulate a separate world, as if the world were not a living organism.

The answer to fulfillment lies in activism, involvement, and personal participation as part of the learning process. Bob Cross, of Port Jervis, New York, a young correspondent who is starting his second year at Orange County Community College, exemplifies what I mean. "The work I have been doing, besides the Teach-In activities," he writes, "has been mostly concerned with getting the minimum flow increased down our Neversink River and protecting the Delaware from possible future thermal additions. I continue to do my environment column in our college paper, the *Citadel*. We are also fighting the continued use of Sevin to control the gypsy moth. Finally, I have been writing to the State Health Department in hopes of getting them to clean up the sewage which is being discharged into the Delaware watershed. I am a member of the Fontinalis Flyfishers Club, Tri-State Rod and Gun Club, Federation of Sports-men's Clubs of Sullivan County, P.U.R.E., and the Agassiz Society at College." Bob is majoring in biology, with the hopes of someday teaching at the college level, but whatever he becomes I feel this is one fellow who will find his way as a useful member of the life society.

I recently attended the annual meeting of the American Association for Conservation Information, which featured a panel program of four college students, all action-oriented, alert, confident, and fearless. Such young people constitute an immense resource in the environmental crusade. The Wyoming Game and Fish Department recognized this to the point of already having hired one of the participants, Colleen Cabot, president of the environmental action group at the University of Wyoming, as a summer intern. She spoke her own mind, nonetheless.

Another panel member, Steve Dominick, of Colorado State University, who plans to become a veterinarian, reckoned that many of the intelligent, energetic independent-minded students are going into teaching rather than to the government agencies they distrust. Bill Lietch, of the University of Montana, bore this out; he's inter-ested in teaching basic ecology to environmental activists through outdoors experiences. More power to him, for one must study life through living to understand it. John Muir, you may recall, quit the University of Wisconsin to pursue what he called the "University of the Wilderness." Carl Alwin Schenck, who directed the pioneer

Biltmore School of Forestry, was no pedagogue but a fellow searcher after truth in the woods, and thus loved by his students. The tragedy is that now many professors are not working *with* the young in the field, but are concerned with their own pedigrees and with grants from assorted special economic interests.

"We're not concerned with our immediate future, for the normal jobs are stultifying. We want to do something useful, of lasting value," said Scott Fisher, of the University of Montana, who is going into teaching, too. "However, I look ahead with mixed emotions, for I feel the hopelessness facing the next generation."

On this count the old professor must disagree. I think back to my visit with Robert Frost, who told me about his years of wandering, in this country and in England, his disappointments and poverty (when he baked the family bread, kneading dough and all) on the difficult, determined road to personal fulfillment. You know, he never finished college, but was a master of the classroom, as well as a poet with abiding belief in nature. Americans by their heritage, he said, are "splendid risk takers, like good gamblers."

Achievement sometimes comes hard, but it tastes better in the long run. Individually and collectively, true believers can work miracles, if we have faith and hang together, studying life as well as school books, taking a few splendid risks based on principle above political expediency and glorified professionalism. Now let the class be seated and the semester begin.

Chapter 21

A Pacifist Spoke to Me on Earth Day

As fate would have it, my first of four stops during the Environ-mental Teach-In Week was at a Quaker-supported college, Earlham, in eastern Indiana, where I picked up to read, and then proceeded to purloin, a pacifist publication called *Fellowship*. The Quakers will forgive me, I trust, particularly considering their odd belief in peace based on love and brotherhood rather than on hatred, distrust and force of arms.

What made *Fellowship* magazine especially appealing to me was its extensive treatment of the environmental crisis, with cogent editorial observations to explain why a pacifist organization should be joining the current upsurge of public interest in this subject. But if indeed the Quakers are thus concerned, why are not the followers of other religious denominations? Why was it necessary for the young to lead the way to "celebrate life," as they say, on Earth Day—when the earth and all of its creatures are children of God? Why is not Earth Day a way of life everyday under the auspices of what we are led to accept as the houses of God?

To the Cherokee Indians environment was the controlling force in their lives. So strong was this conviction that their religious beliefs were based on it; so too virtually all peoples of primitive ages practiced some form of nature religion, experiencing a feeling of holiness for the lands in which they lived.

Human personality and the web of life must be tended with passion and reverence, based on a heritage that is derived from the

From *American Forests*, July 1970.

earth itself. The Cherokee knew this. Every animal, stone and tree was believed to have its own spirit and particular reason for being. Ceremonials were devoted to fulfillment of man's rather small role in the grand design of the universe.

But that was long before churches became palaces of stone and brick, before Gross National Product became confused with God and profitability and self-interest confused with His prophets, before supersonics and superbombs became symbols of progress, and before respect for life-forms went out of season.

Comfort comes from its reassurance of the transcendant importance of each human being, no matter how obscure or difficult life he may be leading, as Alfred Hassler wrote in Fellowship. True enough, the God who marks the fall of a single sparrow notes also and grieves over the suffering of the humblest of his children. But, as Mr. Hassler continued, religion that only comforts is incomplete.

Pie-in-the-sky gospel is simply not enough. Each of us must be inspired to realize the power of his own life and to never sell it short. Our paradise must be fashioned on earth, not only because it is the here-and-now tangible essence but because it is the one part of the infinite in which man can demonstrate himself to be worthy.

"Christ will come—and then the earth will be emptied of much of its population—because the wicked will be destroyed as cleansing fires go before Him," a weekly supplement of the Salt Lake City *Deseret News*, which is owned by the Mormon Church, editorialized recently in denouncing attempts to limit population. Possibly so, but when Christ comes he may be accompanied by Moses and Muhammad, and he may be black, and he may have tough standards for judging wickedness, asking Latter-day Saints and all others not only how well they have conquered the earth, but how well they have husbanded its resources and cared for all the living tribes.

"God has commanded us to 'multiply and replenish the earth.' At no time has He abrogated that law," according to the Mormon editorial. Yea, verily, one can find ample directive of God's will that man exploit nature for his own ends, and may thus conclude that the roots of our eco-disaster are largely religious. But this is only partly true—the Bible abounds in choices. In the first chapter of Genesis, man is instructed to populate and subdue the earth; in the second chapter, he is instructed to take care of it. Moreover, one may read,

"What should it profit a man if he gains the whole world and loses his own soul."

One of the most fascinating examples of environmentalism I know in America is based entirely on religious principles. This is Shakertown, at Pleasant Hill, Kentucky, the village that was intended to be God's kingdom on earth. It was built by the sect called the United Society of Believers in Christ's Second Appearance, who are known to us as the Shakers.

Though their order (which once settled colonies in seven states) has virtually disappeared, Pleasant Hill remains as a monument to their beliefs and good works. They are remembered principally today for the multiplicity of their practical arts and for the disciplined austerity of their lives, including celibacy. Yet more important were their advanced social and ecological concepts. They were pacifists. They were humanitarian toward animals, forbidding the wearing of spurs, kicking of beasts or keeping of pets. They believed in equality of the sexes; they were free of racial prejudice. They practiced the communal existence where no man was richer or poorer than his neighbor. They considered themselves withdrawn from the evil, sinful world, but opened their homes to orphans and unwanted children and, during the Civil War, cared for hungry and wounded soldiers of both sides. They were patient craftsmen, marvelous architects and builders and farmers, who wasted nothing and sustained fertile, productive fields.

The Shakers urged naturalness, because a poor diamond is better than an imitation, and humility, because God, the foremost proponent of biotic diversity, made a million spears of grass for every tree. They were a people who lived in orderly simplicity, piety and harmony with heaven and earth, as we all should.

Conservation of natural resources and true belief are indivisible, whether or not one joins in church-house prayer or in any accepted concept of God. What counts is an appreciation of the mysteries of common origin and common destiny that binds us all together, and a search for a world society wherein (as *Fellowship* notes from the pre-Confucian Chinese) "not only a man's own family is his family and his own children his children, but all men are his family and all the earth's children, his children."

As I travel the country and see the handsome architectural piles of stone and brick rising upright in God's name amidst terrible social decay, I wish sometimes they could be turned into schools and hospitals to serve a useful purpose and that the preachers would renounce the better life to serve the poor and the young who shall inherit the earth. During my contacts with students during the Teach–In, I learned many lessons. "This is not the time to assess guilt," a student said to me at Ohio State, "but to assign responsibility." In this spirit, I will ask: Wouldn't it be wonderful if all the churches and synagogues and mosques conducted an Earth Day and enrolled throngs of their faithful in this great cause?

Now, let us pray!

Chapter 22

Saving the Wilderness

While vacationing in August 1871, the celebrated Horace Greeley arose one morning at sunrise, but not to fish as was his custom. He sat thoughtfully, admiring the lake and absorbing the quiet environment. Presently his guide joined him, but neither spoke, preferring to share in silence the blaze of fresh sunlight spreading across the waters. "John," Greeley said finally, "I suppose when the season ends, like John of old, you will be left alone in the wilderness. But, bear this in mind. God and John French will not be as isolated as Horace Greeley in the living wilderness of New York City."

When I ran across this story in my readings recently it reminded me that the Wilderness Act is now almost 10 years old. In Greeley's time, of course, there was no need for such a law. The wilderness of the wide open spaces was superabundant, in contrast with the limited urban concentrations, such as New York. The theme of the nation was expansion and growth. In our time, however, it requires determination and deliberate design to preserve the few remaining shreds of the American earth that have come down to us essentially as God (or the forces of nature) made them.

The Wilderness Act has always impressed me as one of those epochal instruments of law and social policy, but more so now than ever. At a time when so many people have thrown up their hands in despair over the failures of government, and perhaps our own inadequacies in self-government, this Act reinforces what is right and hopeful about America and the American system. The bill was

From *Field & Stream*, August 1973.

eight years from introduction to passage, a long, uphill fight. Howard Zahniser, the late executive director of the Wilderness Society, who sparked it all the way, never lost patience or hope. Not even the most bitter enemies could resist his honest expression of belief that "We deeply need the humility to know ourselves as the dependent members of a great community of life."

The National Wilderness Preservation System, established by the Act, is a reality. The fifty million acres originally envisioned as the total available for inclusion may now be substantially surpassed. With the heightened tensions of crowded urban life in a super-technological age, people need the release that only wilderness can provide. The recent roadless inventories conducted by the Forest Service showed that many millions of acres, now unprotected, could qualify under terms of the Act. Moreover, one of the most encouraging aspects to me is the upsurge of interest and activity among state and local governments, among private and public agencies alike, in the identification and protection of wilderness and natural areas; for man is at his best when nature is part of his daily environment, rather than some distant dream.

The movement that led to the Wilderness Act began in the years following World War II. Conservationists had become disturbed over unrelenting commercial exploitation and encroachments on the nation's remaining open spaces, particularly on Federal lands— forests, parks, and wildlife refuges—protected in theory but no longer in practice. In 1956 the first Wilderness Bill was introduced. In due course it was rewritten over and over again. Though it passed the Senate, the bill was bottled up in the House by a crusty Colorado political ally of the vested interests, Wayne Aspinall, occupying a seat of power on the basis of seniority alone.

Finally, the groundswell of public support, expressed at Congressional hearings, through hundreds of newspaper editorials, and in thousands of letters directed to Congressmen from all sections of the country, became irresistible. Aspinall recognized that he could not delay action any longer and allowed the bill to come before the House on July 30, 1964. Only one negative vote was cast. In all the long tableau of civilization, the United States thus became the first country on earth to proclaim through legislation a recognition of wilderness as part of its life-style and its legacy to the future.

The Act represents an achievement of democracy at its finest. It was the upsurge of concern by the people that overcame indifference and antagonism in Congress to push it through. It gives a clear direction and firm legal foundation to Federal agencies responsible for protecting wilderness. But, even more important, it delineates a process for public participation—through hearings, on-the-ground surveys, and reviews of official proposals—in determining the feasibility of adding additional areas of Federal forests, parks, and refuges to the wilderness system.

The public concern expressed in the Wilderness Act subsequently led to other laws. In 1966, the Rare and Endangered Species Act declared a national policy to protect species of native fish and wildlife threatened with extinction, and to save their habitat as well. Two years later, in 1968, the National Trails System Act gave protection to the Appalachian Trail in the East and Pacific Crest Trail in the West, and designated fourteen other trails as study areas for potential additions to the Trails System. In the same year Congress also adopted the Wild and Scenic Rivers Act in order to preserve in natural condition prized free-flowing streams and their land borders.

Then the states moved ahead. Virtually half the states have established wild and scenic river systems of their own. In 1970 the Michigan Natural Resources Commission adopted a resolution calling for a study of Porcupine Mountains State Park in order to determine the true value of wilderness and to develop an effective management plan. The Porcupines, covering 58,000 acres along Lake Superior on the Upper Peninsula, had long been the jewel of the state park system, but in recent years were plainly suffering from overuse and conflicting use—something had to be done. No sooner was the study resolution adopted than citizen groups throughout the state volunteered to furnish specialized inputs of knowledge on geology, wildlife, birdlife, botany, hiking trails, history, and other values. As a result, last year the park was renamed Porcupine Mountains Wilderness State Park and carefully zoned in order to protect the fragile wildlands. The legislature also voted to establish Michigan's own wilderness and natural areas system.

New York State offers a preeminent model for the nation and the world in its Adirondack Plan. This includes almost one million acres, in fifteen separate tracts, to be designated as wilderness and administered along lines of the National Wilderness Preservation System; a wild, scenic, and recreational river system; propagation of rare indigenous species of wildlife, such as marten, lynx, loon, and raven, and the reintroduction of extirpated species, which may well include the wolf along with the moose. No Federal program has gone this far.

"The Adirondacks are preserved forever," declared Governor Nelson Rockefeller in May as he signed a new law placing 3.7 million acres of private property within the boundaries of the Adirondack Park under land-use restrictions. Together with 2.3 million acres already owned and protected by the state, this entire composition of valleys, lakes, rivers, and mountain peaks is the largest area in the country to come under comprehensive land-use control, including wilderness designation.

All kinds of people are involved in such efforts. For example, the Western Pennsylvania Conservancy and the noted Carnegie Museum of Pittsburgh have joined forces to identify and preserve significant natural areas in Western Pennsylvania. On a state-wide basis, the Bureau of Forestry in the Department of Environmental Resources is working with many conservation organizations to set aside wild areas within the two million acres of state forest land.

Such places make ideal classrooms. Many professors in botany, biology, and ecology have told me that primeval reference centers are essential to their teaching programs. The University of California in 1965 became one of the first higher educational institutions to insure its learning resource. It established a Natural Land and Water Reserves System, incorporating some land it already owned and seeking to acquire or share other land. "The University is attempting to acquire an adequate number and wide variety of natural areas before they disappear permanently," said Dr. Kenneth Norris, heading up the "outdoor laboratory" project. "The diversity of this terrain is a strong asset in the kind of teaching and research that contributes to human betterment by adding to man's knowledge of the living world."

Education, of course, takes diverse forms. Because it believes that wilderness environment heightens the living-learning process, the University of Oregon is conducting a new program called Cooperative Wilderness Adventures, with river-running, backpacking, rock climbing, and snowclimbing. Each individual is expected to become totally accountable for his own learning and for helping develop learning experiences. And what better place to acquire and share knowledge than in God's outdoors?

The wilderness movement had advanced as a positive expression of people rather than of government. The National Park Service deliberately dragged its feet, fell behind schedule, and concentrated on promoting "enclaves" and "buffer zones" rather than wilderness. The Forest Service placed timbermen in charge of wilderness reviews and concentrated on the most restrictive interpretations of the Act, alleging that even the faintest trace of man's activity would disqualify a candidate area.

When the Act was passed in 1964, it provided immediate protection for 9.1 million acres which had been classified administratively as wilderness in the national forests and set up a review of wilderness potential in 5.4 million acres classed as primitive, to be completed by 1974. But it said nothing about the remaining unprotected roadless areas, or de facto wilderness, covering a substantial, though unmeasured portion of the 186 million acres in the National Forest System. Prodded by law suits and other pressures, the Forest Service undertook an inventory it completed early this year. It found no less than 1,448 roadless areas totaling 56 million acres (including 18 million in Alaska). Though it recommended for wilderness study only 174 areas totaling 6.3 million acres, the stage is now clearly set for a second generation of wilderness reviews, extending well beyond 1974.

In the 23 million acres of national forestland east of the Mississippi, there are only three small units of the Wilderness System: Great Gulf, in New Hampshire, and Linville Gorge and Shining Rock, both in North Carolina. Citizens have nominated scores of candidate areas, but the Forest Service has always been able to come up with some remnant of man's activity—if only a graveyard or trace of an old road—to disqualify them. The wilderness criteria, the agency insists, do not fit conditions in the East.

Others disagree. Representative John P. Saylor, of Pennsylvania, who introduced the original Wilderness Bill in 1956 and has championed the cause ever since, declared early this year: "I fought too long and too hard, and too many people in this House and across this land fought with me, to see the Wilderness Act denied application over an entire half of the country by this kind of obtuse or hostile misinterpretation or misconstruction of the public law and the intent of Congress."

Representative Saylor is one of the principal sponsors of the Omnibus Eastern Wilderness Bill, which would designate twenty-eight new national forest wilderness areas, totaling 471,185 acres, in sixteen states stretching from Maine south to Florida and across the Appalachians to the Ozarks and Ouachitas. Outstanding natural areas are involved, such as the rugged Cohuttas, between Atlanta and Chattanooga. This area is probably the largest mountain wilderness in the East outside of the Great Smokies, with rare plants and high magnificent cascades.

The Omnibus Bill would designate about 2 percent of the Eastern national forests as wilderness, but some conservationists are setting their sights higher, in the conviction that the basic function of the Eastern national forests should not be commercial, but educational, recreational, and scientific. Someone has figured that the total volume of all the timber in Eastern national forests equals only one year's growth on combined private and public forestlands in the East, strongly suggesting that it could be spared the chainsaw and never be missed.

William Penn wanted one acre of forest left wild for every five that were cleared. Thoreau proposed a 500-acre woodlot behind every village or town. "A town is saved," he observed, "not more by the righteous men in it than by the woods that surround it." If Horace Greeley were with us today, he would probably note that it isn't necessary to do a single thing in order to derive the bounties of wilderness: no planes to catch, phones to answer, newspapers to read, conferences to attend, and no television noises either. Time changes meaning, expanding dimensions so you can see and feel more; the mind is unloosed from manipulations and machines. You don't have to travel in a straight-line mile if the crooked mile across some little stream seems more appealing, and who cares if it's a mile, or more?

Wilderness adventure breeds enthusiasm, idealism, and love of life. Man acquires a new perspective in his relationship to others and the American environment around him. It's the very kind of psychic reinforcement that people of all ages and classes need in these trying times. "Nothing great is ever accomplished without enthusiasm," as Ralph Waldo Emerson once wrote. Enthusiasm and involvement have made the Wilderness Act work. Let optimism prevail!

Chapter 23

Forestry: Fallacy and Failure of Dominant Use

If the United States is to endure and prosper as a nation, all land policy must henceforth be based on the foundation of environmental respect. The goals must be to provide a continuing supply of clean air, clear water, stable soil, natural beauty, and open space, including wilderness. These must be recognized as the rights of all people sharing a common environment in this generation and generations hence. The only alternative will be the continuing decline in natural resources and ultimate national collapse.

Thus we need to break with the past when land values were determined in narrow economic terms. The public interest must be superior to the forces of self-serving commodity production which have spurred exploitation of the public lands, as well as their own. Now we need to shape a new image of responsibility and respect for the total land resource.

The need applies quite critically to forests, which even now cover one-third of the country's land area. As sources of raw material, they play a significant part in determining the physical standards of American life. But this is only a fraction of their total role. They are absolutely necessary as conservers of soil and water if we are not willing to watch this nation become as denuded and flood-swept as the Chinese hillsides and valleys. The forests serve as barriers to hot polluted air and restore the atmosphere with oxygenated volumes of air. As environment for the highest type of recrea-

From *What's Ahead for Our Public Lands; A Summary Review of the Final Report of the Public Land Law Review Commission* (Natural Resources Council of America, 1970).

tional and esthetic enjoyment, they are essential to the happiness of millions of human beings.

Economic, physical, and social considerations demand that we maintain a bountiful forest resource. Yet the prolonged failure to protect and enhance these forests has contributed directly to the environmental crisis we face today.

The continued abuse of forest resources on public lands derives from the focus of the power center in American politics. Instead of developing a long range ideology for the well being of land and humankind, the combination of economic and political forces has promoted resource exploitation for the sake of securing raw materials and short-term profits.

This condition is revealed in a review of the national budget. Bureaus and agencies charged with maintaining and protecting public lands have been the weak sisters of the federal family. Even when the administrations of Lyndon Johnson and Richard Nixon joined the chorus of environmental awareness, they gave scant rearrangement of budgetary priorities. For example, the National Forest Development Program, a 10-year project of the Forest Service, was intended to cover the period of 1963-1972. During the years of 1963-1970 the proposed level of spending for "timber sales administration and management" was fulfilled by Congress to 95 percent of the total. Other phases, however, did not fare as well: planned "reforestation and stand improvement," "recreation-public use," "wildlife habitat management," and "soil and water management" were financed at levels of only 40 percent, 45 percent, 62 percent, and 52 percent, respectively. Then came the 1971 budget, for which the administration proposed an increase of $5,000,000 in timber sales and management to a total of $52,000,000—more than twice as much as for all other forest land uses combined.

By providing for timber only, both the executive and legislative branches have given *de facto* sanction for the emphasis on short–term consumption at the expense of long-term protection. Simply stated, the current pressures for greater timber supply and a "high timber yield fund," by whatever name, are only recent manifestations of a longstanding policy of dominant use, or environmental failure and neglect.

The timber industry is now pressing to legalize this concept. Whenever the industry speaks of an approaching timber "famine," it casts the blame on: (a) the refusal of small landowners to let their land be logged; (b) the withdrawal of timberland for national parks and wilderness areas, and (c) the failure of the government to cultivate the national forests more intensively. The given solution is plainly to cut more heavily on public lands.

Such is the design of the timber section of the Public Land Law Review Commission report. It impresses this reviewer as probably the most disappointing part of the entire document. The proposal that federal timber be managed "primarily on the basis of economic factors so as to maximize net dollar return" must be considered as a very bad joke; certainly it has no relevance to pledges and protestations of environmental concern found sprinkled through the report.

Of course, this is not the only suggestion current for dominant timber use. The National Timber Supply Bill, which a wrathful outcry of protest from people everywhere has thus far prevented from being considered in Congress, would establish timber as the primary role over 97 million acres of the national forests.

Then there is President Nixon's unfortunate directive of June, 1970, to the Interior and Agriculture Departments to intensify and increase softwood timber harvest, ostensibly to meet the housing needs of the nation. The President was misled by the Secretary of Agriculture, the Secretary of Housing and Urban Development, and his own advisers. They should have urged him to block the timber industry from its uncontrolled export of logs to Japan, and, further, to expose firms holding purchases of 26.6 billion board feet of national forest timber—a backlog equal to twice the annual cut—which they refuse to harvest. Instead, he ordered the departments to exercise "reasonable flexibility to take account of anticipated swings in demand" in determining the level of timber to be offered for sale in any given year. Despite the usual codicil of environmental concern, the net effect is the surrender of public values for private profit.

The dominant use principle, which stands out as a basic objective of the PLLRC report, is hopelessly lopsided and totally irreconcilable with environmental protection. "Is it unfair," asks Milton

Pearl, the director of the Commission, "in return for all the no-cutting zones that are established to assure that the growing need for wood products will have some 30 to 40 million acres of high timber production land available from federally owned forests?" The answer to Mr. Pearl is that it's quite impossible to equate protection of endangered species of plantlife and wildlife and of vanishing types of ecosystems in the no-cut zones with the allocation of all-cut zones for the benefit of the timber industry.

The actual, or contrived, timber shortage could be overcome in many ways other than overcutting the public forests. The PLLRC might have stressed better management of private forests, prohibition of log exports, elimination of the scandalous waste of wood on both private and public lands, recycling of paper products, control of power transmission lines that destroy 30,000 acres of forest a year, an end to promotion of disposables (whether paper tablecloths, evening gowns, or tuxedos), and a curse on the practice of wasting good trees for telephone poles.

It accented none of those points, but rather proposed creation of "dominant use production units" comprising half the commercial forest in federal ownership, to be run by a federal timber corporation and financed directly from timber sales. This may hardly come under the heading of multiple use, but neither does the call for rapid liquidation of the surviving old growth timber in the Northwest relate to providing homes for the poor. "These large sizes are not required to meet the increasing demand for pulpwood and kindred products, for which shorter rotation periods and younger trees are more suitable." So the report observes in language that echoes industry demands; it may also be added that pulpwood and kindred products furnish the greatest immediate profit return.

The dominant use theory is predicated upon measurement of land values in narrow economic terms, which may appeal to the timberman, or forester, who insists that trees can be harvested and cultivated like any farm crop. This is inconsistent with genuine multiple use, which dictates that values of timber yield, whether on a short or long cutting cycle, must be balanced with protection of soil, water, wildlife, and scenery, and with assurances that harvested areas will grow more trees for future timber needs. It tends to deny the ecological interrelationship of life-forms and thus sanctions the elimination of elements in the land which lack commercial value, but which are essential to its well being. The first rule to guide those who determine land use policy, and who administer the lands, as I suggested at the outset, should be that economic parts of the biotic clock will not function without the uneconomic parts.

Unfortunately, the timber section was written without ecological foundation. The rest of the report shows much the same deficiency, failing to recognize the impossibility of managing a biological community by statute or formula, without due consideration for scientific laws. Had it been otherwise, protection and perpetuation of biotic diversity in the nation's forests would have been accorded a high priority. The fact is the more complex and diverse a community of living things, the greater its stability. A cornfield has but one species and therefore is unstable to insect pests; it has none of the checks and balances to accommodate dry years or the invasion of strangers. Compare this with a prairie, complete with its hundreds of herbs and grasses, thousands of insects, and many other animals and plants. Or with a tropical rain forest, embracing as many as 400 different tree species per square mile, but with three or four trees of any one kind; it is very stable and if one species dies out, the web of life will not be disrupted.

In our own land, the mixed hardwood or hardwood-and-pine forest is a complex, diverse and relatively stable association of plants, with a tendency to maintain its ecological norm. There is plenty of room for manipulation within the norm, along with growing timber on long rotations. Drastic changes outside the norm—such as farm-lot forest management—may be efficient in terms of technology and industrial economics, but they are likely to be disastrous in the long run.

As with any land use that simplifies life communities, farm-lot forest management favors the irruption of pests and disease. Infection is rapid and direct from tree to tree; if one species is destroyed there is nothing left. A monoculturally managed forest therefore creates the need of herbicides and pesticides, which destroy biotic diversity, including the soil nutrients, leading to unending applications of chemical poisons and fertilizers, and steadily decreasing productivity.

Unfortunately, most forms of wildlife will be unable to distinguish between dominant use production units and other areas of public forest. They will become victims and transmitters of poisons. Even fertilizers and coated seeds often thought harmless to wildlife are now found to affect adversely song and game bird populations. Both indigenous and migratory birds are threatened by the entire milieu of persistent poisons and other chemical agents. Meantime, the use of poisons is never successful in totally eliminating rodents. Wise silvicultural practices, based on appreciation of a stable ecosystem, accomplish more effective purposes.

"The preservation of forests and game go hand in hand. He who works for one works for both," wrote Theodore Roosevelt in 1893. This point is not in the timber section and I failed to find it elsewhere in the PLLRC report. Timbermen and foresters insist the silvicultural practice of clearcutting opens the woodlands, increasing the growth of herbs and shrubs for game, giving the impression that "deer" and "game" are synonomous and failing to mention that when one species moves in there is apt to be a mass exodus of many other species. The key idea in forest wildlife management is diversity of habitat, yet vast areas that once supported mixed forests are being reduced to "even-aged" stands with few plants desirable for game. When this leads to destruction of young trees by deer, sportsmen are subjected to demands to "bring the deer into balance." This is another way of saying that forest managers have reduced the carrying capacity of the range, and therefore the public must accept a reduction because the deer are costing money.

The grizzly bear and wolf have been wiped out of the forests; the elk is confined almost entirely to the western states. Actually, the wolf might still survive in the wilderness areas of the Northwest had it not been for the dominant use accorded to the grazing industry. But should wolves, coyotes, and cougars, part of the heritage of the nation, be destroyed on public land so that sheep may graze safely and the sheepman, a guest on the land, profit thereby? As for elk, the dominant use assigned to timbercutting on the steep slopes of the

Fallacy and Failure of Dominant Use   201

Rockies cuts off elk calving grounds, reduces the summer range, making the areas vehicle-oriented rather than wildlife-oriented, destroying the scenic environment that lends zest to sport. Little wonder, considering the timber budget of the Forest Service is *ten times greater* than the budget for fish and wildlife habitat.

The report is lacking in its omission of support for the concept of conserving timberland in wilderness or for the principles established in the Wilderness Act of 1964. It should have stressed that wilderness is never single-use land, that it provides watershed protection, hunting, fishing, hiking, and other forms of quality recreation in solitude and sanctuary removed from urban congestion. Wilderness constitutes a preserve for rare species of plants and animals and for endangered ecosystems. Innumerable laws of nature can never be thoroughly understood without some access to conditions of the primeval. The preservation of forest plant communities is of the utmost value to scientists and ecologists throughout the world. In fact, one century hence others may look back and think how little we of this age knew about soils, plants, animals, air, and life itself. One of the key roles of this generation may well be to insure the availability of resources to the researchers of tomorrow.

Thus, in practical terms, there is now need to assure deferral of all timber cutting on the unclassified forested wilderness units of the national forests and the Bureau of Land Management until they can be reviewed (under the Wilderness Act and Classification and Multiple Use Act) for permanent protection. In addition, the Wilderness Act itself should be amended to eliminate the provision that permits mineral prospecting in the slender remaining vestiges of the original America.

The transcendant shortcoming in the PLLRC report is the manifest lack of unity and cohesion. Ambiguities abound. It speaks in continually changing voices, as though a cast of actors in one single performance was trying to please a host of different audiences. "Congress has not established a clear set of goals for the management and use of public lands," the report quite correctly observes. "This is particularly true for the national forests and lands administered by the Bureau of Land Management." But Congress cannot do so as long as land policy and legislation are characterized by immediate pragmatic problem-solving rather than any long term commitment to conservation. This basic point the report fails to make.

Nevertheless, it does contain a number of constructive proposals, which must not be lost. For example, we are told that greater emphasis needs to be placed on fish and wildlife values in public lands, that game and nongame species should be given equal attention (including protection of wild horses and burros), that agencies should institute positive programs to control hunter and fishermen density, that predator control programs should be eliminated or reduced. These are all overdue and welcome.

The report recommends that policy enhance and maintain a high quality environment both on and off public lands. This means first that areas in need of environmental rehabilitation would be inventoried and the government undertake such rehabilitation—inviting treatment of millions of the most ransacked acres on earth. In addition, Congress would require public land agencies to condition the granting of rights or privileges with environmental quality adherence *off* the public lands, including the denial of timber to pulp mills causing air and water pollution.

Even the Commission's proposed transfer of the Forest Service from Agriculture to Interior carries with it a proviso that research on environmental quality management of the public lands be intensified through the existing Forest Service research program and that cooperative programs be expanded to embrace financial assistance to public land states to aid in planning. These ideas add new dimensions to the historic debate over the idea of a Department of Natural Resources, although this hardly provides an adequate solution when the need is plain for a policy of environmental concern to govern and guide all departments.

Perhaps most essential of all is the Commission's idea for public participation in land use planning, including a provision for mandatory hearings on public land projects. The only hope for breaking with narrow economic determination is through public involvement in the process of decision-making. Ferdinand A. Silcox made this plain when he became chief of the Forest Service in 1933. He warned his colleagues they must keep open the channels by which citizens would see and judge decisions, actions, processes, and their effects. "Then, and not until then," he emphasized, "can you and I and all of us honestly say we are conducting a federal agency on a truly democratic basis, with people and communities having a real and actual voice—not merely a gesture—in vital questions of policy and practice that affect them." If the mechanism for bringing this about can be achieved, it will be a major accomplishment of the PLLRC.

In short, the challenge before the people is to ferret out the useful and desirable features of this report and build on them. In an age when furnishing timber is only one use of the public forests, internal reorganization of the Forest Service and Bureau of Land Management should be designed to bring ecologists, biologists, landscape architects, and trained recreation specialists into decision-making positions in the hierarchy. And, contrary to the PLLRC proposal, the budgets of these agencies must no longer be tied to revenues earned or payments to local counties through timber sales, for such is the antienvironmental basis of land management.

In time past the proponents of dominant use blocked federal regulation of timber cutting on private lands, but they did not eliminate the need. Considering that three-fourths of the nation's forests are in private hands, it is more essential than ever to establish the principle that no land owner, large or small, should be able to control land use without regard for what his actions do to others. Ownership must be defined as a trust rather than a right, for land is an integral part of all life and its resources remain part of the environment. There is need of public ownership and management of more forest land by communities, states, and the federal government, and extension of public cooperation with private owners. Protection and wise use have hardly begun on the small woodlots which comprise three-fourths of the nation's timber supply. There is need to bring scientific management to more watershed lands, to increase wildlife concern in forest management plans, to furnish technical and financial assistance to forest cooperatives, and to offer small woodland owners long-term loans at low interest rates in order to insure both softwood and hardwood for the future.

Above all, the pace for environmental protection should be set on the public lands. On these diverse units it is still possible to observe the genius of earth forces which are greater than those of man. They constitute the living, tangible heritage of the American people, a recreational and scientific resource, our last great roving room. These lands are the treasure of the nation. Now is the crucial hour to appreciate and defend them as such.

Chapter 24

To Lucy: "Unlock Your Dreams and Courage"

I have here a letter from Lucy P., who is about to get more reply than she expected. Lucy writes to tell me about herself and to ask my advice on whether, and how, to make a career in environmental writing. My first reaction is that I have heard from Lucy before, although in some previous correspondence her name may have been Luke, or John, or whatever, searching for guidance and a beginning in what might be called "the environmental field."

On the face of it, Lucy appears qualified, at least qualified to ask. She was graduated from the University of Tennessee in 1978 with a major in environmental studies. For the past six months she has worked as a reporter for a daily newspaper with occasional chances to cover environmental events and issues. Moreover, her letter is well composed and neatly typed—which in itself is something these days, believe me.

> At this point [writes Lucy] I would like very much to go to work on the staff of a publication that deals with the environment or to do graduate work in science writing.
>
> My questions for you are: What general advice would you have for someone in my position? Are there trade journals or other sources where job opportunities in science or environmental writing might be included? From your experience, do you think there is a demand right now for people who can write well about environmental concerns?

From *Defenders of Wildlife*, August 1980.

My first word of wisdom is that earning a living out of writing independently is about as easy as earning a living out of farming. It can be done, but you have to rise early in the morning and labor in the fields until the sun goes down. There is said to be lots of money in turning out racy novels, for those who can and care to, but a letter published in the May 1980 bulletin of the American Society of Journalists and Authors reveals the lot of those choosing other themes. (The contents of the bulletin normally are confidential for members only, but there is scarcely confidential disclosure in this case.) Jamie Maxtone Graham writes from Scotland to explain his resignation from the organization:

> I came into the Society as a reformed farmer. Today I regard myself as a reformed writer, and I look back without much regret on half a lifetime spent in two callings where the producer is, most of the time, had for a mug.
>
> In farming, the grain merchant and the meat packer name the price of the product, which has no relationship to the cost of producing it. In the writing trade, the editor and publisher name the price—for a type of product whose supply always exceeds demand.

So Mr. Graham decided to better invest his $65 annual dues in half a dozen bottles of Scotch. His report is offered not to discourage, but to caution that writing—especially on the environment—is for the brave, bold, and determined.

Practical experience is imperative. A university degree is like a license for employment rather than a testament of knowledge and skills gained. It is one thing to train as a professional by defined rules and rote for a career and then be devoured by a creaky, worn-out system; it's quite another to learn from life in a way that enables one to serve society usefully and to challenge the system.

I recall the fervor of youth in the period leading to Earth Day of 1970. Young people were rocking the boat as it had not been rocked before. Even the staid American Association for the Advancement of Science felt constrained to allow students a share of participation at its annual meeting. The students proceeded to criticize the "misuse of science and technology" which has brought about pollution and a mode of production based on waste; they charged that science is controlled by the federal government and large corporations. But their elders were largely unmoved. As one official retorted, "The AAAS has been concerned about this before these kids got into high school."

Perhaps so, but galloping environmental decay bespeaks the need of something new and different than the recital of accomplishment by an older generation that has failed—even more now than in 1970. The answer, however, has been a spate of environmental programs at some of our best and worst educational institutions training people for careers in planning, resource analysis, and writing impact statements for federal and state bureaus.

Yes, Lucy, the environment is a field with employment opportunity, but more jobs in making paperwork than social change. Because few, if any, courses teach activism, young careerists can say, "The recommended course, after all, is the lesser of several evils," or, "Environmental education will solve our problems," and feel satisfied. There are all kinds of museums, indoors and outdoors, with professional interpretive naturalists at work, studiously avoiding the real world across the fence. Or as the director of the Palm Springs Desert Museum (a Southern California oasis filled with lovely natural science exhibits, but surrounded by a degraded and polluted environment beyond it) told me coolly, "Our board doesn't want us to be involved."

Professional training tends to teach one to conform and direct his ambitions into safe channels. Think for a moment, however, of some of those who came along through experience and experiment. John Bartram, for one, was the plainest of men, a plowman whose curiosity was stirred by observing the interaction of life-forms on his farm and who then taught himself to become a natural scientist, scholar, and principal figure in the botanical discovery of America. Or Mark Twain, who had a fourth- or fifth-grade education, yet drew from life and real people to open new horizons in literature. Or John Muir, who left the University of Wisconsin for what he called the University of the Wilderness, living more outdoors than in, perceiving the landscape in terms of both poetry and science, and who conceived the movement for preservation.

What we need today is a revolution of thought to sweep the world and to challenge the old institutions: medicine, religion, economics, education, science, communications, body politic, established ideas and ideals over a wide spectrum. In our country the challenge demands a critical examination of old national goals measured in sheer economics and of traditional personal goals focused on owning a home in suburbia, working toward retirement, and making money grow. To find one's place in the search for new social standards, to participate in shaping an order based on humanism and naturalism—that might not be what you'd call the best job opportunity, but those who succeed find their own reward.

This kind of idealism can be difficult to incorporate in technical courses. If you attend a graduate school of journalism the underlying objective will be employment in newspaper work, television, public relations or advertising, preferably where the action and money are, rather than at the country gazette back home. Likewise, those in schools of forestry and wildlife management generally look ahead to jobs in federal and state agencies and in the timber industry. Throughout their training and after graduation, they will deal largely with others in their own fields. As with any group of technicians, the competence of foresters and wildlife managers is judged within the bounds of their professions.

Despite the narrow scope of their training and professional employment activity, resource managers chronically resent and resist the active interest of the public. Notwithstanding the manifest issues of public policy affecting public lands and of wildlife that are the trust of all the people, anyone critical of professional management, or mismanagement, must be "uninformed," an "extremist," or an "uninformed extremist." Such is the substance of a manifesto issued several years ago by officials of three old-guard organizations allied with the bureaucratic and economic establishment—William E. Towel, of the American Forestry Association; Daniel A. Poole, of the Wildlife Management Institute; and Thomas L. Kimball, of the National Wildlife Federation. As they charged, emotional reaction rather than professional understanding misdirects the involvement of citizens in conservation affairs:

Our new generation of city-raised young adults is running on the land they have not known and claiming it as their own. Few understand the dynamism of living things and seek to arrest natural succession.

Most oppose hunting, mining, tree cutting, recreational-vehicle use, livestock grazing or the use of any renewable resource, for that matter.

The news account of this enchanting declaration was sent to me by Dr. J. Frederick Bell, of Hamilton, Montana. While recognized in his own field of virology, Dr. Bell during his years at the Rocky Mountain Laboratory of the Public Health Service also became interested in forest matters, particularly in the large-scale devastation of forest and wildlife wrought in the name of professional management throughout the Bitterroot Mountains bordering Hamilton. Dr. Bell enclosed along with the news clipping a copy of a letter he had written to the editor of *Science* magazine urging that he investigate the firing by the American Forestry Association of an outspoken environmental columnist in its monthly magazine—namely me.

The controversy [wrote Dr. Bell] that brought about Mr. Frome's dismissal from *American Forests* is discussed in the enclosed "A University View of the Forest Service" [the report of an investigation of Bitterroot mismanagement by faculty members of the University of Montana]. Those of us who have been involved consider the issues extremely important. Basically, we believe that management practices on public lands should be on a sustained yield basis with adequate provision for recreation, esthetics, prevention of siltation and, above all, watershed protection. The industry-dominated American Forestry Association and U.S. Forest Service personnel tend to think of the national forests as timber "mining" areas that are to be exploited as rapidly as possible for the benefit of industry and without serious concern for adverse effects or for replacement.

We feel that a larger segment of the scientific community should be made aware of the controversy and especially of the punishment meted to a reporter by officers of a supposedly respectable society, when he tried to inform the members, and the public in general, of the despoliation.

The editor of *Science* magazine did not pursue Dr. Bell's plea. It would have been surprising if he had.

The media are as much a part of the entrenched establishment as the AAAS, the American Forestry Association, and our most august educational institutions. So they could hardly be a force for social change, or for treating fairly forces for change or for providing the audience adequate data on truly critical issues.

The main purpose of television is to sell things—a few that people may need, but not many. Programs are designed to keep people entertained between commercials. Considering the essence of mass merchandising, the common denominator of taste in programming can't be very high. News broadcasters and commentators are like actors, and the bigger the audience the more restrained they must be with their thoughts and words.

Real-estate scandals and polluted atmosphere are everywhere, but newspapers that expose them are few and far between. In my own area, the *Washington Post* consistently promotes the cause of builders and boomers while treating local environmental issues as though they didn't exist and concerned citizen groups as though they didn't exist either, or at best as kooks.

Newspapers and wire services cover "stories." If one nation invades another and kills many people, that becomes a story. If black people erupt in urban ghettos and burn enough buildings, that becomes a story. The Love Canal tragedy is the rare environmental episode that has made a story. Members and supporters of the Clamshell alliance have produced a story too big to ignore, but the media treat it as one of confrontation rather than of nuclear warning at Seabrook, New Hampshire. The pall of smoke that hangs over the country, the poisons in soil and water, the vanishing open space, soaring over-population, disappearance of species—these threats to the future of the nation and human race are not sufficiently vivid to constitute much of an ongoing story.

When the media do cover environmental matters, reporters are dispatched directly to the main source of news: the Public Relations man. He knows how to provide the news releases and good quotations that make a story, while serving the interests of those who can afford to pay him. It may be the mayor, plant manager, forest supervisor, or the utility company president. The PR man in *The China Syndrome* was drawn from life and so were the words of his boss in ordering him to cover up the nuclear leak: "Take care of the press— that's what you're paid to do."

China Syndrome is an environmental document of powerful dimensions. Jane Fonda's boss at the TV station didn't want her to get involved in the nuclear-plant controversy, but to stick to her knitting as a well-coiffed doll covering entertaining features like the tiger's birthday at the zoo. Jane, however, insisted on following her reporter's nose on a course that led her and Jack Lemmon, against all odds, to evoke the truth.

I think of *China Syndrome* as a classic of our time in the same sense as *Silent Spring*. Jane Fonda and Rachel Carson demonstrate the opportunity and challenge awaiting young hopefuls like Lucy P. There is so much to be done and damn few who are doing it. Lots of bodies are rattling around and drawing paychecks. They are good people who largely have been institutionalized. The movers and shakers are scant.

I can't give Lucy all the answers in her quest for a career—she must find them for herself. When she asks for my advice, I can say as follows: Set aside fear and apprehension and chart your destiny. Don't wait for it to come to you but shape your own future writing about the environment, if that's what you want. You may not prove to be another Rachel Carson, but then again you may. That's really not as important as making some positive contribution to society in your chosen field. As I said earlier, however, this kind of thing is reserved for the brave, bold, and determined. Now unlock your dreams and courage and get to work.

Chapter 25

When Fishermen
Save the World

During the summer of 1971 I noted a rather chilling newspaper report concerning an accident at the Dow Chemical Company plant located at Midland, Michigan. A workman there had apparently misread a gauge. As a result, he had released caustic soda into the Tittabawassee River, killing between 2,000 and 3,000 fish.

Such tragic blunders do not happen every day, thank heaven. At least, they're not reported in such a manner as to be part of our daily consciousness. But how widespread are they in actuality? Are they fundamentally "accidents" affecting only fish, or are they inescapable by-products of our highly technological society and our super-standard of living which embrace all species?

Fish kills of significant consequence now occur to an alarming degree in every section of the country. On October 24, 1972, for example, a tank truck overturned in a remote area near Cimarron, New Mexico, spilling about 7,000 gallons of diesel oil into the Cimarron River. According to the New Mexico Game and Fish Department, the oil killed 18,500 fish, mostly brown trout, in a nine-and-a-half-mile stretch of river, and also destroyed most of the trout food organisms for 84 miles downstream. The trucking company involved agreed to pay compensation for the fish loss and the cleanup expenses. "Unfortunately," commented Ladd Gordon, director of the Game and Fish Department, "money cannot completely correct the environmental damage to the stream and fish

---

The epilogue to *The Experts' Book of Freshwater Fishing*, edited by Steve Netherby (New York: Simon and Schuster, 1974).

habitats. And it will require several years to restore this fishing water to its natural condition."

Meanwhile, more than 100 men already were battling to contain oil from another accident in New Mexico, this time in the northwest corner of the state. A 16-inch pipeline had ruptured on October 10, releasing an estimated 38,000 gallons (but possibly as much as 200,000 gallons) of crude oil into a dry wash in the desert. Then rain had washed the oil through an irrigation canal and down a Utah arroyo into the San Juan River, which flows into Lake Powell, one of the nation's largest recreation areas and the most popular fishing hole in the Southwest. It spread into a slick reported to be more than 80 miles long, threatening a resource where anglers have taken catfish weighing over 20 pounds and largemouth bass, rainbow trout and German browns of 6 pounds or more.

Turning eastward, the Big Piney River once was queen of the Ozark Highlands of Missouri, in the heart of America. It was known as a stream of green-blue beauty, pure enough to drink from, the epitome of the Ozark float river, as restful and rewarding as they come anywhere. By mid-1972, alas, the entire river was afflicted with serious sewage pollution, principally from the communities of Cabool, Houston and Licking and from the Fort Leonard Wood military reservation; all, in fact, were under orders from the Missouri Clean Water Commission to cease discharges by December 31, 1973. Then came an "accident" from quite another source, killing 110,000 fish, as well as all other aquatic life, in a 15-mile section below Cabool. The cause was seepage from the saturated soil around a chemical/bulk-oil complex. Heavy rain and snow had forced highly toxic materials into the stream; the major killing ingredient was pentachlorophenol, a chemical which is mixed with fuel oil and used to treat fence posts and telephone poles. Included in the kill were many minnows and sunfish, carp and small bass; suckers, always sensitive to contaminants, were among the quickest to die. When it was over, state biologists foreclosed any chance of early fishing on the Big Piney; it would take a rise of several feet of water, they said, to flush the oil off the rocks and clean out the stream so that it could begin rehabilitating itself.

Perhaps the most massive fish kills in America occur in Florida's lakes, canals, rivers and estuaries and on both coasts, almost summer after summer. The causes are principally pollution from sewage and industrial "wastes" discharged into public waterways. South Florida cities along the Gold Coast dump 116 million gallons of virtually raw sewage into the ocean every day. Beaches at such playgrounds as Miami Beach often are so contaminated that they are unsafe for body contact (though rarely, if ever, posted). Ocean game-fish populations have been drastically reduced—partyboat skippers say they must now travel 50 miles from Miami to find good fishing. Annual sailfish catches have dropped from an average of 4,000 fish in the years before 1948 to only 900 in those since 1962. Even more disturbing, sick fish with cancers, tumors, lesions and fin and tail rot have been showing up in Biscayne Bay; but sick fish have also been increasingly observed in the Florida Keys, Tampa Bay and Escambia Bay at Pensacola, and doubtless are present in other grossly polluted waters.

"Every year it seems to get worse," a Florida sportsman wrote to the editors of *Field & Stream* magazine in the fall of 1972. "Not only are fish dying in old areas, but they are turning up in new areas as well. I've seen beautiful game fish—sheepshead, mullet, speckled trout, croakers, redfish and black drum—that any angler would give his right arm to catch lying rotten on the beaches."

This fisherman expressed his despair soon after the latest tragedy had struck. In the period from August 26 to September 15, 1972, a 22-man municipal crew working along Bayou Texar had carried off more than forty tons of dead fish, averaging more than two tons per day. The whole area was pervaded by the stench of dead and decaying fish. Most were menhaden drawn to the bayou waters by prolific algae blooms, where they soon exhausted the oxygen supply of the water and died. The algal growth resulted from an overflow of raw sewage into the bayou from inadequate sewage lines in an area of accelerated real estate development and construction. On September 15 the bayou was closed to swimming and water skiing, but three days later another major kill struck East Bay, site of major oyster beds and the last relatively unaffected estuary of Escambia Bay. The dead menhaden stretched five miles long in a strip one-half mile wide, and more were still dying by the millions.

Fish of different species were seen floating in distress, swimming in circles upside down.

Still, some of the worst disasters escape attention because they're not immediately self-evident. They deal with tragedies of a deteriorating environment shared by fish and fishermen, and therefore are the most frightening of all. This was plainly revealed in the case of Lake Apopka, in Orange County, Florida, in early 1971. Sixteen alligators were found dead; so were many fish, snakes and fish-eating birds such as egrets and gulls. A study team from the University of Georgia arrived on the scene with expectations of investigating illness and mortalities of wildlife populations.

But the team found something else instead: that Lake Apopka was paying the toll of uncontrolled effluents from municipal sewage, muck-farming operations, citrus groves and citrus-processing industries. Moreover, organic debris from water hyacinth and "trash-fish" control programs—promoted in the name of better fishing—had added to the excessive enrichment of Apopka's waters. The team concluded the dead and dying animals were sounding an alarm. The evident catastrophe was essentially a symptom of something much deeper. What needed study and treatment was the sickness of the lake itself.

There is little time to lose, for people can be afflicted too. After all, when birds, or fish, or any living species, succumb to an unhealthy environment, how can man be expected to prosper or survive? Within a three-year period, at least five persons died from a newly recognized disease, amebic meningoencephalitis, contracted from swimming in the central Florida lakes. Authorities concluded that some unknown factor in polluted waters causes virulent strains of a certain organism, *Naegleria gruberi*, to develop suddenly, then to strike, most typically, young swimmers. The organism enters the nose, then eats its way up the olfactory nerves into and through the brain. Each of the five recorded victims perished in agony.

In order to save the fish, we must save the fishing environment. If the fisherman wants to enjoy his sport, and to be sure that there will be sport for his sons to enjoy, and for their sons following them, he can no longer devote himself solely to the techniques and pleasures of fishing, but must also concern himself with the protection and perpetuation of the fishery against the harsh challenges of a technological age.

The degradation of aquatic systems, including the fisheries, is under way everywhere in the world—caused by industrial pollution, pollution from human and livestock "wastes" and pollution from inorganic-fertilizer technology. The sickest aquatic systems, quite paradoxically, are found in the richest, most advanced, most civilized nation on earth, where rivers and lakes have been severely impacted by dams; channelization; herbicides and pesticides; erosion from uncontrolled logging, mining and road building and thermal pollution. All this in the name of progress, profitability, "increasing the tax base," attracting industry and a thousand other explanations that essentially serve a few and go unchallenged by the many. We need to reassess our equation of values, to weigh more closely losses against gains within our supercivilization, then to incorporate values based on the quality of life as part of the process of doing business.

For example, the blessings of the motorcar are indisputable. All America moves on wheels. Nevertheless, highways constructed to the highest technical standards have been endowed with culverts that block fish passage. Siltation resulting from dredging and filling for new roads has destroyed fish habitat on a broad front. The widening of stream channels by highway builders has created warmer, shallower water—a condition that prevents the growth and movement of desirable game species, notably trout, and completely alters the stream ecosystem. Is it really worth the price?

Dr. George Cornwell, professor of wildlife ecology at the University of Florida, has pointedly discussed the question of values with reference to production of food. "Which do you want, fishing for fun or food for life?" demand proponents of herbicides, pesticides and channelization, all in the name of food for more people. But Dr. Cornwell has written: "With our aquatic systems destroyed, the food we produce becomes valueless. We can't separate one part of our life-style from the others and still have an existence worth living. We are not making any headway if we sacrifice our aquatic systems to produce food. A great many Americans value their aquatic systems sufficiently to place food production in a more realistic perspective."

More than a billion acres of cropland, pastureland, and rangeland, plus another 637 million acres of forests, are treated with fertilizers, pesticides and herbicides that drain into our waterways. Normally a large store of humous nitrogen is maintained in the soil by the organic remains of plants and animal manure. But when the soil is intensively cultivated and the natural crop stripped from the land rather than fed to animals, the supply of humous nitrogen declines. The answer of agri-industrial corporations, with vast holdings devoted to single-crop production, is to add artificial inorganic nitrogen to the soil. Once it reaches the lakes and streams, fertilizer stimulates the growth of algae.

Even now, the fertilizer industry is doubling production of artificial nitrogen in the United States about every six years—thereby doubling the load the ecosystem has evolved to carry and process. A surplus of nitrates is definitely harmful to both plants and animals, and this explains the natural cycle of their release into the atmosphere. The alternative, through overloading, is eutrophication— literally the "enrichment" of water. Spread over many centuries, the gradual accumulation of nutrients and sediments ages a lake so that it ultimately changes from an aquatic to a terrestrial ecosystem—or from water to land. In the past few decades, however, the aging process has been accelerated through man's interference, including the use of fertilizers. Ironically, even with the additional applications, agriculture on a national scale is now no longer increasing crop yields; the environment is being overloaded without receiving even the promised short-term returns.

The finest fisheries are being affected by poisons used broadscale in agriculture and forestry. Pesticides are present today in every major river system in the country. Coho salmon in Lake Michigan have accumulated concentrations of DDT which are believed to be largely the reason for reproductive failure. In December 1969, widespread deaths of immature catfish occurred in Southern and Midwestern states. Analysis revealed contamination by endrin, dieldrin, DDT and toxaphene. Fish life is very sensitive. The poison may enter the body of the fish through the gills. It then may act on the blood, the nervous system or the organs.

Some poisons are transmitted up the food chain from "loaded" insects; others from microscopic aquatic plants eaten by small invertebrates and subsequently by small fish. Small fish are eaten by large fish; large fish are eaten by birds such as the osprey and the eagle, transmitting the poison to the top of the aquatic chain. Pesticides may not kill on the first go-round, but they may appear in milk and eggs or accumulate in animal fat.

Some herbicides and pesticides are used by fish managers themselves in enormous quantities for control of aquatic plants and to kill off carp and other species that are considered undesirable. The theory is to make the waters more productive; yet poisons are scarcely selective, and the total effect on the environment is unknown. Too little effort has been made to understand the flow of plant nutrients and energy in the aquatic ecosystem and food chain, the interdependence of plants and food organisms. The urgent need among resource managers is to "think in ecosystems," relating every decision and every action to the total life community, rather than to a single, isolated component, or to a production of a commodity, even when it's sport fish; the challenge to the sportsman is to encourage them to do so for the long-term benefits.

Federal agencies committed to commodity production have demonstrated a singular inability to "think in ecosystems." This is notably true in the Department of Agriculture, where agencies such as the Soil Conservation Service and Forest Service have spread environmental pollution and ecological disruption over rural America in the name of furnishing food and fiber to a growing nation; in the process, they have diminished the quality of life, and certainly the quality of fishing in particular.

The Soil Conservation Service, under Public Law 566, has "improved" thousands of miles of waterway through channelization and claims that no fewer than 11,000 streams still need to be channeled. The standard treatment involves clearing all vegetation a distance of 100 feet from the bank, then deepening the stream channel and eliminating all natural curves in order to speed the flow of high water. The objective is to drain adjacent wetlands so that they can be used to grow more crops and to reduce local flood damage. These goals are usually achieved (at considerable public cost for private benefit), but channelization is equally liable to shift the flood damage downstream and to induce erosion along the banks.

According to a 1970 study by the Tennessee Game and Fish Commission, a proposed channelization project on the Obion and Forked Deer rivers would result in an annual loss of $3 million in fish, wildlife and recreational values. Why so? The studious fisherman can look at a stream and appreciate its relation to the surroundings: Trees and other plants along the banks plainly exercise great effect on the living river by contributing organic matter to its food energy. Leaves that fall into the river provide the primary food source for many microorganisms, such as bacteria and fungi, which are eaten by higher organisms; mayflies, stone flies, caddis flies and blackflies obtain most of their food energy from dead leaves, algae, moss and other particles in the stream before they, in turn, are eaten by fish. Likewise, spiders, crickets, beetles and grasshoppers either fall, crawl, hop or are blown from trees and plants into the water, where they too become important food for fish.

Insects are denied a place by modern farm- and forest-commodity producers, regardless of the roles they play in the food chains for fish and birds. Entomologists of the Forest Service have directed a major portion of their time to finding ways of eliminating insects. Their concern has been for timber production. The Forest Service consequently has sprayed millions of acres with ecologically crude insecticides—and still has failed to eliminate the pests.

Timber-cutting practices permitted on national forests have also been anything but favorable to the fishery resource. Trout and salmon especially demand clean, cold waters for survival, yet silt and sedimentation have been widespread as a result of erosion from logging on slopes that should never have been disturbed. The South Fork of the Salmon River, as one of many examples, has historically contained Idaho's largest salmon run, composed entirely of summer chinook, a species endangered in the Columbia River system. This river runs through steep, mountainous terrain constituted almost entirely of granitic materials in various stages of decomposition. Such terrain simply will not tolerate modern logging and roading without unleashing havoc on the drainage system. Nevertheless, logging did take place, with the inevitable consequences. In 1971, a Forest Service fisheries biologist, William S. Platts, conceded very serious devastation of the aquatic habitat—to such an extent, he said, that it would take the river an estimated eighty-five years to recover and regain reasonable conditions.

Other Federal agencies—the Army Corps of Engineers, the Bureau of Reclamation and the Tennessee Valley Authority—have impacted classic fisheries with massive dam-building projects in all parts of the country. One has only to look at the Pacific Northwest to recognize the disastrous effects. Once the clear, rushing waters of the Columbia and Snake hosted the finest runs of salmon and steelhead trout in the world. Since the dam-building orgy of the past three decades, all in the name of profit and progress, a chain of more than twenty dams stands between the Pacific salmon and their spawning grounds on the Upper Snake.

The mighty Columbia, once the proudest river on the continent, is only a shadow of itself, almost entirely bottled up by eleven main dams. The Snake has been plugged by twelve major dams of varying sizes, shapes and purposes. Millions of dollars have been spent on ladders to aid adult fish to reach their spawning grounds in the mountains and their offspring to return to the Pacific Ocean, but still the fishery is declining. Many fish cannot make it. Even when they do manage to get upstream, their young have great difficulty in swimming downward to the sea. They follow the bottom contour of a river, not the surface. When they reach the upstream side of a dam, they mill about near the base; they have lost their way, and many die. In recent years, young and adults by the millions have also been killed on the Columbia by nitrogen gas, which is caught from the air and concentrated as excess water falls over the dams. Under great pressure in the basins below the dams, the nitrogen supersaturates the water and blinds, cripples and kills fish swimming in large schools.

Is all this justified by the alleged benefits in terms of progress and growth? A reading of *The Experts' Book of Freshwater Fishing,* I believe, will convince even the most casual observer that the enjoyment of life cannot be measured in material terms alone. What a sterile world it would be without the wonders of the outdoors and the mystery that waits to be solved with each cast over the ripples of a clear natural stream! How inadequate by comparison is the ultimate prospect provided by the endless exploration and exploitation of energy sources for commodity production and growth unlimited. Who needs it all?

Industry and government officials insist we must extract increasing volumes of coal by surface mining. They don't deny that damage to the earth is inevitable, but allege that it can be repaired and the land reclaimed. It scarcely is, in fact, except for public relations purposes. But even if it could be, damage is never limited to the mine site. Strip miners widen streambeds, drain lakes, divert surface flows, bury and remove spawning gravels, cause siltation and sedimentation, bring about chemical changes in soil and water quality. The damage in all cases extends miles downstream from the source. As Bernard T. Carter, Director of Fisheries in Kentucky, reported in 1963, following a comprehensive Federal/state study on the Beaver Creek Watershed in the eastern mountains of his state: "The entire fish population and nearly all the bottom fauna—the little animals fish feed on—were completely eliminated from the stream receiving drainage from the strip cut."

The boomers of strip mining in Washington and on Wall Street are now threatening to devour the surfaces of valuable, productive cattle country of Wyoming and Montana just because coal lies beneath them—to give these states the old Appalachian treatment. The irreplaceable environmental, cultural, scenic and social values of the great Western Plains stand to be scarred beyond recognition, or lost altogether.

"Of initial concern is the nationally famous fish and wildlife resource," as the Montana Department of Fish and Game has protested. "But even more important is the land, air and water on which this resource depends. This high-quality aquatic and terrestrial habitat could disappear forever from Montana's landscape, leaving fish and wildlife as unfortunate victims and Montanans as the 'biggest losers of all.' " This must not happen. When Montana—or any state—is critically affected, we are all losers.

But who can make the losers into winners? Who can reverse the tide of degradation that threatens not only the fisheries but the environment at large? The challenge, as I see it, rests with the people—especially fishermen who care—not to depend on experts, but to mobilize their own forces and to express their concern for the quality of life with vigor, to demonstrate their influence in the body politic and, when necessary, to carry the environmental issues before the courts. This, happily, is already taking place. The most promising aspect of the whole scene is the maturing of the American fisherman as an environmental activist.

It's encouraging to observe the aggressive involvement and growth of anglers' organizations everywhere. Trout Unlimited, for one, is gaining influence because it doesn't avoid confrontation on tough issues; its members have learned they must stand up and be counted for the fisheries if they want their share of the fish. TU chapters have been on the firing line to save the free-flowing Delaware River from the Tocks Island Dam; the Little Tennessee from the Tellico Dam; the Middle Snake River as it flows through Hells Canyon from the Hells Canyon Dam and the Teton River from the Teton Dam. TU is an effective advocate of better fishing, encouraging the average angler to "Limit your kill, rather than kill your limit"— in other words, to release most of the fish he catches, in the spirit of true sport.

A key role is also being played by the Bass Anglers Sportsman Society (BASS). In one recent year it filed over 200 antipollution suits in the courts and is carrying the message to the people with fishing and environmental seminars. "The mercury crisis that closed 51,000 acres of fishing waters in Alabama is evidence enough that if we don't have stronger laws and regulate what's dumped into our streams, our fishing will vanish," Ray Scott, BASS president, has declared. "If we do not act now, we can blame only ourselves when our favorite fishing spots die."

I should also mention the Hudson River Fishermen's Association, the essence of grass-roots activism. The meetings, as Robert H. Boyle describes them in his book *The Hudson River*, are something of a cross between a technical seminar at Woods Hole and an old *Duffy's Tavern* program. "I have seen factory workers stand up and put their jobs on the line," writes Mr. Boyle, "by reporting their own employers as polluters. 'Don't check on the company during the day,' one man said. 'They keep the stuff downstairs and let it out after midnight.' " This demonstrates beyond doubt the gutsy character of the American fisherman.

A great deal of progress has been made; or perhaps I should say the foundations have been laid for progress. Congress and state legislatures have enacted a variety of promising protective legislation—the Wilderness Act, the Wild and Scenic Rivers Act, the National Environmental Policy Act, the Water Quality Act—but it's up to the people to make them work.

Water pollution is still worsening; the environment continues downhill. About 500 new chemicals are added every year to the 13,000 "potentially toxic" ones already used by industry. Thanks to its friends in Congress, the petroleum industry can pump its pollutants via injection wells under the soil, threatening to contaminate the most valuable water storage. These trends must be reversed.

"One could be an ecologist regardless of what he calls himself," wrote Paul Sears in 1964. I agree. The true test is in the breadth of perspective—whether one knows what he is up to in terms of the great patterns of life and environment. In this respect, I think of Senator Alan Cranston's heroic proposal to establish a 35,000-acre Pupfish National Monument in the California desert devoted to an inch-long fish which few people have heard of or seen. Except for scientific value, the desert pupfish are useless to man. They're too small to eat, don't make pets and won't survive in home aquariums.

Still, I believe that saving the pupfish would symbolize our appreciation of diversity in God's tired old biosphere, the qualities that hold it together and the interaction of life forms. When fishermen rise up united to save the pupfish, they can save the world as well.

Chapter 26

Freedom of the Press—
For Those Who Own One

I never realized my importance—or influence, or the extent of my following, if you wish—until I was fired in October, 1974. Environmentalists picketed. Congressmen protested. *Time* devoted almost a full page. The Society of Magazine Writers investigated, leading the chairman of its Professional Rights Committee, Patrick M. McGrady, Jr., to declare: "The circumstances surrounding the dismissal of Mike Frome as a columnist for *Field & Stream* pose a threat to the intellectual freedom—the freedom of expression—of every independent writer in this country." Imagine, I told my wife, all this over me.

Most rewarding personally, I have since been flooded with warm and wonderful messages from former readers—primarily hunters and fishermen—clearly demonstrating that little people are indeed concerned about the future of this planet and desperately crave the truth about how to rescue it while there is still time. The whole episode has enriched my life, and deepened my conviction and commitment. As far as I am concerned, the fight for a better environment has just begun.

But I have learned not to be carried away with my own importance—that is not what it's all about. The larger issue involves openness, or the lack of it, in the channels of public information in this country. On the basis of the censorship and suppression that I have experienced, I am apprehensive about the conglomeration and increasingly centralized control of the mass media. Where and how

From *The Center Magazine*, July/August 1975.

is the public to obtain the knowledge it needs—knowledge now being denied—so that it can form sound judgments on crucial national issues? In my own field, the media may touch now and then on one phase or another of the environmental crisis, but only as a passing fancy, never in depth or breadth. I doubt there are more than ten newspapers in the entire nation that regard conservation of natural resources as being half as worthy of coverage as (with due deference) collecting stamps.

This is no accident. I read recently that the city council of Portsmouth, Virginia, voted to permit construction of a $350 million oil refinery, with financing by Cox Enterprises, Inc., better known for its newspapers and broadcasting outlets in Miami, Atlanta, and Dayton. I cannot envision any Cox medium investigating and exposing the inevitable pollution and ecological degradation deriving from oil refineries. Whatever is a newspaper chain doing in the oil business? Oil production and newspaper production should never mix. However, the media are not only big business in their own right, but have ventured afield into other big businesses, and are also a component of even bigger ones.

The need for the press to occupy a constructive adversary role led the founding fathers to make freedom of the press the keystone of the Bill of Rights. Without insuring press freedom, they knew that other freedoms would fall. Thomas Jefferson reflected that if he had to choose between government without newspapers, or newspapers without government, he would not hesitate to choose the latter. That quotation is well known and often cited by the big media, but their entangling industrial and commercial alliances ill fit the image they may like to present as today's John Peter Zengers courageously at work.

In the book field, Random House is now owned by R.C.A.; Little, Brown is owned by Time, Inc.; and Holt, Rinehart & Winston is owned by C.B.S., Inc. And there are other cases. Among the three major outdoor magazines, from which millions of hunters and fishermen presumably learn what is going on in their world, not a single one is independently owned: *Sports Afield* belongs to Hearst; *Outdoor Life* to the *Times-Mirror*; and *Field & Stream* to C.B.S., Inc. I think the country should be concerned and frightened about the continuing conglomeration of the outlets of public expression by powerful private interests. *Field & Stream* for years stood on its own. Then it was acquired by Holt (itself a merger of two publishing houses). Then Holt was devoured by C.B.S.

Today, when every company appears to be owned by some other company, it is virtually impossible to say anything of importance without stepping on somebody's toes and irritating the financial nerve, directly or indirectly. In conglomerates, each part is bound to all other parts. Can there be any single element of the American scene that more insidiously threatens our liberties and freedom of speech?

I was engaged as conservation editor of *Field & Stream* in 1968. This was not a full-time position, to be sure. The magazine has a small staff of five or six editors in New York, plus ten or twelve part-time editors who are engaged in other work or are free to engage in other work. On the masthead I was listed as a department editor. When I joined the staff the editor at that time, Clare Conley, wrote a memorandum of understanding which included the following:

> Naturally, the most important thing in the conservation editor's work is his monthly department; but in addition to this, some of the behind-the-scenes work includes answering mail to do with conservation, consulting with me on story ideas and on the correctness of manuscripts, attending press functions, and in general representing *Field & Stream* as the major conservation magazine that it is.

I qualified for my position at *Field & Stream* not through prowess in either hunting or fishing, but because I had developed some small reputation writing books on conservation themes (including *Whose Woods These Are* and *Strangers in High Places*) and contributing to other magazines. I knew the scene in Washington, where I have lived for thirty years; and I was acquainted with the environmental *dramatis personnae* in Congress, the Interior and Agriculture Departments, and the national conservation organizations.

Franklin S. Forsberg, the publisher of *Field & Stream* (the man responsible to the C.B.S. corporate infrastructure), interviewed me closely. He impressed me as being rather cautious, but not timid; in due course he proved essentially supportive and appreciative of a strong conservationist line in the magazine.

Mr. Conley was something else, an Idaho-bred outdoorsman, an accomplished writer, and a fierce activist in defense of the outdoors. The contents of the sportsmen's magazines generally focus on "how-to-catch-'em, how-to-kill-'em," material written by experts, many of whom learned the secrets from an old guide named Joe. The advertising promotes fishing tackle, high-powered rifles, telescopic lenses, outboard motors, trail bikes, snowmobiles, and game preserves which preserve game for the kill. Mr. Conley, however, had set his sights on protection of the sportsman's environment, as well as enjoyment of the true sport.

Our motivations and backgrounds differed, but we shared common goals. During the period of our collaboration the magazine was more than a monthly journal; it was a crusading force. I doubt that any magazine took a tougher environmental line or involved its readers more. We tackled critical issues in all parts of the country, dealing with logging, mining, grazing, land use, pesticides, and pollution. I wrote about the Corps of Engineers (a three-part series called "Dam the Rivers, Full Speed Ahead!"); about Hells Canyon on the Snake River; Alaskan oil; the waterfowl crisis in the prairie states; eagle killings in Wyoming. In 1970, we established the *Field & Stream* Environmental Action Group, designed to recognize and stimulate citizen involvement on grassroots issues. Then I started an addendum to my column called the Environmental Action Line, mostly short items and tips of regional interest. These all proved popular; outdoorsmen who had felt helpless found encouragement and direction.

We dealt with the political issues at the heart of America's environmental decay. The magazine was read and recognized in Washington. For the issue of January, 1972, I wrote a column on the first year in office of Rogers C. B. Morton as Secretary of the Interior. It was a critical one and Mr. Conley headlined it as follows:

3 Quarters Played
Nixon 0
1 Quarter Played
Morton 0

Shortly after the issue appeared, the Undersecretary of the Interior, William J. Pecora, telephoned me, feigning high dudgeon and exclaiming, "We demand equal time!" I had known Mr. Pecora well over the years. We disagreed on basic issues but were friends. He had formerly been the director of the U.S. Geological Survey and was an adept bureaucrat who never broke off communication. I was all in favor of granting equal time and in the April issue that year we carried a column by Secretary Morton (titled "Let's Recount the Score"); it was so weak and ineffective I almost offered to rewrite it as a public service.

In the September, 1968, issue we published a new feature, "Rate Your Candidate," evaluating fifty incumbent members of the House and Senate in six categories (from "Out in front—deserve cheers and support" to "The Expendables—won't be missed"). The feature included a questionnaire covering thirteen key issues which could be clipped and sent to candidates, with extra copies available for the asking. The following excerpt from the text shows the fare we served our readers:

Most Congressmen know little about conservation, and care little. They are content to go along with the crowd, to vote the party line, to follow the piecemeal course charted by the leadership. Sure, they all favor conservation in the abstract because they feel the swelling tide of emotional concern among the people. But when the chips are down many are apt to cast their votes with the special interests. For instance, after no less than fifty years of prodding, Congress finally voted last year to establish an Indiana Dunes National Lakeshore—*that* was a token for the people. But the boundaries were established in such an emasculated manner that they mean little and will take long efforts to shape into substance——and *that* was for the industrial giants who exploit the lakeshore and call the tune for the Indiana congressional delegation.

The special interests are alert, up-to-date, working all the time. One can hardly help but admire the real estate boomers; industrial developers; logging, mining, livestock, and petroleum industries; highway builders; chambers of commerce; the economic power structures of city, county, and state able to create a grand illusion that what serves them best serves the community best. Often they control the press, or intimidate it. For instance, during the intensive promotion for the Rampart Dam project (which would have destroyed wildlife and water-fowl habitat on the Yukon flats while making an artificial lake as large as Lake Erie) not one Alaska newspaper dared to speak out against it, although individual editors were personally opposed. Likewise, in Arizona, newspapers were caught up in the frenzy for damming the lower Colorado river where it flows through the Grand Canyon, without adequately presenting the alterna-tives or analyzing the fearful consequences of these dams on the Southwest; yet some of them were quietly relieved when the project was defeated.

I mention these pressures to show that a congressman cannot always, perhaps not even often, be his own man. True enough, some members of Congress are bought and paid for by the special interests, either through campaign contributions, legal fees through their law firms, or other such handy devices. A few don't have to be paid; when they pick up inside informa-tion on new reservoirs and other government land projects, they buy real estate and make the killing themselves by selling it to the government at high prices. Most, however, are trying to get along by doing the right thing for the people they represent. They are subject to a continual barrage by the economic power structure and special interests and barely enough from the ordinary public, whether organized in sportsmen's clubs or other conservation groups, or as unorganized individuals, to provide a countervailing pressure.

Since a congressman's first mission is to stay in office and get himself re-elected, he walks a tightrope. He may be tough on issues away from home, but he is apt to get slippery when his own political fate is concerned. He weakens, compromises, behaves like a frightened pawn in a chess game. Few members of the House have the self-assurance of a man like John Saylor of Pennsylvania to do what is right and feel he can get away with it. Few members of the Senate follow their own conscience to the extent of Wayne Morse of Oregon, the brilliant, unpredictable maverick. But I think the wise conservationist must forgive an occasional deviation and endeavor to build a better and broader base of support, freeing the honest congressman from the power of the special interests.

The technique of congressional rating is not exactly new, but I believe *Field & Stream* was the first to apply it to the conservation field. The idea of the ratings and questionnaires to candidates has since been used by a number of state conservation organizations. Our effort may also have paved the way for the excellent activities of the League of Conservation Voters (which not only rates congressmen on their voting records but raises money to influence key campaigns) and of Environmental Action, which targets the "Dirty Dozen" in the House of Representatives, and works to defeat them.

In 1970, we expanded the feature, rating all one hundred members of the Senate and more than one hundred members of the House, this time using a point system (from Excellent, 85-100 points, to Poor, below 40 points). Our judgment was based not simply on voting records, but also on degree of understanding, degree of commitment, extent of involvement, and effectiveness in getting things done. Determinations were made on the basis of interviews with national and grass-roots conservation organizations, as well as other research. I exercised complete charge, but I did so as a thorough nonpartisan, favoring neither liberal nor conservative, neither Democrat nor Republican, but always sticking to the environmental issues.

Early in 1972, I discussed with Mr. Conley plans for a new Rate Your Candidate feature. I proposed this time to rate every member of Congress and I asked for a special assistant. Mr. Conley approved and I hired Gail Hayes, a brilliant young woman who had been with Environmental Action and the Highway Action Coalition. We decided to tackle the tough ones and to ignore the consensus votes, though it is difficult to pin down clear-cut definitions through legislation. Congressmen tend to obscure their tracks. Through amendment and emasculation the soundest legislation is apt to lose its meaning by the time it goes through the mill. But we tried. And this time we sent a questionnaire to every member of Congress inviting each of them to tell us about his or her environmental policies and performance. Almost three hundred replies were received from members of both houses.

Rate Your Candidate covered eight pages in the September, 1972, issue. Ratings covered a spread from Excellent to Very Good, Good, Fair, and Marginal, to Poor and Very Poor. Representative Wayne Aspinall, of Colorado, the powerful, crusty chairman of the House Interior Committee, was listed as follows: "In a class by himself—the man who must go." Alan Merson, Mr. Aspinall's primary opponent, at once ordered ten thousand reprints; he said later that our pungent classification was the most decisive factor in his victory. (Unfortunately, he was defeated in the general election.)

Readers responded warmly and gratefully; they simply had not known the facts before. One reader in Virginia, noting that a disproportionate number of the "Poor"-rated congressmen came from the Southeast, implored: "Put a little heat on Dixie; we've got sportsmen down here as well as moonshiners. Prod us up a little. From our legislators' records, we could use it." District No. 2 of the Idaho Wildlife Federation issued a bulletin urging all its members to read our September issue: "With the tool Mr. Frome has given us we may be able to curtail some of the farces being foisted upon us and be much more effective in reaching our objectives."

There was plenty of criticism, too, principally on the gun-control issue. Some readers were upset about the high ratings given to senators favoring registration. As one wrote: "Of the seven senators up for re-election this year rated 'good' to 'excellent' by Mr. Frome, five of the seven have consistently supported anti-gun legislation, including national registration and licensing (Case, Pell, Percy, Brooke, and Mondale). Thirteen of the fifteen rated 'inadequate' to 'very poor' have consistently opposed such legislation, and certainly deserve some recognition in this regard."

I suppose in a sportsman's magazine the opponents of gun control deserve some recognition, which they did receive in separate editorials. But we tried to separate the environment and gun-control questions. It has always seemed lamentable to me that some of the worst political opponents of wildlife habitat should be allowed to wear the label of sportsmen's friend for their position on gun ownership. Some readers, however, were carried away. A sporting goods dealer in Kansas issued an irate bulletin: "Those advertisers who do not wish to promote the anti-gun position should refrain from advertising in *Field & Stream*. We dealers should refrain from selling the products of those who do advertise in *Field & Stream*." From a friend in the industry I received this admonition: "Stick to conservation, Mike—not controversy."

Then there were the complaints from congressmen. The low-rated vented their wrath upon the publisher, the editor, C.B.S., the advertisers, in letters and through the press. I was called on to write endless letters to congressmen, explaining our project, both in general and on specific questions.

None seemed more upset than Representative Bob Sikes, of Florida. On September 25, 1972, he attacked *Field & Stream* on the floor of the House. He said the rating contained so many surprises that it had become the subject of much comment around the Capitol—"little of it favorable." He criticized the selection of issues, including the supersonic transport ("It is hard to understand how a vote for or against the S.S.T. affects conservation and the sportsmen's interests in America)" Cannikin, the Aleutian Islands atomic test; the Reuss water pollution amendment; and the confirmation of Earl Butz as Secretary of Agriculture. Then he concluded:

> Let us be charitable and say *Field & Stream* used poor judgment. I am reluctant to say they do not know any better. Congressmen are accustomed to harsh treatment from 'experts' who pre-empt for themselves the exclusive right to judge performance. It is not new for us to be rated by handicappers who measure our work against their views and not in light of the interests of the public. Fortunately, campaigns are decided by separate constituencies who consider the issues in their entirety and who are not bound by the one-sided views of the handicappers.

> After all, Congress has been around much longer than *Field & Stream* or C.B.S.

By this time, alas, Mr. Conley was no longer on the scene. First, Mr. Forsberg had retired and had been replaced as publisher by a former advertising executive, Michael J. O'Neill. Mr. Conley had been deeply concerned about possible editorial interference and about slickness creeping into the magazine. He had clashed with the new publisher and been dismissed.

The new editor, Jack Samson, had been on the staff for about two years as managing editor. We had good rapport; he gave reason to hope the crusading days would continue. For one thing, Mr. Samson wrote to critics defending the magazine's tough environmental line, warning that without protecting the woods and clear streams from the ravages of strip mining, clear-cut logging, and the like, there would be no place remaining for hunter and fisherman to enjoy their sports. And I felt I had his support during the Rate Your Candidate flap.

This was evident in a number of communications he sent me. One was a tear sheet from *Business Week* (September 23, 1972) headed "How the Ecologists Defeated Aspinall," with reference to *Field & Stream's* role. It bore a handwritten notation, "Great! Jack." Then there were letters from congressmen and others sent to me for response, with such written comments as: "Mike, you could have fun with this guy." "Mike, have fun. Best, Jack." "Mike, here's another missile for you. How's the old arm holding out?" There was a sharp letter from Warren Page, president of the National Shooting Sports Foundation, demanding: "Doesn't Frome know that the majority of these gentlemen have either authored restrictive gun bills of the worst sort or have stumped for badly designed restrictions which must have the eventual effect of eliminating those excise tax and hunting license funds which have contributed roughly two billion bucks to modern conservation?" Mr. Samson wrote across the top, "Mike, maybe you could try an answer to Warren. I tried last time and it didn't work."

Then, following the 1972 election, he wrote this encouraging word: "You are an excellent conservation editor and we sure as hell will continue to back you, as we have done during the past few months of heated controversy over politics." Could any writer ask more?

The first sign of a breakup came in 1973. Following up on confidential reports, I went to New Mexico to investigate questionable land transactions conducted at the state office of the Bureau of

Land Management, an Interior Department agency that administers millions of acres of domain throughout the West. Staff personnel were deeply disturbed (but fearful of speaking openly) about many areas of land being transferred to private ownership. Land studies by the agency were inadequately performed and records scantily kept; exchanges were being conducted without public review.

I had pursued other B.L.M. land problems in Arizona, Wyoming, and Idaho and had found the public estate being divested of choice acreage without, shall we say, prior full disclosure of value to be lost. Some of these cases became known through confidential warnings, which may be the most frightening aspect of all; why should whispers be necessary when the Interior Department is charged with protection of public interest, not the promotion of profiteering private interest?

In New Mexico I learned that a prominent real estate outfit, the Crowder Investment Company, had completed a series of major land exchanges with B.L.M., obtaining title to more than half a million acres of federal land. Two key areas—one adjacent to El Paso and another midway between Albuquerque and Santa Fe—held high real estate potential. Additional cases were pending even while I was in New Mexico. (Moreover, in March, 1973, Secretary of the Interior Rogers C. B. Morton appointed Willard Lewis, a business consultant associated with the Crowder Investment Company, as the Department's Southwest field representative.)

I learned further that a powerful political figure, Tom Bolack, had entered applications to B.L.M. for purchase of ten tracts, averaging about 750 acres each, in the northwest part of the state. He had held meetings in Washington with political officials including Curt Berklund, Deputy Assistant Secretary of the Interior, who later became director of the B.L.M., seeking to obtain approval for these applications without following established B.L.M. procedures. Staff professionals, however, had recommended that at least three tracts in the flood plain of the San Juan River be retained in public ownership to protect wildlife values and public access. The Navajo tribe, owner of adjacent land to the south, termed Mr. Bolack's approach "a direct attempt to circumvent the federal policies and law with respect to land within the public domain."

I wrote a report on my findings for publication as my regular column in the June, 1973, issue. That never appeared. Nor did I receive any valid explanation. It was my first taste of censorship. I tried to attribute it to the fact that Mr. Samson had lived and worked in New Mexico for a number of years, and so I hoped it would be my last taste of censorship. In June, while traveling in Montana, I met Ted Trueblood, a longtime *Field & Stream* associate editor and columnist. He shared my concern and subsequently sent a letter of inquiry to Mr. Samson. "I consider Mike Frome an asset to *Field & Stream* and the best writer in the conservation field," wrote Mr. Trueblood. "I have a number of friends who read his column first— even ahead of Zern or me!" On July 3, Mr. Samson replied: "Glad you ran into Mike Frome. I agree he is one of the best conservation editors around. Nothing was amiss about his June column not running. It was just a priority matter and I think we have our priorities ironed out."

However, in the publication of my column for the July, 1973, issue, dealing with the unhappy state of our national forests, I found key expressions deleted and the article cut abruptly. The reader was left hanging in the midst of the adventure on Admiralty Island, Alaska. The following three paragraphs were omitted:

I fear for the future of the eagles in Southeast Alaska. The Forest Service doesn't have enough people to inspect logging shows, nor people sufficiently qualified to observe damage to habitat, whether of eagles or other wild species, nor people with enough courage to speak out. Insofar as Admiralty goes, the country is allowing a timber-oriented agency to manage one of the finest wildlife areas on this continent.

I have dwelt on Alaska because the Forest Service there has made timber sales of immense proportion, committing the public resource to single use over long periods of time. The errors are plainly evident. They point up a basic deficiency prevalent throughout the National Forest System. Two years ago, the Forest Service published a study of six national forests in the West, called the Stratification Report. It revealed that land classified 'available for commercial logging' had been overestimated by an average of twenty-two percent. These figures may even be modest. Severe overcutting is widespread.

A tragedy of awesome consequences is at hand. Secretary Earl Butz should be replaced by someone with environmental concern. The Chief of the Forest Service should either exercise some muscle and leadership or quit. Without basic change in direction, generations still unborn will be required to pay in depleted resources for the exploitation of our public forests which this Administration has decreed. Sportsmen and all other citizen conservationists must demand a reversal in this fearful course.

In the course of the next several months the space for my column was cut and my secretarial allowance eliminated, but these steps were explained as resulting from a drop in advertising revenue and economy measures dictated by C.B.S. In addition, I was instructed to write in generalities without naming names. Mr. Samson scrapped plans for a Rate Your Candidate feature. In a memo to me he wrote: "I feel this is definitely not the year of the environmentalist. The energy crisis has caused a backlash which I don't want to subject *Field & Stream* to at this time." Still, on April 9, 1974, he congratulated me warmly on being nominated for the board of the Outdoor Writers Association of America and gave approval to attend meetings on the expense account.

In late September, 1974, I submitted my column for the December issue, dealing with the Forest Service's new Environmental Program for the Future, which struck me as nothing more than a scheme of accelerated exploitation of forest resources. So, I wrote as follows:

> The document, I fear, does not fulfill the promise. The emphasis in the text is not on sustaining land health over the long run, but on gaining maximum production of commodities over the short run, without fundamental concern for the future. Three levels of operation are offered to the public: low, moderate, and high. However, the low level of timber cutting, 16.4 billion board feet, is just a shade below the moderate level and not much below the high (of 20 billion board feet). There is no choice of indicating that today's cutting is already too high, that foresters should revert to a sensible dimension in order to insure perpetual yield. . . .

Reading this document carefully convinces me that my friends of the Forest Service have found a new package for the old sales pitch. What they really want to generate is not public involvement in decision-making but public support for increased appropriations to cut more trees, build more roads, spread more chemical poisons, graze more livestock. The draft Environmental Program supposedly represents the basis of furnishing public input, but page after page is filled with the most suggestive comments on why the low-level alternative will not do, and why the high-level alternative will best meet "national production goals for 1984." Almost as an afterthought, hunters and fishermen are promised greater access, but in many cases there is too much access already for the game and the true sportsman.

This column was never published. Within a week after I had sent it to the office in New York I received my letter of dismissal. (My wife, who opens and sorts my mail, said, "Have a double Scotch before you read this one." And the time was only 10:00 a.m.). It was marked "Personal and Confidential"—presumably Mr. Samson expected that I would keep my discharge a secret and that it would all blow away. This attitude subsequently characterized his and C.B.S.'s response to inquiries; they simply did not want to talk about it. Mr. Samson's letter gave no real reason. "We contemplate handling our conservation department in a slightly different manner. This will not only require a modification in the editorial approach," he wrote, "but will mean a change in editorial personnel."

Thus my relationship with *Field & Stream* came to an end. However, no one, I daresay, could have foreseen the trend of things that followed.

I notified one person, Joe Stephens, a close friend and ardent environmentalist of Alexandria, Virginia, and the dominoes fell. He in turn advised the national conservation organizations in Washington, D.C., across the Potomac. Marion Edey, spark plug of the League of Conservation Voters, was incensed; she urged a picketing action before the Washington headquarters of C.B.S. And in a few days fifty citizens produced a highly unusual happening, even for Washington, toting posters with such slogans as "Fairfax Loves Mike Frome" (carried by a member of the Board of Supervisors of my own county); "Friends of the Earth Love Mike"; "C.B.S.—Censored Broadcasting System"; and "Does C.B.S. Front for Polluters?" Almost concurrently a dozen national organizations directed statements of protest to William S. Paley, board chairman of C.B.S. So did several members of Congress; Representative Guy Vander Jagt, of Michigan, went so far as to issue a news release endorsing the picketing.

Soon the media coverage began. Jeff Stansbury and Ed Flattau, columnists for the *Los Angeles Times* syndicate, reported on asking Mr. Samson why he had let me go. He declined to respond, declaring, "We don't want to wash our linen in public. It was strictly an editorial decision." So he wrote inquiring readers as well, with a statement that "Mr. Frome's removal concerns only him and *Field & Stream*." This was a curious posture for someone in the public arena to assume on an issue of public concern.

Mr. Paley's replies likewise dismissed inquiry and protest. He wrote that he had looked into the decision. He had determined that I was not a full-time employee of *Field & Stream* but "did submit articles to our senior editors for publication"—when, in fact, over a course of six and a half years I contributed seventy-five monthly columns and a dozen major articles in this magazine, and was given business cards and stationery by his organization. He said *Field & Stream* was now going to engage a full-time conservation editor, when this was not to be the case at all. Such is the insensitive blight of bigness, whether in government, industry, media, or any other form of institution; bigness and bureaucracy render review or reversal of course extremely difficult.

Time magazine apparently also had difficulty in getting C.B.S. or *Field & Stream* spokesmen to open up, though Mr. Samson spoke enough to denigrate my competency. Nevertheless, in its issue of November 4, 1974, *Time* said I had been fired because I made enemies in big business, the gun lobby, and on Capitol Hill. The last two paragraphs of its feature read as follows:

> Rhode Island Senator John Pastore was cited [in our Rate Your Candidate feature] as "marginal"—a particular concern to C.B.S. Pastore chairs the Subcommittee on Communications, with jurisdiction over broadcasting regulations. His committee

hearings are often an ordeal for the networks, and broadcast executives are always fearful of restrictive legislation. Clare Dean Conley, then *Stream's* editor, recalls: "We got vibes from C.B.S. that they didn't want trouble with Pastore. The word was 'Do what you have to do, but take it easy.' "

That Frome refused to do, with the result that he lost his biggest platform. Says Congressman Reuss: "If *Field & Stream* has no place for Frome, then we have come to a time when the voice of conservation is, quite literally, a voice crying in the wilderness."

Presently Mr. Samson disclosed "the real reason," for my dismissal: that I was anti-hunting. Well, I had never thought of myself as such and certainly had never submitted a line of anti-hunting material to *Field & Stream.* But the editor explained his action in a letter sent to a number of people:

> I personally fired him because—while I have no objection to anyone freely expressing an opinion in this great country—when someone writes anti-hunting material in another publication and also submits a monthly conservation column to this eighty-year-old hunting and fishing magazine, it is more than sufficient grounds for dropping that column. No one who is anti-hunting will remain on the masthead of *Field & Stream* as long as I am editor.

As evidence of my anti-hunting bias, Mr. Samson disseminated a photocopy of a page from Cleveland Amory's new book, *Man Kind?* On this page Mr. Amory quotes from my latest book, *Battle for the Wilderness,* in which I wrote:

> Although hunting plays a valid role as an outdoors experience, the rightness of one being to kill another for sport is now extremely moot. The need to hunt for food is gone. Much of sport hunting has scant relevancy to primitive instincts or old traditions. It does little to instill a conservation conscience. Blasting polar bears from airplanes, hunting the Arabian oryx—or deer—from automobiles, trail bikes, or snowmobiles, tracking

a quarry with walkie-talkie radios, killing for the sake of killing annihilate the hunt's essential character. There can't be much thrill to "the chase" when there is little chase. At one end of the spectrum, "slob hunters" shoot farmers' livestock, road signs, and each other. At the opposite end are the "superpredators": jet-set gunners whose greatest goal is to mount on their walls one of everything that walked Noah's plank.

If that is an anti-hunting statement, my critics are free to make the most of it. In our time, sportsmanship and appreciation of outdoor life constitute the real meaning in hunting. I decry poor hunting practices of all sorts; those who violate the basic rules of outdoor sportsmanship give hunting and hunters a bad name. Dale A. Burk, outdoor editor of Montana's *Daily Missoulian*, stressed this point in his column of February 11, 1975:

> Samson is incorrect in assuming that this statement is anti-hunting. It is simply anti-bad-hunting practices and any responsible sportsman would share Frome's point of view that hunters must deal responsibly to eliminate from their ranks those who cause the sport much trouble and lend fire to the anti-hunting forces. . . ."
>
> Representative Conte [Silvio Conte, of Massachusetts] put it in these terms: "With the dismissal of Mike Frome, the media barons have tarnished the C.B.S. halo. It appears that when the chips were down, the public interest was sacrificed to the corporation's self-interest. If so, then the firing of Mike Frome must be interpreted as a selfish and hypocritical act."

The *Field & Stream* editor's justification for my dismissal disturbed the Society of Magazine Writers [later renamed American Society of Journalists and Authors], too, but for another reason. On the Barry Farber radio program in New York on March 6, 1975, Pat McGrady, chairman of the Society's Professional Rights Committee, explained his concern:

> I was once told by the editor of a women's magazine that he would never contemplate an article suggestion that would expose the cosmetics industry, for the logical, if not good, reason

that the cosmetics industry supports heavy advertising revenue with almost all of them. That editor never told me that if I could find a magazine or a broadcasting outlet where I could talk about how the public was being bilked by cosmetics manufacturers I couldn't say it there—and also continue to write for his magazine. Now what we have here is a very interesting case because the editor of *Field & Stream*, Jack Samson, in effect has laid down an edict that writers for that magazine in no other media are permitted to voice any quality or degree of anti-hunting sentiment. I find this a colossal presumption. . . . Where a man is chastised for expressing, not an anti-hunting opinion, but an anti-slaughterhouse opinion, in *another* publication, I think they've got a lot to answer for.

Mr. McGrady reported in this same interview how he had talked with Mr. Samson and John Suhler, president of C.B.S. Publications, about my dismissal. " . . . Jack said, 'Well, you know he wasn't doing the kind of job we wanted, that's really why—I didn't want to embarrass the guy—that's why we fired him. And there were other things.' I said, 'What wasn't he doing the way you wanted him to?' He said, 'Well, when he was doing those exposés—I mean he was going too heavy on the exposés. . . .' And he said, 'Above all, the thing I really objected to when he was doing those exposés—I mean filling the whole article with names of people. He didn't have to do that! I don't mind an exposé every now and then, but when you start putting the names in, embarrassing people, you're going too far.' "

All this illustrates why the media serves such bland fare—the mass media, I mean, to which millions of Americans are chronically exposed daily, nightly, weekly, and monthly, complete with color pages and with dazzling living television color. Challenges to society are restricted or simply sanitized out.

One of the principal challenges of our time revolves around energy. Americans have been led to believe that we desperately require the exploration and exploitation of new energy sources. But energy is much less needed for the true needs of the people than to furnish voltage for television commercials promoting another year of ever-changing automobile taillights. Industries insist they are furnishing materials for growth, but never say that the depletion of resources circumscribes the true potential of the nation. Yet, the people are not informed because most channels of information are controlled by the same forces.

Newspapers, broadcasting outlets, motion pictures, and even school textbooks are like advertising. The main purpose of television is not to educate; if it were, there would be no need for off-brand educational television. The principal function of the commercial channels is to keep the public abreast of highly important items for modern living, such as detergents and deodorants. Performers fill time leading into the commercials. So do newscasters and commentators. How could they possibly alert the public to the environmental crisis when they are part of the pattern that spurs waste and overconsumption and that drags down the taste of the American people?

The media are deeply committed to the syndrome of growth and energy exploitation, not simply because of reliance on advertising for survival, but because it is woven integrally into the system. The media are related both by blood and marriage to the establishment that runs things. Thus the sources of news in this country are largely big business and big government.

"To say that Idahoans are on the whole rather poorly served by the press—which means radio and television as well as daily and weekly newspapers—is to put it mildly," wrote Sam Day, in the *Intermountain Observer* in 1969. One aspect, he noted, is that most news media in Idaho do not even bother to cover the meetings of major state boards, including those concerned with natural resources. They are under the impression the job is being done for them. But this is an illusion, for the wire service reports upon which they rely are based for the most part on material prepared by publicity men of the agencies themselves, reflecting the official point of view.

"The inadequacy of news coverage in Idaho actually goes deeper than that," wrote Mr. Day. "Too often the reporter goes no further than official news sources, or sources where the news has been neatly packaged for him." Consequently, most newspapers are lookalikes, feeding the same fare, serving the same power structure, rarely digging out and exposing real-estate scandals, industry-caused air or water pollution, or a thousand other abuses of the environment and the common man's dignity. The public relations man, promoting the interests of those with funds to pay him, has become more a source of news than the public itself.

Highly respected newspapers are as corruptible as the obscure. The Scripps-Howard newspapers have crusaded against billboards, the highway lobby, and the trucking lobby; they even present an annual national award for the best newspaper writing on conservation. But in Memphis, Tennessee, when the chips were down during the nineteen-fifties and nineteen-sixties, in dealing with a local wilderness standing in the way of commercial profitability, it was quite another story. In that city Scripps-Howard holds a monopoly over morning and afternoon newspapers and owns major radio and television stations. It could have used these media to defend Overton Park as a priceless possession of 342 acres with seventy-five varieties of trees, one of the few urban forests left in the world today. Alas, downtown merchants and developers became convinced that a freeway through the park would jingle coins in their pockets. For years Scripps-Howard led the battle in their behalf, suppressing news, slanting and distorting news, ridiculing park defenders, browbeating the city council, belittling any politician who dared to stand up in behalf of the park. Scripps-Howard sought time and again to create the impression that the issue had been settled irrevocably beyond salvation through public interest or public action.

I wrote about this case in 1970, and one year later was quoted in a booklet on Overton Park written by Irma O. Sternberg. She described the issue as it evolved;

> So severe had Memphis brainwashing been that local businessmen, engineers, other professional men in various areas, speak *at their peril* against desecration of the park and distortion of expressway facts. Much of the same accusation as that made by Frome was printed in an editorial in a local professional journal (*Memphis Architecture,* published by the Memphis Chapter of the American Institute of Architects). Highly respected locally and nationally, the editor nevertheless received from several members of the highway-promoting establishment scathing letters of rebuke—as might be expected. But worse: he

was severely censured by many of his own associates, who apparently value the continued patronage of the local establishment above the preservation of the democratic tradition and free speech in Memphis. . . .

Pity our community, where truth has become a villain and an outlaw, and the only socially and economically acceptable 'facts' are those approved by the media! This is *not* the benign dictatorship of a Crump regime.

The *Washington Post* offers another case in point. The news copy in its weekly real estate section is little more than pure puffery designed to dignify the advertisements. If the presentation of news is the paper's basic function, why not a weekly section on human rights or on natural resources conservation, which are burning issues of the Washington metropolitan area?

The *Washington Post* has carried notable editorials on conservation in distant places, such as the Grand Canyon, Alaska, and the redwood country of California. But on the home front it has shown itself as part of the establishment promoting development for profitability's sake. Sam Smith, editor of the *D.C. Gazette,* a struggling spunky monthly which gives hope and heart to the inner city, is a bitter critic who writes: "As a local power, the *Post* has not only been conservative, it has been dangerously reactionary, serving the economic interests of the most greedy of the powerful. Urban renewal, freeways, convention centers, the multi-billion-dollar subway fiasco, all owe a deep debt to the long loyalty of the *Washington Post.* . . . To the city, the *Post* is Big Business first and journalism second."

A typical *Post* editorial, titled, "Our New Satellite Cities," published July 6, 1968, reveled in "the dramatic burgeoning of new business centers in the Washington suburbs." It cheered the prospect of a new skyscraper city, with buildings up to thirty stories, which, in fact, would destroy qualities of living in the Virginia section called Tyson's Corner. It urged the debasement of rural counties with a promise of "enormous profits that will result from rezoning of this land." More recently, on September 30, 1972, the *Post* editorialized in support of construction of four nineteen-story towers that would disfigure and destroy the shoreline of suburban Alexandria, Virginia, where I live, at a time when citizen conservationists were mustering every effort to block it. "It will bring more people and life to the nearby historic old town which is being most intelligently renewed," advised the *Post*. "It sorely needs more life and business, however." Curiously enough ,"Save Charleston" was the title of an editorial published soon afterward supporting South Carolina citizen efforts to keep high-rise development out of just such an area.

What the *Post* failed to mention was its own vested interest in commercial exploitation of the Alexandria waterfront, through its subsidiary, the Robinson Terminal Warehouse Corporation, and the strong likelihood of a windfall profit. Indeed, on October 5, 1973, the Secretary of the Interior, Rogers C. B. Morton, asked for a court injunction to halt enlargement by the Robinson Terminal and in- fringement on lands claimed by the federal government. Robinson agents were driving pilings to double the size of the warehouse, even after receiving written objections by the Interior Department. Such action, according to Secretary Morton, placed the *Post* in "a very hypocritical position."

We ought to know who owns what and to banish such hypoc- risy. The *Washington Post* has often demanded, and quite rightly, that public officials make full disclosure of their financial stakes. If the *Post* is to use its editorial columns to influence public opinion to better its own financial position it must do no less.

But how do we make certain this will really be done?

"No experiment can be more interesting than that we are now trying, and which we trust will end in establishing that man may be governed by reason and truth," Jefferson said. "Our first object should therefore be to leave open to him all avenues of truth. The most effective hitherto found is the freedom of the press. It is, therefore, the first shut up by those who fear the investigation of their action."

As I read the First Amendment, protection goes to the owner or operator of the press. Nevertheless, there is a need for Congress to enunciate a sound public policy to insure that the media themselves do not restrict the avenues of truth through the influence of con- glomerate control or non-media-related business activities. A me- dium of communication should not be owned by another corporation, certainly not by a corporate conglomerate, because of the strong possibility that the medium's undertakings will be subverted to the service of interests other than the dissemination of truth.

C.B.S., Inc., as a case in point, owns radio and TV stations; it makes records and musical instruments (including Steinway pianos); publishes books (both through Holt and Popular Library, a paperback house) and magazines; conducts research and development for industry, the military, and space technology. C.B.S. must tirelessly woo congressional backing for license renewals, as well as for its policies on cable TV and equal time. As Stansbury and Flattau pointed out, these concerns make C.B.S. far more sensitive to the politicians' wrath than an independent publisher of *Field & Stream* would be.

It is easy to say, I suppose, that I still have every right to speak and to express myself, just as I had before, that the only change is that I no longer enjoy the privilege heretofore accorded to express myself in the pages of *Field & Stream*. Maybe so. But as Peter Harnik, of Environmental Action, declared in his letter of protest to C.B.S.'s Mr. Paley:

> Mike Frome's removal is but another step in the polarization of our society, something C.B.S. should have a great stake in minimizing. Mike was reaching a large "middle-of-the-road" audience with perceptive commentary on controversial issues that all Americans should be aware of. Now he may be forced to write for environmentalist publications, in effect preaching to the converted, while his *Field & Stream* audience will continue to be fed bland and unstimulating material which can only further remove them from critical issues which all Americans are or soon will be facing.

For myself, I feel imbued with hope—too much support has come my way to feel otherwise. I will follow the course of William Lloyd Garrison, who wrote: "I am in earnest. I will not equivocate. I will not excuse. I will not retreat a single inch. And I will be heard." I believe in the democratic system, and that I am part of the human machinery that will make it work.

Chapter 27

Forestry: Only God
Can Make a Tree, But . . .

The practice of clearcutting timber on public and private forests has
become the subject of heated debate, both nationally and in various
regions of the country—as well it should, considering the high stakes
in economics, ecology, and esthetics. Controversies have arisen over
the management of the California redwoods, the Douglas fir forests
of the Pacific Northwest, spruce forests of southeast Alaska, lodgepole and ponderosa pine forests of the Rocky Mountains, the hardwood forests of the Northeast, and the mixed hardwood-pine forests
of Appalachia and the South. Within the past three years, hearings
on clearcutting have been conducted before committees of both
houses of Congress. Reports and studies have been made by the
Council on Environmental Quality, the United States Forest Service,
deans of forestry schools, and concerned citizen groups. Yet there is
still no resolution of the debate.

What is clearcutting? In an editorial appearing in its April 1972
issue, the magazine *Field & Stream* presented this blunt appraisal of
the practice:

"It is a method of harvesting trees which causes complete
devastation. It is more harmful than a forest fire. The land is churned
up over vast areas by big machinery. *Every* tree is cut down and most
of the surface plants are killed. Until grasses and shrubs can get
started again, the land is wide open to extreme erosion. Timber
companies prefer this method of harvest because it is cheaper than

---

From *Business and Society Review,* Summer 1973.

cutting selected mature trees and leaving the remainder unharmed and because having once destroyed a mixture of kinds of trees on a certain tract they can plant one type of tree, which they prefer. These trees are planted in neat little rows, all standing the same height and all reaching maturity at the same time for another cutting. But it is no longer a forest any more than an orchard is a forest. There are no open grassy glens, no bushes, no aspen or alders. Everything is crowded and shaded out by the trees, and for the major part of the growth years of the trees there is little food for animals or birds. It is a sterile sort of forest designed by a computer."

Quite different descriptions of clearcutting are offered by its advocates, who include, in addition to most of the forestry profession, large corporations, holding investments in timber lands or in mills.

"It is efficient, economic, and in general produces forest products and resources useful to man," declared Dr. Kenneth P. Davis of Yale University, president of the Society of American Foresters, while testifying before a Senate committee in 1970. The immediate consideration was a proposed moratorium on clearcutting in the national forests, as urged by citizen conservationists. To halt clearcutting, he warned, "would place an unwarranted and disruptive restriction on using a proper and, in many situations, necessary method of managing forest lands."

Edward P. Cliff, Chief of the Forest Service, addressing the National Council of State Garden Clubs in May 1965, declared that the practice "is something like an urban renewal project, a necessary violent prelude to a new housing development. When we harvest overmature, defective timber that would otherwise be wasted, there is bound to a temporary loss of natural beauty. But there is also the promise of what is to come: a thrifty new forest replacing the old. The point is that there often must be a drastic, even violent upheaval to create new forests. It can come naturally—and wastefully— without rhyme or reason as it has in the past, through fires, hurricanes, insects, and other destructive agents. Or it can take place on a planned, purposeful, and productive basis."

Mr. Cliff served as Chief Forester from 1962 to 1972. Under his aegis clearcutting came of age; he defended and promoted it with fervor. "For the young 'citified,' articulate part of our citizenry," he declared before the Pacific Logging Congress of 1966, "it is especially easy and natural to get stirred up about outdoor beauty, recreation, wilderness, vanishing wildlife species and environmental pollution. It is not likely that very many know or even particularly care much about how timber is grown, harvested, and used to meet their needs." The Chief likened accelerated timber cutting through modern technology to gardening, or farming of field crops. "Wild old stands have pristine beauty which is instantly felt and appreciated," he wrote in the 1967 *Yearbook of Agriculture*. "But a newer forest, man-planned and managed and coming up sturdily where century-old giants formerly stood, also has its brand of beauty— similar in its way to the terraced contours and the orderly vegetative growth upon well-managed farmlands."

The clearcutting concept, as enunciated by Dr. Davis and Mr. Cliff, plainly emphasizes the anthropocentric—the design of nature for the use of man; it rejects the notion that resource managers must "think in ecosystems"—that they must relate every decision and every action to the entire complex picture rather than to an isolated component of the ecosystem, let alone to considerations of expediency or short-term economic returns. It denies the principles evoked by Aldo Leopold, forester of another generation and yet a pioneer of today's ecological movement, who wrote: "The land is one organism. Its parts, like our own parts, compete with each other and cooperate with each other. The competitions are as much a part of the inner workings as the cooperations."

Clearcutting's bias toward commodity production in the short run, rather than toward protection of the resource in all its aspects for the long run, is often the main basis of attack in the media. Strong criticisms along these lines in *Field & Stream* and other publications (notably the *New York Times, Reader's Digest, Atlantic Monthly, Des Moines Register and Tribune* and *Montana Daily Missoulian*) have been summarily dismissed by spokesmen for the timber industry, the forestry profession, and the Forest Service with such epithets as "sensationalism," "hit-and-run reporting," and "yellow journalism." In a speech on "The Nature of Public Reaction to Clearcutting," delivered in February 1972, an official of the Forest Service, John R.

Castles, declared: "Probably the most frustrating and insidious form of pressure is that generated by irresponsible or ill-informed news media people who seize on unsubstantiated reports, half-truth rumors, misinformation, or outright distortions without checking them further."

But the evidence, even from timber-forestry witnesses, appears to substantiate charges that clearcutting is environmentally pollutive and ecologically disruptive, as well as designed principally for immediate profit. In an article in the February 1972 issue of the *Journal of Forestry*, for instance, Dr. David M. Smith, professor of silviculture at Yale, described the emergence of the new synthetic forest: "Combinations of herbicides, prescribed burning, and powerful site-preparation machinery made it possible, almost for the first time, to start new stands entirely free of the competition of preestablished vegetation. In some localities, it has become possible to contemplate deliberate efforts to eliminate natural populations and replace them with the planted products of conscious genetic selections. . . . It takes no great wit to see that within this frame of reference, the optimum cutting practice will be that which removes nearly everything that will pay its way out of the woods. The future benefits which might be derived from growth on reserved merchantable trees are quite intangible from this point of view."

Professor Smith went further, joining the critics in their concern over damage done by heavy machinery used in logging and site preparation. "The vegetation can be swiftly repaired," he wrote, "but it may take centuries or millenia to repair the kind of damage to the soil that can result from deep gouging or scraping action. It is time there was more concern for adapting the machinery to the silviculture and less resignation to the idea that soil damage is an inevitable consequence of practical forest operation."

John McGuire, who succeeded Mr. Cliff as Chief of the Forest Service, also conceded, in an interview published in *American Forests* magazine of October 1972, that: "Roads have been cut where they shouldn't have been permitted. Erosions have followed that make it impossible to get a forest of quality, or even any forest, in that area again." But instead of talking about eliminating roads in order to regain protection of the natural resource, he proposed construction of an additional 100,000 to 150,000 miles of highway in the national forests, thus tending to give credence to charges that the Forest Service is the handmaiden of special economic interests. Or, as Justice William O. Douglas declared in his dissent in the *Mineral King* case (Sierra Club v. Morton), issued April 19, 1972: "The Forest Service—one of the federal agencies behind the scheme to despoil Mineral King—has been notorious for its alignment with lumber companies, although its mandate from Congress directs it to consider the various aspects of multiple use in its supervision of the national forests." In the same message, Justice Douglas likened clearcutting to strip mining.

The most dangerous kinds of chemical poisons, poured into the soil and seeping into streams, are implicit tools of clearcutting. Entomologists warn that a pure stand of timber forms an ideal situation for damage from insects and disease; infection is rapid from tree to tree, and if one species is destroyed, there is nothing left. A monoculturally managed forest, therefore, creates the need for pesticides and herbicides. Ultimately these chemicals do more harm than good, for the biotic diversity is destroyed. Nevertheless, the Forest Service has poisoned millions of acres of public land, encouraged the use of ecologically crude poisons on millions of additional acres, and ignored pleas and protests.

The general fear among environmentalists is that more wood is being cut than grown on both public and private forests. The timber industry called for increased logging of the national forests—even though three-quarters of commercial forest land is in private hands—and the Forest Service responded by trebling its cutting of timber in the period from 1950 to 1970. Still, the industry wants the Forest Service to increase production by accelerated cutting of old-growth forests and by ecologically questionable programs of thinning and fertilizing. It fought enactment of the Wilderness Act of 1964 and now opposes establishment of additional inviolate wilderness, although such areas stabilize soil and watersheds, provide habitat for a variety of wildlife species, and are cherished for recreational pursuits.

Justification of clearcutting is repeatedly attempted on grounds that it produces more game. "Actually, this is the strongest argument for clearcutting, because artificial openings in the forest are a boon to wildlife," wrote William E. Towell, executive vice-president of the American Forestry Association.

It is true that clearcuts produce quail habitat, often where nonexistent before, and that an abundance of deer browse is produced on many clearcut areas. Biologists note that these benefits are temporary, however; before many years, quail habitat and deer browse decline. Within ten years following planting the pine canopy can be expected to close; until thinning, this clearcut is of use only as cover to wildlife. With increasingly short cutting rotations, it is difficult to anticipate how "mast" (foods such as berries and nuts) will be provided in the future for turkeys, squirrels, and deer. Removal of mast trees and cover is now destroying prime squirrel and turkey habitat, and lack of mast may reduce the carrying capacity for deer after a relatively few years. In the sequence of events, the clearing and conversion to pine in natural pine-hardwood areas, or hardwood areas with high deer populations, sometimes induces destruction of planted pines by deer, with the accompanying demand for hunters to "bring the deer population into balance."

Even though logging may improve deer habitat, serious disturbance eliminates such species as spotted owls and pine martens, which require old growth conifers for survival. Birds actually furnish the most efficient and least costly form of insect control in the forest. It is their definitive function in providing balance to the ecosystem. A single woodpecker, for example, has been estimated to be able to consume the larvae of 13,675 highly destructive wood-boring beetles per year. It is fair to generalize that the more numerous and varied the bird population of a forest, the broader the spectrum of natural insect control. John Smail, executive director of the Point Reyes Bird Observatory, a California research organization focusing on the ecology of nongame species, has reported on an analysis of nine breeding-bird censuses in coniferous forests in California, Colorado, and South Dakota. The analysis showed that 25 percent of the total number of birds using these forests are of species that nest in holes. These hole-nesters require older trees with some decayed portions in order to breed successfully (and feed large broods of young on destructive insects), although they forage on trees of various ages.

"Any forestry practice producing solid stands of trees of the same age reduces the diversity of bird species able to breed, and this in turn severely reduces possible insect control," according to Mr. Smail. "Clearcutting is the most drastic example."

The South is perhaps being hit harder by clearcutting than any other section of the country. Vast areas that once supported mixed forests have been reduced to even-aged stands of pine, like apple orchards or orange groves. The sole purpose in transforming forests into farm lots is to provide pulp and paper for an affluent, throw-away society. "For a paper company, the obvious objective of pine management is to produce the largest volume of usable wood fibre per acre," wrote Henry Clepper in the August 1971 issue of *American Forests*, in describing the operations of International Paper Co., a timberland giant which owns 8 million acres in the United States and Canada—including 5 million acres of the South—and controls an additional 15 million acres under long-term lease from the Canadian government. "To attain this goal, foresters must control the site, which is to say the forest environment."

The *Louisiana Conservationist* in 1971 described how this is achieved. Under a headline, "Flourishing Forests Threaten Wildlife," this state publication noted: "When the stand reaches the desired stage of maturity the entire timber crop will be cut and the whole process repeated. To complete this cycle anywhere from 15 to 80 years may be required, depending upon the wood products desired. Already thousands of acres in blocks, ranging from 160 to well over 1,000 acres, have been stripped of existing timber, bulldozed, chopped, or burned clean, and then seeded or planted with pine. The small stream bottoms which have historically supported hardwoods are now the main targets. They provide a last and most critical retreat for game within the great sea of pine."

The industry's design to transform the rural South into a man-dominated forest, or massive pine factory, is embodied in a highly publicized campaign called "The Third Forest." According to the industry's report, titled *The South's Third Forest—How It Can Meet Future Needs*, there are now 24 billion cubic feet of "cull" trees—unwanted hardwoods—which take space needed for "better" trees. The removal of cull trees in order to provide for future growing stock would constitute the bulk of timber stand improvement on no less than 90 million acres. Dr. George Cornwell, professor of wildlife ecology at the University of Florida, commented on this proposal as follows:

"As wildlife habitat, cull trees usually mean food (mast) and housing (den and nest). In terms of natural beauty, most culls would be more highly valued by the forest recreationist than the 'better'trees planted in their places. Imagine my disappointment on learning that, after several decades of wildlife managers' pleading with forest managers to retain these den, nest, and mast-producing trees for wildlife use, a major Southern forest policy plan would call for their removal throughout the Third Forest. This approach to the cull tree is symptomatic of the recommended silvicultural practices in the South's Third Forest and would appear to reflect a nearly total contempt for non-timber values."

Until the upsurge of recent years, clearcutting had been accepted as a silvicultural practice only in certain short-lived forest types which reproduce easily, such as aspen, jack pine, lodgepole pine, and some southern pines. But it always had been applied in small patches, so that surrounding trees deterred hot, dry winds from desiccating the forest soil, and were close enough to supply the openings with seed for regeneration while providing shade cover for young seedlings. The more prevalent system of silviculture was selective logging, or "selection-cutting." Essentially, this system is designed to follow and fit into nature's pattern of growth, maturity, and decline by selecting individual trees, or very small groups of trees, in order to favor species tolerant of shade, or larger groups up to quarter-acre clearings to favor species intolerant of shade.

With the advent of large machinery, however, clearcutting became a habit. It began in the Pacific Northwest, on the basis of assertions that Douglas fir, the most profitable—and hence most desirable—species, reproduces only in full sunlight. Since then clearcutting has spread to cover nearly all forest types.

What alternatives are there to clearcutting? Dr. Leon Minckler, professor of forestry at Syracuse University, who spent twenty years in research for the Forest Service, insists that clearcutting is not the way to go, that Eastern hardwood trees do regenerate better through other techniques. Other forest technicians are now challenging the idea that Douglas fir must be cut in large blocks. In an article in the *Journal of Forestry* for January 1972 Dr. Minckler wrote:

"For integrated uses (such as timber, wildlife, watershed, recreation, and esthetics), management should aim toward maximum diversity and minimum damage to the environment. This can be accomplished by single tree selection, group selection, small patch cutting of a few acres, or a combination of these. Clearcutting, on the other hand, tends to minimize diversity and makes it almost impossible to avoid damage to the site, to streams, and to esthetic qualities. Most of all, it eliminates the forested character of a particular area for a long time. Ecologically it is a major disturbance. When harvesting mature stands, clearcutting is a cheap and effective way of extracting timber, but the sacrifice of other values may be a poor trade-off for cheap timber harvesting. In immature or partially mature stands, clearcutting may not even be the cheapest way of harvesting timber."

According to Gordon Robinson, a veteran California forester and consultant to the Sierra Club, good forestry consists of growing timber on long rotations, generally from 100 to 200 years, depending on the species and quality of the soil, but invariably allowing trees to reach full maturity before being cut. "It is not enough to have orderly fields of young trees varying in age from patch to patch," he declares. "In looking at a well-managed forest one will observe that the land is growing all the timber it can and that most of the growth consists of high-quality, highly valuable material in the lower portions of the large older trees. It will be evident that no erosion is taking place."

In short, while the corporate forester or timberman may insist that trees can be harvested and cultivated like any farm crop, in a genuine balanced-use forest immediate values must be integrated with long-range protection of soil, water, wildlife, wilderness, and scenery, and with assurances that harvested areas will grow more trees for future timber needs.

Business has a natural and understandable tendency to stress economics rather than ecology when thinking about resources. But land is an integral part of all life, and its resources remain part of the environment. In dealing with them, business needs to blend ecology and economics in its thinking. No landowner, large or small, should be able to control land use entirely for his own benefit without regard for what his actions do to others. Ownership is a trust which must be exercised in the interest of all—and one of the prime ingredients of that interest is the quality of the environment.

Dealing as we do with a complex earth mechanism which we only partially understand, we should be cautious in tampering with natural forces. Clearcutting has been subject to so many challenges and criticisms, and may do such serious long-range damage to soils and streams of the nation, that it needs to be curbed at once and restricted to experimental uses only, until answers are fully known.

Certainly any system of conservation based solely on commodity production or economic self-interest is hopelessly lopsided. It tends to ignore, and thus to eliminate, elements in the life-community of the land that lack commercial value, but which are essential to its well-being; if the land mechanism as a whole is good, then every part is good, whether we understand it or not. Perhaps the first rule to guide those who use and administer the land should be that economic parts of the biotic clock will not function without the uneconomic parts. Once that rule is learned and applied, then and only then can we sustain healthy, productive forests for the long-term future.

Chapter 28

Thoreau's Glad Tidings

One evening at dusk, I had gone paddling and fishing from my campground on the shore of Lake Umsaskis, about midway along the Allagash Waterway. A bronze sheen of fading sun spread over the water. Across the lake a lone moose raised his dripping antlers, then submerged them to browse the roots of water lilies. Instinctively I thought of the words of Henry David Thoreau, which I had reread that very afternoon.

"It is all mossy and moosey," recorded the master of the Maine wilderness. "In some of those dense fir and spruce woods there is hardly room for the smoke to go up. The trees are a standing night, and the general stillness is more impressive than any sound, but occasionally you hear the note of an owl farther or nearer in the woods and, if near a lake, the semi-human cry of the loons at their unearthly revels."

How astonishing that the scene, and the sounds, around me should parallel so closely Thoreau's description of more than a century ago! Such is the marvel of the Maine Woods. More than 80 percent, possibly 85 percent, of the state is covered with forest. No other state possesses so great a proportion. The towering white pines that once stood as high as 240 feet and were three centuries old are now gone, though even they could return in time, given human wisdom and appropriate self-restraint. Still, Thoreau through the printed page is as valid a guide and companion as the day his words were written.

"What is most striking in the Maine wilderness," he declared, "is

From *Vista*, Fall 1973.

the continuousness of the forest, with fewer open intervals or glades than you had imagined." Such is the impression in the deeper recesses of the Allagash, the finest canoe stream in a state noted for its canoeing, and in Baxter State Park surrounding Katahdin, the gray granite monolith that is Maine's highest mountain. From a plane you can see 10 million acres of wild forest land, flecked with hundreds of gleaming lakes, a great natural frontier of the Northeast, without towns or local government, and still very few roads. As cities grow and the megalopolis spreads, surely the North Woods become a more valuable treasure to both Maine and the nation.

So does Thoreau. During his lifetime he published only two books (*A Week on the Concord and Merrimack Rivers* and *Walden*), but his collected works, or daybook, run to 20 volumes, a mine of observations and discoveries about small and great things. He held neither dream, hope nor design that his works would ever be recognized for what they are: classics of ageless prose that speak simply, directly and upliftingly. Anyone who approaches Thoreau with any natural feeling will never again view nature as a thing wholly apart from himself or herself.

"He illuminated the humblest of subjects by intense scrutiny and faithful reporting," writes Joseph Moldenhauer, the editor of an important new authoritative edition of *The Maine Woods*, a faithful restoration of the original, first published in 1864, two years after Thoreau's death. "He asks the reader to take nothing for granted, nothing on authority or on second hand—but to look closely and independently at what is to be seen." For, as Plato said, "Science is nothing but perception."

As an author, Thoreau's style at times is wryly humorous, or satirical, his composition replete with imagery, philosophical themes and human drama, but always demonstrating personal integrity and clarity of purpose. He had no quarrel with civilization, but defined wilderness as a necessary component, warning against having "every part of man cultivated," which must only warp, diminish and, ultimately, barbarize him. His ecological lesson is plain: If we do not permit the earth to produce beauty and joy, it will not, in the end, produce food either. If we do not value it as beautiful in its own right, as well as useful, it will ultimately cease to be even useful. "In wildness is the preservation of the world"—little wonder this quotation from Thoreau has become the motto of the Wilderness Society.

Thoreau kept his life simple, flexible and immediate, bewaring of collecting possessions that might soon possess the possessor. The citizens of his home town, Concord, Mass., were baffled by his propensity to spend an hour in the rain, lost in introspection over the sight of wild ducks on a pond, yet counting it a waste to engage in "practical" activities. Nevertheless, he was probably the most intelligently industrious man at his calling, and, I daresay, the most optimistic and tolerant. "I do not propose to write an ode to dejection," as he once declared, "but to brag as lustily as a chanticleer in the morning, if only to wake my neighbors up."

His hopefulness and positivism are spread across the pages of *The Maine Woods*, "What a place to live, what a place to die and be buried in! There certainly men would live forever, and laugh at death and the grave." So he exulted following his exploration of Katahdin. The idea was clearly not to hoard the treasures but to share them. Thus in the appendix he advised the potential tourist of his day on what to wear, carry (in the way of compass, axe, pocket-map and the like), the necessary provisions, the fee of an Indian guide and the cost of the 12-day excursion starting from Moosehead Lake.

In a brief essay on *Walden*, E. B. White calls it the best youth's companion yet written by an American—"for it carries with it a solemn warning against the loss of one's valuables, it advances a good argument for traveling light and trying new adventures, it rings with the power of positive adoration, it contains religious feeling without religious images, and it steadfastly refuses to record bad news." Exactly the way I feel about *The Maine Woods.* The more you know about Thoreau and his three trips to the north country, the more provocative the whole subject becomes. Follow Thoreau and Joe Polis, his trusted Indian guide, master of the woods and woodcraft. Many of the sites he visited and the camps he made can still be located. In some cases, the surroundings have been drastically altered; in others the mood is Thoreauvian.

Thoreau made his journey on the Allagash in the summer of 1857 with his cousin Edward Hoar and Joe Polis, in a slender canoe of birchbark sewn with the thread of black spruce. The entire trip from the presently popular starting place at Telos Lake (Thoreau actually started from Moosehead Lake) down the north-flowing Allagash takes about ten days to two weeks, ending at the splashy rendezvous with the St. John's River on the New Brunswick border. It demands poling over rocky waters, portaging around waterfalls and paddling across broad lakes. Each section of the 100-mile route is different, the waters flowing at times softly through dark pools, then cascading in a white froth and exclaiming their power in a thunderous roar.

Here the elements assert themselves. The route leads up Telos Lake into Chamberlain Lake, where stiff winds blowing out of the northwest produce waves that can be dangerous. So it was in Thoreau's time, too. "After reaching the middle of the lake," he wrote, "we found the waves as usual pretty high, and the Indian warned my companion, who was nodding, that he must not allow himself to fall asleep in the canoe lest he should upset us, adding that when Indians want to sleep in a canoe, they lie down straight on the bottom."

Thoreau located his campsite for the night where you may locate yours, about midway on the south side of the lake, "where there was a broad, gravelly, and rocky shore, encumbered with bleached logs and trees," within sight of the only clearing in these parts, called the Chamberlain Farm.

"The lakes," he continued, "are something you are unprepared for: They lie up so high, exposed to the light, and the forest is diminished to a fine fringe on their edges, with here and there a blue mountain, like amethyst jewels around some jewel of the first water." That's how Thoreau saw it. Each traveler will find his own image to record and revere—perhaps rolling out before sunup, with sleeping bag stiff with frost; to be greeted by a thousand stars still bright in an immense, endless heaven; then paddling and peering ahead through steaming fog, so dense that even the near shoreline is difficult to see, and finally emerging into a sunrise that bathes fir, spruce and white birch with brilliant tints of red and orange.

On entering Eagle Lake, deep in the wilderness, you can spot Soper Mountain off to the north, crowned by a lookout tower, then approach Pillsbury Island, where Thoreau camped on the southeast side. "Somebody had camped there not long before," he noted, "and left the frame on which they stretched a moosehide, which our

Indian criticized severely, thinking it showed but little woodcraft." Which makes me wonder, what would Thoreau say about some of our outdoor practices today? Indeed, what should we say?

This was Thoreau's northernmost camp on his Allagash expedition. From here he turned back toward Bangor by way of Webster Brook and the East Branch of the Penobscot. But the determined traveler (or reader) can still follow him onward, shifting from canoe to shank's mare, picking up the tracks of moose, bear, rabbit and a host of other creatures to the summit of Katahdin. On the way up through forest and brush he scrambled, rolled, bounced and walked. Finally, he came to a high flank, "where rocks, gray, silent rocks, were the flocks and herds that pastured, chewing a rocky cud at sunset. They looked at me with hard gray eyes, without a bleat or low."

Thoreau's feelings in this primeval setting? He said it was fit for heathenism and superstitious rites, then continued:

"Nature was here something savage and awful, though beautiful. I looked with awe at the ground I trod upon, to see what the Powers had made there, the form and fashion and material of their work. This was that Earth of which we had heard, made out of Chaos and Old Night. Here was no man's garden, but the unhanselled globe. It was not lawn, nor pasture, nor mead, nor woodland, nor lea, nor arable, nor wasteland. It was the fresh and natural surface of the planet Earth, as it was made forever and ever—to be the dwelling of man, we say—so Nature made it and man may use it if he can."

Though exercising scant influence on men and events while he lived, Thoreau's philosophy has been increasingly felt with passing years. Surely it was in the mind and heart of Percival Baxter, the son of a wealthy Maine family who became governor. With his own money, he purchased, and presented to the state, Katahdin and 200,000 surrounding acres—now known as Baxter State Park—with a proviso that the region "forever be kept as sanctuary for wild beasts and birds . . ."

Thousands in search of natural sanctuary now march the Appalachian Trail to the summit of Katahdin, a massive uplift 30 miles in length, offering different vistas from every angle and in every season. The final climb comes on the famous Knife Ridge, extending along a narrow ridge where you can stand astride almost vertical walls and stare down on either side into great basins, gouged out of ancient glaciers. Whenever dense clouds roll in, you must crawl the Knife Edge to hold your footing. But if the clouds should leave, the sweeping scene from Baxter Peak will make it worthwhile; for here is the place to appreciate the earth as Thoreau did—as living poetry, more wonderful than convenient, more beautiful than useful.

This glowing picture of the Maine Woods, I fear, is not quite complete. Baxter State Park is overrun with far more visitors than it can support. Some campgrounds and trails are barren, subject to accelerated erosion, quite unlike the rough country Thoreau was obliged to penetrate. Such an area can support limited use at best; once overrun, it no longer imparts a sense of wilderness. The same is true of the Allagash. In 1965, the National Park Service reported the area "had preserved its wilderness characteristics to a remarkable degree." The following year Maine voters approved establishment of the Allagash Wilderness Waterway in order to "protect and enhance the natural beauty, character and habitat of a unique area." But since then nearby logging roads have been expanded, and behind the bulldozers have come more people than this area can support.

Fortunately, public groups, led by the Maine Natural Resources Council, and the State of Maine are moving to save the Maine Woods. The first steps to regulate use have been taken at both Katahdin and the Allagash. New areas, such as the spectacular Bigelow Range, are being studied for protection and public use. The promising new Maine Wildlands Law provides a system of zoning and planning, with special emphasis on lakes, rivers, streams and mountains, thus preserving more of our woodlands for hiking and relaxed enjoyment of nature's beauty.

"Who shall describe the inexpressible tenderness and immortal life of the grim forest," asked Thoreau, "where Nature, though it be mid-winter, is ever in her spring, where the moss-grown and decaying trees are not old, but seem to enjoy a perpetual youth; and blissful innocent Nature, like a serene infant, is too happy to make a noise, except by a few tinkling, lisping birds and trickling rills?" Some future Thoreau? Perhaps. In the meantime, let us love it wisely and save it for him and for her.

Epilogue

Reflections

In mid-1988 the editors sent me the typescript for final review before production. Shortly I found myself swept up by remembrance of times past. I laughed while learning anew that in 1962 room rates at Canyon Village in Yellowstone National Park were $13.50 for two persons, $18.50 for four, which I had reported then as "horribly overpriced." I found once again that I'd been given an award by the National Society of Colonial Dames for my book *Battle for the Wilderness.* It was nice of the ladies, especially since I had no idea they cared. I reread the statement of Stewart L. Udall, from an interview while he was Secretary of the Interior, that "all of us overcompromise and therefore fall short of our ideals." Jeepers, I hope not *all* of us, for without ideals what else is left? On the other hand, I felt uplifted by Miss Lucy Morgan's words, "Education doesn't put brains in your head," which she spoke to one of the many mountain women she encouraged to pursue their talents in crafts work. I thought of Miss Lucy's brother, Reverend Rufus Morgan, hiking the hills into his nineties and seeing so much to share with the rest of us though he was virtually blind.

I reflect on friends like Miss Lucy and Reverend Rufus who are gone, and lovely little places mentioned in the text that are gone, too, like George W. Vanderbilt's Black Forest lodge and the Pisgah Forest Inn. There is another facility on the site of the inn, a modern motel, but it doesn't match the setting or provide anything like the atmosphere that visitors of today and tomorrow need and deserve. I rediscover in these pages the beauty of the Southern highlands, the mountain region extending from Virginia and West Virginia south through North Carolina, Tennessee, eastern Kentucky, South Carolina, Georgia and Alabama, and the good qualities of native mountain people. I reread my proposal to double the size of the Great Smoky Mountains National Park, which still strikes me as a valid idea, despite all the difficulties involved. The best thing we can do is to save whatever remains, through the Appalachian highlands, recognizing that what's good for the land is good for the people. Otherwise both land and people will be lost in the mad scramble of growth and greed.

As I wrote in my plea to fishermen to save the world, a lot of damage has been done in the name of progress, the tax base, and other gimmicks that essentially benefit the few while penalizing the many. Society needs to reassess the equation of values with more emphasis on quality of earth, water, sky, and life.

I relive by reading this book tough conservation battles. There is no end to them, no matter what the outcome. While on a visit to Knoxville during the mid-1980s, I met an old friend who had been active to the bitter end in the fight to save the Little Tennessee River. We shared a tear, then agreed that for us both the Little T would never die. In other words, this is only the beginning, folks. I may not be around for the great 21st century awakening and renaissance, but Lucy P. will. Lucy P., where are you now?

Index

Acadia National Park, Maine, 22–24
Adirondack Mountains, N.Y.,
    121–22, 146; *see also* New York
Adirondack Plan, 192
Admiralty Island, Alaska, logging in
    eagle habitat, 236
Alabama, 81, 84, 122; mercury crisis
    closes fishing waters, 223
Alabama Conservancy, 73, 81–83,
    107
Alabama Department of Conserva-
    tion, 84
Alaska, 54, 79, 123, 165, 193, 245;
    Arctic slope, 106; forests, 248; oil,
    228
Albany, N.Y., 122
Albright, Horace, 25–27, 29, 30, 33,
    154
Albuquerque, N.Mex., 235
Aleutian Islands, Alaska, 179
Alexandria, Va., 237, 245–46
Allagash Wilderness Waterway,
    Maine, 258–63
Allanstand Cottage, Asheville, N.C.,
    15, 50–51
Allegheny Plateau, eastern United
    States, 88
American Association for Conserva-
    tion Information, 183
American Association for the

Advancement of Science, 207–8,
    211
American Automobile Association,
    145, 151
American Forest Institute, 61
American Forestry Association,
    209–11, 253
American Forests, 34n, 153n, 176n,
    185n, 210, 251, 254
American Institute of Architects,
    151; Memphis, Tenn., chapter, 244
American Nature Association, 151
American Pulpwood Association, 35
American Society of Journalists and
    Authors, formerly Society of
    Magazine Writers, 207, 225, 241
American Society of Landscape
    Architects, 25
Amory, Cleveland, 240
Anderson, Clinton, 161
Appalachia. *See* Southern Appala-
    chian Mountains
Appalachian Development Act, 162
Appalachian National Park,
    committee, 27; proposed, 71
Appalachian regional aid program,
    37, 72
Appalachian Trail, 42, 56, 94, 100,
    121, 191, 262; conference, 44; to be
    "spared" from road by tunnel, 96

Appalachian Trailway News, 42n
Arizona, 146, 160, 163, 165, 230, 235
Arkansas, 122
Asheville, N.C., 3, 6, 13–14, 16, 30,
    32, 51, 57, 77, 129
Asheville Citizen-Times, 113, 115
Asheville Gazette News, 10
Aspinall, Wayne, 161, 163–64, 190,
    232, 234
Association to Save the Little
    Tennessee, 36, 75, 128; *see also*
    Little Tennessee River
Atlanta, Ga., 61–62, 64, 177, 194, 226
Atlantic City, N.J., 133
Atlantic Monthly, 250
Attakullakulla. *See* Cherokee Indians
automobile, 98, 136, 139–40, 144–46;
    blighting influence in parks, 45;
    marvelous monster, 144; worst
    enemy of the parks, 76, 100

Baker, Lamar, 110
Balsam Range, N.C., 59
Bandelier National Monument,
    N.Mex., 100
Bangor, Maine, 262
Bankhead National Forest, Ala., 73,
    81–82
Bar Harbor, Maine, 23, 25
Barkalow, Frederick S., Jr., 123
Bartram, John, 208
Bartram, William, 6, 127
Bass Anglers Sportsman Society, 223
Battery Park Hotel, Asheville, N.C.,
    32, 33
Battle for the Wilderness, 81n, 116,
    240–45
Baxter, Percival, 262
Baxter Peak, Maine, 263
Baxter State Park, Maine, 259, 262–63
Bayou Texar, Fla., 215
Beadle, Chauncey Delos, 18
Beal, Merrill Dave, 111–12
Beall, J. D., 28–29

Beans Creek, Tenn., 69
bears, 88, 91, 109–10, 112, 121, 126,
    135, 162, 201; badly treated in
    North Carolina, 15–17; drinking
    cola as tourist attraction, 137;
    grizzly, 201; *see also* wildlife
Beaucatcher Mountain Tunnel,
    Asheville, N.C.,104
Beaver Creek watershed, Ky., 222
Becking, Rudolph W., 166
Bee Branch Scenic Area, Ala., 81–82
bees, 61, 64, 67, 69
Bell, J. Frederick, 210
Bellah, James Warner, 22
Bemis Tract, N.C., 108–10
Berea College Student Industries,
    Ky., 49
Berklund, Curt, 235
Bible, abounds in choices,186
Big Bend National Park, Tex.,154
Big Piney River, Mo., 214
Big South Fork, Cumberland River,
    Tenn.,128
Bigelow Range, Maine, 263
billboards, 134, 138, 145–47, 162,
    167–8, 244; absent on Blue Ridge
    Parkway, 55, 105; all over Florida,
    139; blight, 151; control in
    Wisconsin, 158
Biltmore Estate, N.C., 4-5, 17–18, 51;
    National Game Preserve, 15;
    School of Forestry, 9–10, 184; *see
    also* Vanderbilt, George
Biltmore Industries, 15, 32, 51
birds, 63, 65–66, 112, 253–54;
    adversely affected by chemicals
    62, 201; nurtured in Sipsey Valley,
    Ala., 83; sanctuaries rare in
    Colorado, 158; *see also* wildlife
Biscayne Bay, Fla., 215
Bitterroot Mountains, Mont., 210
Black Brothers range, N.C., 77
Black Hills, S.Dak., 146; Badlands
    and Lakes Association, 140

Black Mountain, N.C., 129
Black Warrior River, Sipsey Fork, Ala., 81
blacksmithery, 48–49, 51
Blowing Rock, N.C., 52
Blue Ridge Mountains, 3, 14, 30, 51, 55–57; front range, 114
Blue Ridge Parkway, 5, 14, 29–33, 51, 105, 118, 120–23, 148–49; greatest road in the world, 54–59; *see also* Southern Appalachian Mountains
Bluffs Lodge, Doughton Park, N.C., 58
Bogachiel watershed, Wash., 80
Bolack, Tom, 235
Bonds, Hoyt, 63–64, 67
Boone, Daniel, 70
Bowaters Southern Paper Corporation, 60–63, 66, 68–69
Boyle, Robert H., 223
Bradwell Bay, Fla., 92
Brandborg, Stewart M., 93, 99
Brasstown, N.C., 51
Breathitt, Edward T., 158–9
Brevard, N.C., 14
Bronson, Jim, 108
Brooke, Edwin, 232
Broome, Anne, 79
Broome, Harvey, 77, 79–80, 103, 110, 110-11n
Bryson City, N.C., 42, 76, 94–96
Buckspring, N.C., site of Vanderbilt family hunting lodge, 5
Bureau of the Budget, 35
Bureau of Indian Affairs, 162
Bureau of Land Management, 168, 202, 204; questionable land transactions in New Mexico, 234–35
Bureau of Outdoor Recreation, 98
Bureau of Public Roads, 74, 150, 167; *see also* Federal Highway Administration
Bureau of Reclamation, 165, 173, 221

Bureau of Sport Fisheries and Wildlife, 61–62, 64, 69, 150; *see also* U.S. Fish and Wildlife Service
Burk, Dale A., 241
Business and Society Review, 248n
Business Week, 234
Butz, Earl, 233, 237
Bybee, Ky., 49

Cabool, Mo., 214
Cabot, Colleen, 183
Cades Cove, Tenn., 29, 126
Cahalane, Victor, 65
California, 148, 159, 166, 253; open space law, 158; Natural Land and Water Reserves System, 192
California Agriculture Experiment Station, 66
Camisa, Louis, 63
Cammerer, Arno B., 20, 23, 27, 100–1
Campbell, Olive Dame, 51
Canada, 118, 121
Cannikin, Aleutian Islands, Alaska, atomic test site, 233
Canyon Village Motor Lodge, Yellowstone National Park, Wyo., 141
Cape Lookout National Seashore, N.C., 159
Carnegie Museum, Pittsburgh, Pa., 192
Carney, Champlin, 120
Carolina Mountain Club, 125
Carroll, Roy, Jr., 151
Carson, Rachel, 149, 212
Carter, Bernard T., 222
Case, Clifford, 232
Castles, John R., 250–51
Cataloochee Valley, N.C., 112–13, 125
Cate, Garth, 103
Caudill, Harry, 159
Cedar Creek, Va., 136
Center Magazine, The, 225n

Central Intelligence Agency, bigger than the law, 114
Chamberlain Lake, Maine, 261
Champion Fibre and Paper Company, generally highly regarded for forestry practices, 14
Changing Times, 133n
channel straightening, 81, 150, 182, 217, 219; *see also* dredging; U.S. Army Corps of Engineers
Chapman, David, Col., 20
Charleston, S.C., 246
Charlottesville, Va., 55
Chatooga River, Ga., 128
Chattanooga, Tenn., 19, 60, 64, 129, 138, 194
Chattanooga News-Free Press, 36, 63
Chattanooga Trout Association, 67
Cherokee, N.C., 48, 50
Cherokee Indians, 17, 39, 74, 82, 91, 113, 124, 127–28, 137, 185–86; double-walled baskets, 48; Green Corn Dance, 170; North Carolina reservation, 162; Overhill Indians, 19
Cherokee National Forest, Tenn., 108, 113, 130
Chesapeake and Ohio National Monument, 30
chestnut tree, American, 5, 6, 124
Chicago Motor Club, 151
Chickamauga Dam, Tenn., 19
Chickasaw Indians, 82
Chimney Tops, Great Smoky Mountains, 79, 110
China Syndrome, The, 212
Chorley, Kenneth, 21, 23, 26, 28
Christ, remembered at tourist stops, 137–38, 140; second coming, 186
Chrysler Corporation, 147
Church of Jesus Christ of the Latter-Day Saints, 186
Churchill, Winston, 11

Cimmaron River, N.Mex., 213
Civil War, 142, 187; Battle Above the Clouds, 138; centennial, 134
Clamshell Alliance, 211; *see also* Gettysburg, Pa.
Classification and Multiple Use Act, 202
clear-cut logging, 73, 82, 234, 253-57; defined, 248–49; environmentally pollutive, 251; likened to mining, 252; *see also* Forest Products Industry
Clement, Frank, 147
Clemson University, S.C., 120
Clepper, Henry, 254
Cliff, Edward P., 73, 84, 91, 92n, 109; under whom clear-cut logging came of age, 249–50
Coastal Management Act, N.C., 105
Cohutta Mountains, 194
Cohutta Wilderness, Ga., 129
Colonial Williamsburg, Va., 21–23, 25–26
Colorado, 158, 161, 253; Open Space Action Committee, 167–68
Colorado River, 156, 160, 163, 173, 230
Colorado Springs, Colo., 158, 163
Colorado State University, 183
Columbia Broadcasting System (CBS), 226–27, 233, 237–41, 247
Columbia River, 220–21
Combs, Bert, 148
Commerce Department, 67
Conasauga River, Ga., 129
Concord, Mass., 260
Coney Island, N.Y., 133
Conley, Clare, 227–28, 231, 233–34, 240
Connecticut, 158
conservation, 156–69; definitions, 157, 168, 172, 177; of energy, 107; of water, 162; summary of issues,

165–67; wears a thousand faces, 156; *see also* environmentalism

Consolidated Edison Company, 158

Conte, Silvio, 241

Cooper, John Sherman, 147

Cooper, Prentice, 20

Copper Hill, Tenn., 126

Cornwell, George, 217, 255

Cottam, Clarence, 65

Council on Environmental Quality, 248

Cox Enterprises Incorporated, 226

crafts, 46–53; craft business established at Biltmore Industries, 15; demonstrations on Blue Ridge Parkway, 58. *See* weaving; pottery; blacksmithery

Craggy Mountains, N.C., 77

Cranberry Back Country, W.Va., 88, 89

Cranston, Alan, 224

Craters of the Moon National Monument, Idaho, 99

Cross, Bob, 183

Crowder Investment Company, 235

Cumberland Plateau, Tenn., 68, 82, 129

Cumberland River, Tenn. *See* Big South Fork

D.C. Gazette, 244

Daily Missoulian, 241, 250

Dale, E.M., 30

damming, 38, 74–75, 81, 83, 114, 128–29, 156–57, 160, 165, 173, 217, 221, 228

Daniels, Josephus, 28

Daughters of the American Revolution, 36

Davis, Kenneth P., 249–50

Davis, Willis P., 20, 26

Day, Sam, 243

Dayton, Ohio, 226

DDT, 69, 218; *see also* pesticides

deer, 83, 88, 91, 117, 119, 125, 253; fawn farm at Pisgah National Forest, 15; as tourist attraction, 137; *see also* wildlife

Defenders of Wildlife, 65, 206n

DeHart, Ray, 121

Delaware River, 183, 223

Democratic National Committee, 160

Department of Agriculture, 9, 69, 86, 198, 219, 227; Forest Service transfer to Department of the Interior considered, 203; secretaries, 70, 87, 165, 198

Department of the Interior, 69, 86, 115, 128, 160, 164, 171, 198, 227, 235, 246; Forest Service transfer to Department of the Interior considered, 203; secretaries, 105, 155, 165

Des Moines Register and Tribune, 250

Dickerman, Ernest, 110–11n

dieldrin, 218; *see also* pesticides

Dimmick, Ralph, 62, 65

Dingell, John, 150, 161

Disney, Walt, 134

Disneyland, Calif. *See* tourist industry

Dolly Sods Scenic Area, W.Va., 88, 89

Dominick, Steve, 183

Dorr, George B., 25

Doster, Merrimon R., 115

Doughton Park, N.C., 31, 58

Douglas, William O., 79, 252

Dow Chemical Company, 213

Downing, Robert L., 120

Doyle, William E., 85

dredging, damages fishing streams, 150; *see also* channel straightening; U.S. Army Corps of Engineers

Droop Mountain State Park, W.Va., 121

Drury, Newton B., 20

Duck River, Tenn., 114
Duffy's Tavern, program, 223
Duke Power Company, 126–27

Eagle Lake, Maine, 261
Eakin, J. Ross, 20
Earlham College, Ind., 185
Early, Jubal, 135
Earth Day, 185, 188, 207
East Bay, Fla., 215
East Meadow Creek, Colo., 85
eastern panther. *See* panther
Eastern Wilderness Areas Act, 92–93, 110, 129; Omnibus Eastern Wilderness Bill, 194
Echota, ancient Cherokee Indian metropolis. *See* Cherokee Indians
Ecological Society of America, 102
Edey, Marion, 238
Egler, Frank E., 149–50
Eisenhower, Dwight, 161
El Cacique, Puerto Rico, 92
El Paso, Tex., 235
Elk Park, N.C., 52
Ellenberg, Edward G., 110n
Emerson, Ralph Waldo, 172, 195
Emory University, Atlanta, Ga., 72
endangered species, panther, 122, 160, 199, 211, 250; *see also* Endangered Species Act
Endangered Species Act, 107, 113, 115 , 123, 128, 191; *see also* endangered species
endrin, 218; *see also* pesticides
"Environmental Action Line," *Field & Stream*, 228
Environmental Action, organization, 231, 247
Environmental Defense Fund, 76
Environmental Teach-In Week, 185
environmentalism, 206–12; definition, 116; environmental writing, 207; fishermen as activists, 223; *see also* conservation

erosion, 3, 7, 12–13, 70–71, 77, 83n, 96, 109, 111–12, 126, 196, 217, 220, 248, 251, 256, 263
Escambia Bay, Fla., 215
Eureka, Calif., 166
Everglades National Park, Fla., 79, 117, 125, 139, 165
Evins, Joe, 40
Evison, Boyd, 118, 123, 125
Experts' Book of Freshwater Fishing, 213n, 221

Faces of the Wilderness, 79
Fairfax, Va., 238
Fallon, George, 40
Falls Branch Scenic Area, Tenn., 92, 108-10, 111n
Farber, Barry, 241
Federal Highway Administration, 111n, 162–63; *see also* Bureau of Public Roads
Federal Highway Beautification Act of 1965, 167
Federal Highway Funds, 158, 167–68
Federal Power Commission, 104
Federation of Garden Clubs, 36
Fellowship, 185–87
fertilizers, chemical; adversely affect bird populations, 62, 201; affect fish, 217–18
Field & Stream, 60, 60n, 61, 69, 181, 181n, 189n, 215, 225–42, 247–48, 250
First Amendment to the U.S. Constitution Bill of Rights, 226, 246
fish kills, 69, 213–24
Fisher, Scott, 184
Flattau, Ed, 239, 247
Flattop Peak, Va., 57
Florida, 84, 119, 122, 139, 147, 194; Keys, 215; perhaps most fish kills in America, 214–16
Floyd Plateau, Va., 31

Fonda, Jane, 212

Fontana, N.C., 76, 95, 103n; Conservation Roundup, 103, 103n, 107, 116; Dam, 95; Lake, 44, 95

Food and Agriculture Act, 161

Ford, Edsel, 27

Ford, Gerald, 105–6

Ford Motor Corporation, 147

Forest and Stream Magazine, 119

Forest Hill Park, Ohio, 22

forest products industry, 7, 24, 32, 37, 72–73, 81, 83n, 93, 130, 154, 156–57, 163, 193, 218, 220, 228–29, 234; dominant use theory failure, 196–205; impact on fish, 217; impact on redwoods, 166; impact on proposed wilderness areas, 90; pesticide use, 60–69, 82; "timber mining," 210; timber shortage, 199; *see also* clear-cut logging; forestry; logging

Forest Service, 9, 12–13, 15, 30, 38, 44, 73, 77, 81, 84–89, 92–93, 97, 99, 108–10, 110–11n, 114, 119, 122, 125, 162–65, 173, 177, 193, 197, 202–4, 210, 212, 219–20, 237–38, 248, 250–52, 255; at Admiralty Island, Alaska, 236; establishment in east, 71; influence zones, 90; listening sessions, 72, 107; panther habitat study, 120; waste, 80; *see also* forestry

forestry, profession, 7, 9, 248-57; theory 3, 8, 182; *see also* forest products industry; Forest Service

Forked Deer River, Tenn., 220

Forsberg, Franklin S., 227, 233

Fort Leonard Wood, Mo., 214

Fort Loudoun, Tenn., 39–40, 75

Four Corners, 106

Freedom of Information Law, 65

Freeman, Orville L., 73, 92n

French, John, 189

French Broad River, N.C., 5, 14;

Upper French Broad River, 75, 104

Friends of the Earth, 239

Frome, Michael, 225–45, 247

Front Royal, Va., 55

Frost, Robert, 181, 184

Fry, Hubert, 67

Gales Mine Falls, N.C., 121

Gardiner, Mont., 25

Garrison, William Lloyd, 247

Gatlinburg, Tenn., 29, 50, 93–94, 137

Gauley Ranger District, Monongahela National Forest, W.Va., 89

Gee Creek Wilderness, Tenn., 129

General Motors Corporation, 147

George Washington National Forest, Va., 58

George Washington University Magazine, 170n

Georgia, 56, 59, 95, 122, 129

Georgia Conservancy Newsletter, 108

Georgia-Pacific Corporation, 169

Gettysburg, Pa., 133, 136, 142, 161; *see also* Civil War; tourist industry

"Gettysburg Address," 135

Gift from the Hills, autobiography of Lucy Morgan, 47

Glacier National Park, Mont., 153–54

Gold Coast, Fla., 215

Goodrich, Frances, 15, 50–51

Goodwin, John, 52

Gordon, Ladd, 213

Gore, Albert, 40

Gottschalk, John, 69

Graham, Jamie Maxtone, 207

Graham County, N.C., 108

Grand Canyon National Park, Ariz., 155–58, 163, 165, 173, 230, 245

Grand Tetons, Wyo., 22, 142; Jackson Lake Lodge, 23

Grandfather Mountain, N.C., 29–30

Gray, Asa, 6, 127

Great Gulf Wild Area, N.H., 87, 193

Great Lakes, 84

Great Smokies Recreation Region, proposed, 114
Great Smoky Mountains, 3, 14, 19, 22, 24, 26, 59, 79, 112, 117, 120–22, 125-27, 129, 146, 162, 164, 173, 194; trans-mountain road, 42–44, 94–97, 100, 102–4; tourist attraction, 137, 142; *see also* Great Smoky Mountains National Park
Great Smoky Mountains Hiking Club, 77
Great Smoky Mountains National Park, 17, 20, 21, 28–29, 33, 43, 50, 55, 75–76, 93, 101, 103, 111, 117, 120, 122–25, 130, 137, 154–55; entrance fee considered, 113; panther sighting, 117, 124; purchase fund campaign, 27; *see also* Great Smoky Mountains,
Greeley, Horace, 189, 194
Green Mountains, Vt., 122, 148, 181
Greensboro Daily News, 142
Greer, Taft, 49
gun-control, 232–33, 239
Guyot, Arnold Henry, 172

Hall, E. Raymond, 66
Hamilton, Mont., 210
Hanna's Handbook of Agricultural Chemicals , 66
Harnik, Peter, 247
Harpers Ferry, W.Va., 177
Harrisburg, Pa., 135
Hartzog, George B., Jr., 96–99
Harvard University, Cambridge, 6
Hassler, Alfred, 186
Hathaway, Stan, 105–6
Hayes, Gail, 231
Haywood County, N.C., 126
Haywood County, Tenn., 112
Hearst media chain, 226
Hells Canyon, Idaho, dam, 223, 228
Hendersonville Times-News, 130
Hensley, Bea, 51

herbicides, 67–68, 82, 146, 149–50, 200, 217–19, 251–52; *see also* pesticides; 2,4-D; 2,4,5-T
Hermach, George, 77
Hickel, Walter J., 100
Highway Action Coalition, 231
highways, 76, 157–58, 161, 163; interstate system, 144–47; *see also* Federal Highway Administration
hiking, 43–45; walking most popular form of outdoor recreation, 42; *see also* trails
Hillis, J. J., 67–68
Hiwassee Land Company, 60, 63, 67
Hoar, Edward, 260
Hodges, Luther, 145, 148
Hoey, Clyde, 20
Hoh watershed, Wash., 80
Holiday, 156n
Holshouser, James, 105
Holt, Rinehart & Winston, 226–27, 247
Hoover, Herbert, 26
Horsepasture River, N.C., 127
House, Homer, 10
House Appropriations Committee, public works subcommittee, 40
House Interior Appropriations Subcommittee, 161
House Interior Committee, 85, 161, 164, 232
Housing and Urban Development, 198
Houston, Mo., 214
Houts, Buddy, 63
Hudson, Marzine, 64–65
Hudson River Fishermen's Association, 223
Hudson River, N.Y., 158
Hudson River, The, 223
Humble Oil Company, 169
Humpback Rocks, Va., 56
hunting, 241
Hyde Park, N.Y., 19

Ickes, Harold L., 19–21
Idaho, 235, 243
Idaho Wildlife Federation, 232
Imperial Collection of Audubon Animals, 65
Independence Hall, Philadelphia, 51
Indiana Dunes National Lakeshore, Ind., 229
indians, 134, 170; government thrusting industry upon, 174. *See* Chickasaw; Cherokee; Sioux; Navajo
Interior Department. *See* Department of the Interior
Intermountain Observer, 243
International Paper Company, 254
interstate. *See* highways
Izaak Walton League, 94, 150

Jacks River, Cohutta Wilderness, Ga., 129
James River, Va., 56
Jefferson, Thomas, 39, 136, 226, 246
Jefferson National Forest, Va., 58
Job Corps, 180
John C. Campbell Folk School, Brasstown, N.C., 51
Johnson, Lady Bird, 51
Johnson, Lyndon B., 34–41, 156, 159–61, 163, 166, 197
Journal of Forestry, 251, 256
Joyce Kilmer Memorial Forest, N.C., 73–74, 90–91
Joyce Kilmer-Slickrock Wilderness, N.C., 91–92, 92n, 129; proposals to establish, 74, 90

Kana-Gatoga. *See* Cherokee Indians
Kansas, State Biological Survey, 66
Kelsey, Harlan P., 30
Kennedy, John and Jacqueline, 140
Kentucky, 75, 159, 179, 222; rendered desolate by strip mining, 76; rewarded for complying with

federal anti-billboard provisions, 148
Kentucky Hills Industries, Pine Knot, Ky., 52
Keowee River, N.C., 127
Keowee-Toxaway area, N.C., 126–27
Kephart, Horace, 70
Kerr, Robert S., 163
Kilmer, Joyce, 91. *See* Joyce Kilmer-Slickrock Wilderness
Kimball, Thomas L., 209
King, Martin Luther, 176, 178
Kirchner, Leda and Leslie, 15
Kirwan, Michael, 40, 161
Klamath, Calif., 166
Knife Ridge, Appalachian Trail, Maine, 262–63
Knoxville News-Sentinel, 40, 43, 110
Knoxville, Tenn., 20, 27, 103, 110n, 129

Laitin, Joseph, 41
Lake Apopka, Fla., 216
Lake Chelan National Recreation Area, Wash., 113
Lake Erie, 40, 230
Lake Jocassee, N.C., 127
Lake Michigan, 218
Lake Powell, Utah, 214
Lake Superior, 146, 191
Lake Umsaskis, Maine, 258
Land and Water Conservation Fund Act, 160–61, 163, 167
land use options, 105, 115, 158, 204, 228; H.R. 3510 legislation, 106–7
Lane, Franklin L, 153
Langford, George, 89–90
Langton, Henry, 62–63
Laura Spelman Rockefeller Memorial Foundation, 20–21, 27. *See* Great Smoky Mountains National Park
Laurentian Mountains, Quebec, Canada, 119

League of Conservation Voters, 231, 238
Lee, Robert E., 135
Lemmon, Jack, 212
Lenoir, N.C., 28
Leopold, Aldo, 122, 250
Lewis, Willard, 235
Lexington Herald, 37
Licking, Mo., 214
Lietch, Bill, 183
Lincoln, Abraham, 135–36
Linville Falls, N.C., 22, 29–33
Linville Gorge Wilderness, Pisgah National Forest, N.C., 29, 30, 77, 87, 193
Little, Brown & Company, 226
Little Buffalo River, N.C., 108–9
Little Carpenter. *See* Attakullakulla
Little Tennessee River, 113–16, 118, 165; Fontana Dam, 95; only home of snail darter, 115, 127–28; Tellico Dam 34–41, 74–75, 115, 127–28, 223; *see also* Association to Save the Little Tennessee; Tennessee Valley Authority
Loch Ness monster, 120, 124
Loeb, Henry, 178
logging, 7, 23, 32; along Keowee River, 127; *see also* forest products industry; clear-cut logging
Longstreet, James, 135
Looking Glass Falls and Looking Glass Rock, N.C., 14
Lookout Mountain, Tenn., 138
Los Alamos, N.Mex., 100
Los Angeles *Times-Mirror* Company, 226
Louisiana, 122
Louisiana Conservationist, 254
Lowman, George, 122–23, 125
lumber. *See* forest products industry

McGrady, Patrick M., Jr., 225, 241–42

McGuire, John R., 84, 87, 110, 251
McIlwain, Jerry, 73
McIntyre, O.O., 24
McKay, Alex, 122
McKellar, Kenneth, 20
Maggie Valley, N.C., 17, 137
Maine, 56, 84, 121, 194, 258–63; Natural Resources Council, 263; Wildlands Law, 263
Maine Woods, The, 258–60
Maloney, Andy, 44
Mammals of North America, 66
Mammoth Cave National Park, Ky., 102, 165
Mann, James, 114
Marion , Va., 77
Mark Twain, pen name of author Sam Clemens, 176–78, 208
Martin, Edsel, 52–53
mass media, 225–47; big business, 226; channels of information controlled, 243; deeply committed to syndrome of growth, 243
Massachusetts, 121, 158
Massanutten Mountain, Va., 56
Mather, Stephen T., 25, 27, 153–54, 160
Mattil, O.J., 50
Meade, George C., 135
Memphis, Tenn., 178, 244–45
Memphis Architecture, 244
Merson, Alan, 232
Mesa Verde National Park, Colo., 25
Metcalf, Lee, 150, 161
Miami Beach, Fla., 215, 226
Michaux, André, 127
Michigan Natural Resources Commission, 191
Midland, Mich., 213
Midwest, 178; Great Plains, 94
Mill Creek, Calif., 166
Miller, D. S., 49
Milwaukee Journal, 96

Minckler, Leon, 255–56
Mineral King, U.S. Supreme Court case, 252
mining, 129, 154, 161, 217, 222, 228–29; coal, 89; temporarily exempt from Wilderness Act, 164; *see also* strip mining
Mississippi River, 71, 87, 193
Missouri, 122; Clean Water Commission, 214
Moldenhaur, Joseph, 259
Mondale, Walter, 232
Monongahela National Forest, W.Va., 88–90
Montana, 150, 163, 236; Department of Fish and Game, 222
moonshine, 16, 31
Moosehead Lake, Maine, 260–61
Moosehorn National Wildlife Refuge and Moosehorn Wilderness, Maine, 86
Morgan, Lucy, 46, 51
Mormon Church. *See* Church of Jesus Christ of the Latter-Day Saints
Morse, Wayne, 230–31
Morton, J. Sterling, 8
Morton, Rogers C. B., 228–29, 235, 246
Moses, 186
Moses, Robert, 151
Mostek, Raymond, 151
Mother Goose, as tourist attraction, 135, 142
Mount Cadillac, Maine, 25
Mount Desert Island, Maine, 25
Mount Katahdin, Maine, 259–60, 262–63
Mount Mitchell, N.C., 77, 113, 129, 130; deserves national park status, 113; purchase unit, 13
Mount Pisgah, N.C., 3, 5, 8, 14, 58
Mount Rogers, Va., 57

Mount Rushmore Memorial, S.Dak., 140
Mountain Area Management Act, 109; considered in North Carolina, 105
Mountain View Hotel, Gatlinburg Tenn., 29
mountaineers, 12–13, 15, 48–53, 56–57, 124; role in establishment of national forests in the east, 11
Muhammad, 186
Muir, John, 183, 208

Nantahala Mountains and National Forest, N.C., 73, 109, 113, 117, 129–30; trees cut on slopes, 72
Nashville, Tenn., 61
National Audubon Society, 94; of Illinois, 151; of western Pennsylvania, 149
National Cemetery at Gettysburg, Pa., 135
National Communicable Disease Center, 66
National Council of State Garden Clubs, 249
National Environmental Policy Act, 76, 107, 112, 224
National Forest Development Program, 197
National Forest Products Association, 108
National Forest Wild Areas Bill, 87n
national monuments, 85, 93, 133–34, 154
National Park Service, 5, 23–24, 27, 29, 38, 43–45, 57–58, 66, 76, 80, 85, 93–100, 107, 112–13, 118, 120, 125–26, 129, 134, 140–41, 161, 163, 167, 173, 177, 263; "Back Country Travel in the National Park System," booklet, 99; Blue Ridge Parkway best run unit, 54;

National Park Service, *Continued*
dragging its feet on wilderness,
193; golden anniversary, 153–55;
shabbiness, 143; should push for
elimination of Schedule C
Classifications, 155; symbolizes
the nation itself, 154; wilderness
"thresholds," 98
National Parks, 70n, 124n
National Parks Association, 94, 99
National Parks and Conservation
Association. *See* National Parks
Association
National Pest Control Association,
66
National Roadside Council, 151;
should be developed to coordi-
nate councils in all states, 152
National Science Foundation, 166
National Shooting Sports Founda-
tion, 234
National Speleological Society, 102
National System of Interstate
Highways. *See* highways
National Timber Supply Act, 198;
fought over during 1969, 108
National Trails System Act, 191
National Wild and Scenic Rivers
System. *See* Wild and Scenic
Rivers System
National Wilderness Preservation
System, 77, 81, 85, 92, 94, 99,
164–65, 190, 193
National Wildlife, 172
National Wildlife Federation, 37, 209
national wildlife refuges, 85, 99, 164,
179
Natural Bridge, Va., 136–37
Natural History Museum of Kansas,
66
Natural Resources Council of
America, 196n
Natural and Scenic Rivers System,

N.C., 104; *see also* Wild and Scenic
Rivers System
Nature Conservancy, 94, 109–10
Navajo Indians, 235
Nelson, Gaylord, 158, 161, 168
Netherby, Steve, 213n
Neuberger, Maurine, 147
Neuberger, Richard, 145
Nevada, 147
Neversink River, N.Y., 183
Nevins, Allan, 134–35
New Brunswick, Canada, 119, 122,
261
New England, 59, 70
New Hampshire, 84, 120–21
New Jersey, 158
New Mexico, Game and Fish
Department, 213; questionable
land transactions, 234–36
New River, N.C., 104–5, 128
New York, N.Y., 189, 227, 238
New York, 148, 158, 192; State
Health Department, 183; State
Thruway Authority, 148; *see also*
Adirondack Mountains
New York Times, 96, 250
Nixon, Richard, 197–98
Noonan, Patrick F., 110
Norris, Kenneth, 192–93
North Carolina, 3, 24, 27–28, 30, 39,
44, 46, 54, 71, 75, 90, 94–96, 100,
104–5, 113, 118, 128, 136, 148, 162;
Department of Natural Resources,
126; Highway Department, 95;
State Museum of Natural History,
123; Wildlife Resources Commis-
sion, 17, 137
North Carolina State University, 123
North Cascades National Park,
Wash., 113; federal transfer of
land jurisdiction, 107
Northeast Regional Pest Coordina-
tors, 66

Northwest Trading Post, N.C., 58
nuclear facilities, 114, 212
Nusbaum, Jesse, 25

Oak Ridge, Tenn., 95
Obed River, Tenn., 128
Oberheu, John, 62, 64
Obion River, Tenn., 220
Ocala, Fla., 139
Ocala National Forest, Fla., 139
Oconaluftee Visitor Center, N.C., 55
oconee bells, rare flowers, 127
Office of Economic Opportunity, 52
Office of Management and Budget.
    See Bureau of the Budget
Ohio River, 40
Ohio State University, 188
oil spill, 214
Oklahoma, 122
Oklawaha River, Fla., 138
Old Faithful, Yellowstone National
    Park, Wyo., 80
old-growth forests, 77, 252–53
Olmsted, Frederick Law, 4, 17
Olmsted, Fritz, followed Gifford
    Pinchot into forestry, 9
Olympic Peninsula and National
    Park, Wash., 80
O'Neill, Michael J., 234
1080 compound, used in predator
    control, 161
Orange County, Fla., 216
Orange County Commmunity
    College, N.Y., 183
Ornithological Society of Colorado
    Springs, 158
Otter Creek, W.Va., 88–89
Ottinger, Richard, 36, 40
Ouachita Mountains, 84, 194
Outdoor Life, 226
Outdoor Writers Association of
    America, 237
Overton Park, Memphis, Tenn., 178,
    244

Ozark Mountains, 84, 122, 194; Big
    Piney River, 214

Pacific Crest Trail, 191
Pacific Logging Congress of 1966,
    250
Pacific Northwest, 163, 221, 255;
    forests 248
Pacific Ocean, 221
Pack, Arthur N., 151
Page, Warren, 234
Paley, William S., 239, 247
Palm Springs Desert Museum,
    Calif., 208
panther, 117–26, 130, 201; see also
    endangered species; wildlife
Parents' Magazine, 140
Parkway Craft Center, N.C., 58
Parris, John, 112–13
Pastore, John, 239–40
Peaks of Otter, Va., 51, 56; Lodge, 57
Pearl, Milton, 198–99
Pecora, William J., 229
Pedernales River, Tex., 38
Pell, Claiborne, 232
Penland School of Crafts, N.C., 46;
    asked to weave tablecloths for
    Independence Hall, 51
Penn, William, 194
Pennsylvania, 122, 150, 192
Penobscot River, Maine, 26
Pensacola, Fla., 215
pentachlorophenol, wood preserva-
    tive, 214
Percy, Charles, 232
pesticides, 60–69, 146, 160–61, 171,
    200, 217–20, 228, 252; must be
    controlled, 173, never successful
    in totally eliminating rodents, 201;
    see also herbicides
Pesticides and the Living Landscape, 66
Petrified Forest National Park, Ariz.,
    99
phosphide gas, 67

Pi Beta Phi, Arrowcraft Shop, Gatlinburg, Tenn., 50
Pickett, George, 136
Piedmont area, 54, 57
Pillsbury Island, Maine, 261
Pinchot, Gifford, 4, 7, 10, 13–14, 70–71, 156, 160, 167, 176, 178; defines conservation, 172; differences with Schenck, 11
Pine Knot, Ky., 52
Pisgah National Forest, 16–17, 30, 57, 71, 113, 130, 137; Pink Beds, 7, 10–11, 14; Pisgah Ledge, 15, 58; purchase unit, 13; Ranger District, 14; *see also* Vanderbilt, George W.
Pisgah National Forest Inn, 15, 58
Plato, 259
Platt, Robert B., 72
Platts, William S., 220
Pleasant Hill, Ky., 187
Pocahontas County, W.Va., 121
Pocantico Hills, N.Y., Rockefeller family home, 24
Pocono Mountains, Pa., 146
Point Park, Lookout Mountain, Tenn., 138
Point Reyes Bird Observatory, Calif., 253
Polis, Joe, 260–62
pollution, 83–84, 96, 110, 196, 207, 211, 228, 238; air, 81, 126, 180, 203; antipollution suits, 223; chemical, 126; environmental, 171, 219, 250–51; industrial pollution, 72, 168; noise, 126; particulate, 90; sewage, 214–16; visual, 90; water, 81, 125, 162, 180, 203, 224, 233, 244; we can't afford it, 115; workers report employers' violations, 223
Poole, Daniel, 209
Popular Library, 247
Porcupine Mountains Wilderness State Park, Mich., 191
Port Jervis, N.Y., 183

Portsmouth, Va., 226
Potomac River, Md., 328
pottery, 49
Prigmore, Charles S., 73, 107
Princeton University, Princeton, N.J., 172
Public Health Service, 66; Rock Mountain Laboratory, 210
Public Law Land Review Commission, 196n, 198, 202, 204
Puerto Rico, 93
Pupfish National Monument, Calif., proposed, 224

Qualla Arts and Crafts Mutual, 49
Quarterly News Bulletin, 125

Raccoon Mountain, Tenn., 114
Radio Corporation of America (RCA), 226
Raleigh News and Observer, 28
Rampart Dam, Alaska, 230
Randolph, Jennings, 107
Random House, 226
Rapid City, S.Dak., 140
"Rate Your Candidate," *Field & Stream* feature, 229–34, 237, 239
Reader's Digest, 250
Redevelopment Land Agency, 179
Redwood Creek, Calif., proposed as part of national park, 166
Redwood National Park, Calif., 166; demand for, 158
redwoods, 165–67, 245, 248; make Rockefeller speechless, 22; tallest known, 166
Reuss, Henry, 233
Reynolds, John M., 77
Richmond, Va., 56
rivers. *See* Wild and Scenic Rivers System
Roadless Area Review and Evaluation, 92
Roan Mountain, 129

Roanoke, Va., 56, 136
Robbinsville, N.C., 73–74, 91, 104, 108
Robinson, Gordon, 256
Robinson Terminal Warehouse Corporation, 246
Rock City, Lookout Mountain, Tenn., 138
Rockefeller, Abby Aldrich, 26
Rockefeller, David, 29–32, 58
Rockefeller, John D., 20
Rockefeller, John D. III, 25
Rockefeller, John D., Jr., 20–33, 58
Rockefeller, Laura Spelman, Great Smoky Mountains National Park established in her memory, 20
Rockefeller, Laurance, 25
Rockefeller, Martha Baird, 29, 33, 59
Rockefeller, Nelson, 25–26, 192
Rockefeller Center, New York, N.Y., 26
Rockfish Gap, Va., 55–56
Rocky Mountains, 59, 70, 84, 93, 113, 118, 125, 129, 202; forests, 248
Roosevelt, Franklin D., 19, 161
Roosevelt, Theodore, 12, 70, 119, 153, 157, 160–61, 165, 201
Ross, Smith, 52
Ross Lake National Recreation Area, Wash., 113
Route 100 Association of Vermont, 148
Ruby Falls, Lookout Mountain, Tenn., 138
Rudd, Robert, 66
Russell Sage Foundation, Southern Highland Division, 51

Salmon River, Idaho, 220
Salt Lake City Deseret News, 186
Samson, Jack, 234, 236–42
San Francisco, Calif., site of 1967 Sierra Club wilderness conference, 85, 97

San Juan River, Colo., 214, 235
Sangre de Cristo Mountains, N.Mex., 146
Santa Fe, N.Mex., 235
Sargent, John Singer, portraits displayed at Biltmore Estate, 17
Saylor, John P., 194, 230
Schenck, Carl Alwin, 9–11, 14, 183
Schlapfer, Ted, 108
Schultz, E. W., 109
Schwartz, Carl H., Jr., 36, 39, 41
Science, 210–11
Scott, Ray, 223
Scripps-Howard, 178, 244
Seabrook, N.H., 211
Sears, Paul, 177, 224
Seeley, Ted, 16
Selway-Bitterroot Wilderness, Mont., 173
Senate Committee on Energy and National Resources. *See* Senate Committee on Interior Affairs
Senate Committee on Interior Affairs, 160
Senate Public Works Committee, 114
Senate Subcommittee on Communications, 239
Seney National Wildlife Refuge and Wilderness, Mich., 86
Sequoia National Park, Calif., 154, 165
Sequoyah, created written Cherokee language, 39, 74, 113, 128
Sevin, 183; *see also* pesticides
Shahn, Ben, 46
Shakertown, Ky., 187
Sharptop Peak, Va., 57
Shaw, Luther, 104
Shenandoah National Park, Va., 55, 120, 122, 165
Shenandoah River Valley, Va., 30, 56, 136, 146
Shining Rock Wilderness, Pisgah National Forest, N.C., 77, 87, 193

Sierra Club, 44, 94, 163, 256; *Mineral King* case, 252; wilderness conferences, 85, 87, 97

Sieur de Mont National Monument, Maine, 25

Signal Mountain, Tenn., 60, 64, 67–68

Sikes, Bob, 233

Silcox, Ferdinand A., 203–4

Silent Spring, 212

Silver Springs, Fla., 138–39

Sioux Indians, 140

Sipsey River, 77, 83

Sipsey Wilderness, Ala., 77, 82–83; legislation to establish, 84

Skyline Drive, Shenandoah National Park, Va., 55–56

Slickrock Creek, N.C., 74, 91–92, 129

Slickrock-Joyce Kilmer Wilderness Area. *See* Joyce Kilmer-Slickrock Wilderness

Sliding Rock Falls, N.C., 14

Smail, John, 253

Smith, Anthony W., 99

Smith, David M., 251

Smith, Newt, 74

Smith, Sam, 245

Smithsonian, 79n, 117n

Smithsonian Institution, Washington, D.C., 51–52

snail darter. *See* Little Tennessee River

Snake River, Idaho, 221, 223, 228

Snowbird Mountains, N.C., 108–9

Society of American Foresters, 36, 249

Society of Colonial Dames, 116

Society of Magazine Writers. *See* American Society of Journalists and Authors

Soil Conservation Service, 168, 219

"Song of the Open Road," 144

Soper Mountain, Maine, 261

South Carolina, 114, 122, 128

Southern Appalachian Mountains, 13, 72, 76–77, 84, 91, 103, 106, 113, 118, 120, 122, 124–26, 128, 162, 174, 194, 222, 248; forests 248; need large-scale acquisitions by Forest Service, 109; springtime, 6; *see also* Blue Ridge Parkway

Southern Appalachian Slope National Recreation Area, proposed, 114

Southern Highland Handicraft Guild, 15, 58

Southern Living, 46n

South's Third Forest —How It Can Meet Future Needs, The, 254

Sport Fishing Institute, 150

Sports Afield, 226

Spruce Knob-Seneca Rock National Recreation Area, W.Va., 90

Spruce Pine, N.C., 51

Squires, Mark, 20

St. John's River, Maine, 261

Stamper, Lottie, 48

Standing Indian Natural Area, N.C., 72

Stansbury, Jeff, 239, 247

Stephens, Joe, 237

Sternberg, Irma O., 244–45

Storm King Mountain, Hudson River, N.Y., 158

Strangers in High Places, 19n, 103, 227

Streetman, Clarence, 60–61, 63, 69

strip mining, 76, 81, 222, 234; controlled in Kentucky, 159; encouraged by Tennessee Valley Authority, 75, 114, 162; *see also* mining

Stuckey's, roadside shop chain, 135

Student Conservation Program, 44; newsletter 43

Stupka, Arthur, 25

Suhler, John, 242

Sunburst Lumber Company, 14
Supreme Court of the United States, 128, 252
Sutton, V. J., 61
Swain County, N.C., 76, 95–96
Swannanoa, N.C., 53
Syracuse University, Syracuse, N.Y., 255

Tampa Bay, Fla., 215
Tarrytown, N.Y., 22, 24, 31–32
Taylor, Roy A., 104, 129
Tellico Dam. *See* Little Tennessee River
Tellico Plains, Tenn., 73, 91–92, 104, 108
Tellico uplands, Tenn., 113
Telos Lake, Maine, 260
Tennessee, 24, 27–28, 44, 94, 100, 112, 137; billboards, 146–47; Game and Fish Commission, 60–61, 63, 67, 220; pesticide use, 60–69; political leadership sterile, 178
Tennessee Beekeepers Association, 67–68
Tennessee Farm Bureau Federation, 36
Tennessee Livestock Association, 36
Tennessee Outdoor Advertising Association, 146
Tennessee River, Moccasin Bend, 138
Tennessee Valley Authority, 36–37, 44, 74–76, 95, 104, 107, 113–16, 127, 128, 162, 165, 173, 221; exemplifies bureaucracy unleashed, 35; serious challenge to sound land use, 114; *see also* Little Tennessee River
Teton River, Wyo., dam, 223
Tetons. *See* Grand Tetons
Texaco, 135
Thoreau, Henry David, 194, 258–63
Thorsen, Del W., 109

Time, 225
Time Incorporated, 226, 239
Tittabawassee River, Mich., 213
Tocks Island Dam, Del., 223
Toe River Valley, N.C., 47
tourist industry, 25, 115, 148, 162; attractions, 134–35, 142; Disneyland, 133; *see also* Gettysburg
Towell, William E., 103, 209, 253
Townsend, Tenn., 42
toxaphene, 218; *see also* pesticides
Toxaway River, N.C., 127
trails, 56–57, 82, 88–89, 91, 97, 191, 263; motor, 98; *see also* hiking
trans-mountain road. *See* Great Smoky Mountains
"Trees," 73, 91
Trout Unlimited, 223
Trueblood, Ted, 236
Tryon, N.C., 103
Tuskegee, Tenn., Cherokee Indian village, 39, 74, 128
TVA. *See* Tennessee Valley Authority
2, 4-D, 69, 82; *see also* pesticides
2, 4, 5-T, 69, 73, 82; *see also* pesticides
Tyson's Corner, Va., 245

Udall, Morris, 163
Udall, Stewart L., 45, 96–97, 160, 164
Unaka Purchase Unit, N.C., 13
Unicoi Mountains, Tenn., 73
United Society of Believers in Christ's Second Appearance, 187
U.S. Air Force, 62
U.S. Army Corps of Engineers, 107, 128–29, 165, 221, 228; *see also* channel straightening; dredging
U.S. Chamber of Commerce, 106
U.S. Department of Labor, 52
U.S. Department of Natural Resources, 203

U.S. Fish and Wildlife Service, 66, 107, 120, 171, 202; *see also* Bureau of Sport Fisheries and Wildlife
U.S. Forest Service. *See* Forest Service
U.S. Geological Survey, 229
U.S. Potash Company, 26
University of California, 192; Davis campus, 66
University of Florida, 217, 255
University of Georgia, 216
University of Kansas, 66
University of Montana, 183–84, 210
University of Oregon, 193
University of Tennessee, 62, 128, 206
University of Wisconsin, 183, 208
University of Wyoming, 183
Upper French Broad (River) Defense Association, 75
Utah, 179
Utah State University, 181

Vander Jagt, Guy, 239
Vanderbilt, Cornelius, 3
Vanderbilt, Edith, 51; establishes Biltmore Industries, 15; gives land to government, 14
Vanderbilt, George Washington, 3, 7–8, 11, 18, 58; *see also* Biltmore Estate; Pisgah National Forest,
Venable, Sam, 111
Versailles, palace near Paris, France, 22
Veterans of Foreign Wars, 91
Virgin Islands, site of national park, 54
Virginia, 54, 148, 232
Vista, 258n
voles, 60–61, 63, 65–67

Wagon Road Gap, N.C., 14
Walden, 259–60
Waldens Ridge Sportsmen's Club, Tenn., 67

walking. *See* trails; hiking
Wall Street, New York industrial district, 222
Wallace, George C., 77
Warm Springs, Ga., 19
Washington, D.C., 54, 94, 100, 103, 114, 147, 179, 222, 227, 238; site of 1971 Sierra Club wilderness conference, 87
Washington Post, 211, 245–46
Washingtonian, 54n
Water Quality Act, 161, 224
Water Resources Planning Act, 161
Waterrock Knob, N.C., 59
watersheds, 80, 183, 204, 222; protected by law in Kentucky, 158; Weeks Law enacted in 1911 to protect, 93
Waukegan News-Sun, 146
Waynesboro, Va., 55
weaving, 47, 52
Webster Brook, Maine, 262
Wee Loch Craft Shop, N.C., 52
Week on the Concord and Merrimack Rivers, A, 259
Weeks Law of 1911, 12, 71–72, 84, 93
Weems, Sam P., 30–33, 55, 148
Welder Wildlife Foundation, 65
West Jefferson, N.C., 58
West Virginia, 88, 120, 121; rendered desolate by strip mining, 76
West Virginia Highlands Conservancy, 88–89
Western Carolina University, 74
Western Pennsylvania Conservancy, 192
Westmoreland Sanctuary, N.Y., 44
Westwood, Richard, 151
Wetherby, Lawrence, 159
What's Ahead for Our Public Lands, 196n
White, E. B., 260
White Mountains, 84, 121–22
Whitman, Walt, 144, 146, 152

Whose Woods These Are, 3, 227
Wild and Scenic Rivers Act, 40, 191,
224; *see also* Wild and Scenic
Rivers System
Wild and Scenic Rivers System, 105,
165; Little Tennessee could be part
of, 75; New River as part of, 104,
128; *see also* Wild and Scenic
Rivers Act
wilderness, 76, 81–102 passim, 111,
189–96, 250; criteria, 86; definition,
87–88n, 98; in the east, 72, 82, 84,
90, 94, 111, 193–94; never idle
land, 95; *see also* Wilderness Act
Wilderness Act, 43, 84–85, 87–88,
90–92, 96–102, 107, 110, 129, 161,
163–64, 189–91, 193–94, 202, 224,
252; *see also* wilderness
Wilderness Society, 35, 44, 77, 93–94,
103, 110, 110n., 190, 260; council,
79; motto, 259
wildlife, 15, 150, 209, 255; abundant
along Blue Ridge Parkway, 55;
Biltmore Estate as preserve, 5;
threatened by pine forests in
south, 254; *see also* bears; birds;
deer; panther
Wildlife Management Institute, 209
Wilkes County, N.C., 31
Williamsburg. *See* Colonial
Williamsburg
Wilson, James, 12–13, 70–71
Wilson, Woodrow, 153
Winchester, Tenn., 69
Winchester, Va., 136
Winters, Harold, 52

Wisconsin, 158
Woodcrafters and Carvers, shop,
Gatlinburg, Tenn., 50
Woods, Arthur, Col., 26
Woods Hole, Mass., 223
Woods, Polly, 57
World War I, 153
World War II, 190
Wright, Bruce S., 119, 122
Wyeth, Andrew, 46
Wyoming, 222, 235; eagle killings,
228; Game and Fish Department,
183

Yale University, New Haven, School
of Forestry, 10, 176–77, 179, 251
Yancey County, N.C., 130
Yearbook of Agriculture, 1967 issue,
250
Yellowstone National Park, Wyo.,
26, 133, 141–43, 155; lacking in
wilderness, 80; visited by John D.
Rockefeller Jr. and sons, 25
Yellowstone Park Company,
Yellowstone National Park, Wyo.,
141–42
Yosemite National Park, Calif., 45,
154
Yukon River, Alaska, 165; flats, 230

Zahniser, Howard, 190
Zenger, John Peter, 226
Zern, Ed, 236
zinc phosphide, 60–69; dangerous to
livestock and humans, 63; toxic to
all forms of animal life, 66; *see also*
pesticides

Conscience of a Conservationist was designed by Dariel Mayer, composed at the University of Tennessee Press on the Apple® Macintosh™ SE and LaserWriter II™ with Microsoft® Word and Aldus Pagemaker®, and printed and bound by Thomson-Shore, Inc. The book is set in Palatino. Text stock is 60-lb. Glatfelter Natural Antique. Frontispiece and chapter opening ornaments are by Rudolph Wendelin.